Sine ni Lav Diaz

Sine ni Lav Diaz

A Long Take on the Filipino Auteur

EDITED BY

Parichay Patra and Michael Kho Lim

Bristol, UK / Chicago, USA

First published in the UK in 2021 by
Intellect, The Mill, Parnall Road, Fishponds, Bristol, BS16 3JG, UK

First published in the USA in 2021 by
Intellect, The University of Chicago Press, 1427 E. 60th Street,
Chicago, IL 60637, USA

A catalogue record for this book is available from
the British Library.

Copy editor: Newgen
Cover and frontispiece designer: Aleksandra Szumlas
Production manager: Sophia Munyengeterwa
Typesetting: Newgen

Cover and frontispiece image: Lav Diaz on the set of *Ang Hupa* (*The Halt*),
Antipolo City, 24 January 2019; photography by Cielo Bagabaldo

Print ISBN 978-1-78938-424-6
ePDF ISBN 978-1-78938-425-3
ePub ISBN 978-1-78938-426-0

Printed and bound by CPI.

To find out about all our publications, please visit
www.intellectbooks.com
There you can subscribe to our e-newsletter,
browse or download our current catalogue,
and buy any titles that are in print.

This is a peer-reviewed publication.

Contents

Foreword:
Lav Diaz, Artist

Lav Diaz is a well-known name in independent film-making and film festival circles. Anybody who is interested in Philippine cinema would be familiar with the name. Whether those who profess to know him have seen his films is another matter. The films of Lav Diaz do not attract droves to the theatres (if his films get any screening time at all). They are known to be utterly long and very slow. But Lav Diaz does not care. The audience is the least of his concerns. He does not care if anybody watches his films; he does not care if viewers step in and out of the screening room. However, he would not mind if more people watched his films, which is why his recent films star established actors such as Sid Lucero, John Lloyd Cruz, Piolo Pascual and Charo Santos. He looks at film-making as a cultural struggle for a greater cinema. If popular actors would help him in that struggle, so be it. Lav Diaz is not a communicator. He is an artist. His main concerns are his work and the art of cinema.

I learned more about Lav Diaz, the artist, when we interviewed him for our documentary series *Habambuhay, Remembering Philippine Cinema*, a project of TBA Studios for the celebration of the centennial of Philippine cinema. Lav talked about his family and his younger years in Tupaglas, Maguindanao, a province in Mindanao, the southern island in the Philippines, known for being the hotbed of the secessionist movement. His parents, both public school teachers, exposed their children to literature and, quite interestingly, cinema. The family would make weekend excursions to the town of Tacurong for movie binges in the theatres. They would stay overnight in the town until they had seen the double features in the four second-run theatres – films ranging from Fernando Poe Jr action films to Nora Aunor musicals, from Hong Kong martial arts movies to Italian spaghetti westerns. Sometimes, a classic foreign film would be thrown into the repertoire, like Kurosawa's *Ikiru* showing in the French theatre that was run by a Frenchman. At home, over dinner, Lav's father would proceed to discuss the films. Lav's exposure to literature and cinema would continue during his maturing years in college until the lure of film-making became an obsession.

Like the other film-makers of his generation, Lav Diaz looked for an opening that would allow him to break into the world of film-making. The offer to do a *pito-pito* movie for Regal Films signalled this opportunity. Named after the herbal medicine called *pito-pito*, meaning a concoction from seven wondrous herbs, Regal's *pito-pito* meant seven days of shooting and seven days of post-production. Lav took this opportunity of a lifetime to do a feature film. The plunge into this crazy world of cheap moviemaking resulted in promising movies, if not the promise of things to come (*Serafin Geronimo: Ang Kriminal ng Baryo Concepcion* and *Burger Boys*). His first cut of *Serafin Geronimo* ran for three hours and thirty minutes. Naturally, Mother Lily of Regal Films would have none of it. Lav was convinced or forced, most probably, to cut it down to a 'viewable' length – a little over two hours.

Lav saw the futility of working in the mainstream of the industry. His reflections on what was happening in the industry, on why cinema was so far behind literature and the other arts and on what he really wanted to do resulted in what we know today about the films of Lav Diaz – uncompromising, anti-conventional and subversive, personal but committed.

Lav Diaz's process of doing films does not follow conventions. A semblance of a treatment or a 'dummy' (his word) screenplay is used to guide the production budgeting and scheduling or to give the actors a rough idea of the film; or there may not be a script at all. For example, Lav overhears a typhoon coming to hit a province, and the film muse creates an image in his fertile mind – a pregnant, crazy woman meets a lost, crazed artist in the raging rain. Inspired by this, Lav forms his team – two actors for this particular project – and they travel to the north that will be hit by the typhoon and shoot the scene that would become the ending of a film. The ensuing shoot will be developed day-to-day; Lav works on the material to be shot in the wee hours of the morning, gives a copy to the actors and they shoot. How can one be more unconventional than that? Lav describes the essence of his process as one of discovery. He follows the characters day by day and develops the story as shooting goes along, involving his actors and staff in the process.

Lav's style – long take, one shot equals one scene, slow pace – is definitely unconventional or, more accurately, subversive. One can say that he is harking back to the early years of cinema when the entire film was taken in a single shot, the early years before the idea of editing and the Hollywood style of filming ruled the world of cinema. Moreover, the concept of 'waiting' in Malay culture is crucial to this style. Lav credits the works of film-makers such as Tarkovsky with encouraging him to take the plunge and free cinema from the conventions of film language and the demands of economics. In his attempt to free cinema, he is able to be closer and committed to his ideal of a cinema that reflects the political, social and economic realities of his environment and mirrors the truth as he sees it.

This anthology of essays on Lav Diaz, co-edited by Parichay Patra and Michael Kho Lim, is a welcome addition to the scant material on Philippine cinema and Filipino film-makers. The chapters will not be an easy read, for sure. The films under scrutiny and analysis, after all, are not an easy watch.

Clodualdo del Mundo Jr

Preface

The idea of an edited volume dedicated solely to Lav Diaz germinated during our sojourn in Melbourne, at the time of our doctoral research at Monash University. The city of Melbourne, with its cinematheque, the Australian Centre for the Moving Image, and several film festivals, perpetually exists in a condition conducive to a project like this. It also houses a considerable Filipino diaspora, especially in its universities. Diaz's films have been featured in the various editions of the Melbourne International Film Festival (MIFF) between 2013 and 2016: *Norte, the End of History* (in 2013), *From What Is Before* (in 2014), *Storm Children: Book One* (in 2014) and *A Lullaby to the Sorrowful Mystery* (in 2016). Thanks to the MIFF programmes, we have had the rare and much-needed theatrical experience of Lav Diaz. The cinephilia that has existed in Melbourne for years, well before and despite the advent of cinema studies as a university discipline, contributed significantly to this project.

At the completion of our respective research, we left the Antipodes and took the project with us to various parts of the world. In March 2017, Parichay Patra participated in a symposium and exhibition titled *Lav Diaz: Journeys* in London, organized and hosted by the University of Westminster and curated by May Adadol Ingawanij. Meanwhile, Michael Kho Lim's experiences in and research on the independent film-making landscape in the Philippines, his several meetings and interviews with Lav Diaz and his industry network have shaped some of the most indispensable elements in the volume. The proposal, after several overseas calls, Skype sessions, a trip to Manila, rejections and revisions, has finally found its place in the partnership between Intellect and De La Salle University Publishing House.

We came from two different Asian locations and wanted to situate Lav Diaz in different contexts and domains – the reason why we engaged with a number of contributors from the Philippines and the 'West', mostly Europe. To date, academic and non-academic references to Diaz and his works are scattered over such different platforms as book chapters, journal articles, unpublished dissertations and film festival booklets that are not always accessible to the wider public. For instance, the BOZAR Centre for Fine Arts, the Courtisane Film Festival and the

Cinematek in Brussels have produced a special catalogue on Lav Diaz in the context of their retrospective in 2015. They have reprinted and published articles from various sources, including those by William Brown and May Adadol Ingawanij, the latter being reprinted in this collection. There are also several interviews with Diaz and some chapters by the deceased film critic Alexis Tioseco, published and reprinted across many books and festival souvenir programmes. A more exhaustive list of such publications can be found in our introduction to the present volume.

Apart from these materials, there is no sustained, book-length work on Lav Diaz and his cinema. However, more than the absence of an anthology, it is Diaz's exemplary body of work and contributions to world cinema that make him and his cinema deserving of a space in film studies literature and which also help in filling in a gap especially in the context of Southeast Asian cinema. Since this book is the first of its kind on Lav Diaz, we hope to expand the scope and range of its contents by incorporating writings and responses from various quarters that include contributions from critics, freelancers, creative media enthusiasts, practitioners involved in independent film production, scholars studying or teaching cinema in and outside of the university space and those located in and outside of the Philippines in order to critically explore the works of one of the most significant contemporary auteurs from national and transnational cinema perspectives.

Acknowledgements

We would like to thank Lav Diaz for agreeing to have a prolonged conversation spanning several decades of his life and times. Hazel Orencio made the meeting with Diaz happen, helping him to find some time in his extraordinarily loaded schedule. We would also like to take this opportunity to thank all our contributors for their patience as this project went on for years. Jelena Stanovnik and Tim Mitchell at Intellect must be thanked for their unflinching support through this protracted journey. The suggestions and inputs of the two anonymous reviewers have helped us reshape some of the existing material in the book. David Jonathan Bayot of the Manila-based De La Salle University Publishing House (DLSUPH) helped us greatly with the much-needed intercontinental collaboration because of which the book remains accessible to its Asian readership.

We would also like to acknowledge the support extended by May Adadol Ingawanij in allowing us to reprint her article published in the journal *Afterall*, the help of David Morris and Whitney Rauenhorst as individuals and the University of Chicago Press as an institution for the reprint rights. It is to be acknowledged that the chapter by Alexis Tioseco appeared originally in a Torino Film Festival publication and was reprinted in a booklet on Lav published by the Brussels Cinematek, BOZAR Centre for Fine Arts and the Courtisane Film Festival on the occasion of a retrospective of the film-maker. Therefore, for the reproduction of the chapter in our tribute section, we are grateful to the Torino Film Festival and all concerned institutions in Brussels. We would also like to thank Stoffel Debuysere and Arindam Sen in this regard.

Parichay Patra wishes to thank the University of Westminster for sponsoring his trip to London for the 2017 Lav Diaz symposium and, IIT Jodhpur, his present institution, for supporting his Manila trip in 2019.

This book is dedicated to the undying memories of Alexis Tioseco and Nica Bohinc – murdered in Quezon City, Philippines, on 1 September 2009. They were two more victims of the everyday and eternal violence in the Philippines that categorizes Lav Diaz's cinema.

Introduction:
Lav Diaz: Cinema beyond Time

Parichay Patra and Michael Kho Lim

In recent times, Lav Diaz and his unusually long films have generated considerable interest in the transnational festival space. He has won a number of important international awards over the course of a few years, and his near-complete retrospectives have been arranged in various parts of the world.[1] It is more of a transition from a niche, cult-admiring cinematic secret society to the red velvet and flashlight, something which creates a stir in a cinephilia comprising of his fans and detractors alike. However, his possible penetration into film studies research remains vastly unrealized, which may seem strange given the widespread acceptability of the so-called slow cinema in the festival and film studies circuit.

To date, there is no book-length work on Lav Diaz despite him being one of the most significant auteurs of our time. There are intermittent journal articles and book chapters (Brown 2016; Ingawanij 2015), unpublished dissertations (e.g. Mai 2015) and scattered materials on slow cinema (e.g. Lim 2014; de Luca and Jorge 2016; Çağlayan 2018; Jaffe 2014; Koepnick 2017). Special retrospective booklets coming out of cinematheques or film festivals can also be located, even if they are not for wide circulation (Mazzanti et al. 2015). A bilingual journal has come up with a special issue devoted to slow/long cinema that features some articles on Diaz in English and Portuguese, including a few by some of the contributors to the present volume (Baptista et al. 2017).

Looking more critically into the problem of a dearth of critical engagement with Lav Diaz, we tried to locate its reasons beyond the durational extremity of the film-maker. The problem lies mostly in the ways of constructing Diaz solely as the global representative of a national (Filipino) cinema or in confining him to the problematic global category of 'slow cinema'. The Diaz fanboyism that pervades in European festivals has led to an uncritical adulation of his cinema that does not contribute to the production of research material. The championing of Diaz

1

and his cinema as a representative of the Philippines, its politics, its cinema, especially the 'new cinema', has happened at an opportune moment. But it has often resulted in a championing solely for slowness and the durational principles, something that hardly does justice to his film aesthetics, let alone to the complexity of his engagement with the histories of many colonialism(s), the Malay Archipelago, the Filipino nation and, more significantly, cinema itself.

This collection considers Lav Diaz and his works holistically without being confined to a specific approach or research method. On the contrary, it involves almost all the major contemporary academic approaches to cinema. It focuses on an auteur who has been celebrated immensely in recent times and yet has remained largely unexplored in cinema studies. The book will address this research gap.

As such, this book aims to situate Diaz at the crucial juncture of 'new' auteurism, Filipino New Wave and transnational cinema, but it does not neglect the industrial-exhibitional coordinates of his cinema. The rationale behind this project is to raise questions on the oeuvre of a significant auteur, situate him in and outside of his immediate national context(s), present a repository of critical approaches on him, reconsider the existing critical positions on him, find newer avenues to enter (and exit) his canon that will consciously avoid the time-worn rhetoric of long take and slowness of the proverbial 'slow cinema' camp and find corridors in him that will lead to informed ways of reaching other movements/ auteurs in other times and other places.

We want to explore various other aspects of Diaz and his cinema whose notoriety, as we believe, should not rely solely on its incredible running time. We want to look at Diaz from the perspectives of a national and a transnational critic (one of the two editors is from the Philippines and the other from India), concentrate both on the spatial and the temporal, place him within the intricacies of the culture and creative industries and the distribution practices and politics in his native place, allow space for his 'detractors' who (perhaps rightly) focus on and object to his 'artlessness', and also read him in the context of his fascination for the epic novel and novelistic cinema, his engagement with Dostoyevsky and Jose Rizal, among others. The evolution of Diaz as a Filipino auteur is associated with everything mentioned earlier and, most notably, with his myriad ways of engaging with the histories of colonization and the unending postcolonial/neo-imperial dictatorial experience(s).

The book's title uses Diaz's directorial credit – his signature or branding to a certain extent: 'Sine ni Lav Diaz', which can be translated as 'a film by Lav Diaz' or 'the cinema of Lav Diaz'. We take on the latter notion to refer to his body of works as a form of cinema in itself. However, Diaz notes that beyond the identification of 'his' cinema, he is addressing the Filipino verity – the *Pinoy*,[2] the Malay, the Indio.[3] 'It's something very cultural to me, a signposting, a direction, an embracement of the sui generis nature of Filipino cinema, the way I see it, the way I envision it. It's my claim, that we have our own cinema, the *Pinoy* pride if you may' (Diaz 2015: n.pag.). Correspondingly, we use 'long take' to signify Diaz's cinematic style and to represent the book's extensive look or comprehensive study on Diaz. It presents an expansive or a wide range of views through the contributors' (long) take on Diaz and his works. Lav Diaz often divides his critics into mutually exclusive camps and factions. Hence, this book offers a platform for all and is constructed around three major sections, apart from the foreword, the introduction, an interview with Diaz and a reprint of an article by the late Alexis Tioseco.

The first section, 'Lav Diaz through Cinematic Histories', looks at the evolution of Lav Diaz through national and transnational cinematic and literary histories. This complex cine-literary network will return throughout the volume engulfing the 'Diaz canon' in its way. This is beyond the usual mode of adaptation or the literature-cinema interface even though Diaz has (loosely) adapted the works of Fyodor Dostoyevsky and Jose Rizal. The portrait of an auteur manifests here through national cultures and literatures of the world, primarily because of Diaz's interest in realizing the novelistic or epic novel form in cinema.

Clodualdo del Mundo, Jr.'s chapter sets the stage for the book as he reviews the state of Philippine cinema from the period after Lino Brocka and his contemporaries produced a number of key works that have defined the 'Second Golden Age of Philippine Cinema' in the 1970s and 1980s. From this peak, Philippine cinema dropped to a moribund state in the 1990s – a period that del Mundo refers to as a 'history of footnotes'. No one is significant enough to deserve a main entry in his chapter except for the rise of another generation of film-makers to which Lav Diaz belongs. Del Mundo then situates Diaz in this context, along with other film-makers of his time and another generation that follows them. This chapter thus provides an overview of Diaz's position in and his contributions to the overall landscape of Philippine cinema.

The spectral presence of Dostoyevsky looms large all over the volume, and an exploration into it begins with Tom Paulus, who has his way of coming to terms with his major question only after a long-winding and apparently eclectic introduction that places Lav Diaz within national and transnational cinema histories, invoking seemingly disjointed elements such as Taiwanese and Filipino cine-political histories, Italian neorealism, Godard and the Filipino novel under Spanish colonization. Paulus develops the wider context and then departs rather violently, wondering why the nineteenth-century Russian novel *à la* Dostoyevsky becomes a pivotal point in the world of Diaz despite the existence of a national (Filipino) literature that he has established in his introduction. He evades the temptation of taking the shortest route by exploring the Dostoyevsky adaptations of Diaz; his is a remembering of Dostoyevsky and his elements ranging from his utopian socialism to his ultimate alienation from the Russian radicals. Paulus relocates preconditions for such elements within the Filipino society and its modernism and delves deep into Lav Diaz's increasingly complex engagement with Christianity, redemption, history and the messianic. For Paulus, the suffering of the Filipino in Lav Diaz transcends the problematic question of nationhood by becoming 'a moral problem', and his chapter far surpasses the limiting nation-state framework to launch an inquiry into the ethico-moral.

In contrast to the wider transnational approach and invocations of Paulus, May Adadol Ingawanij offers a rooted, continental and yet holistic view of Diaz in her chapter that appeared first in *Afterall*, a Chicago University Press journal. Locating Diaz within the turbulent politico-cultural-literary histories of South East Asia, Ingawanij includes most of Diaz's primary concerns, such as the Marcos dictatorship, the unending presence of the Great Mothers (mythical rather than biological, like the healer Bai Rahmah in *From What Is Before* [Diaz 2014]), victimization of the nation-body, the reiterated motif of rape and physical realism, and unearths elements from almost all of his major films. However, the chapter does not evade the transnational; instead it places Diaz into a different domain by referring to the Third World revolutionary art and Third Cinema, especially Glauber Rocha.

Michael Guarneri has worked extensively on Lav Diaz and introduced the auteur in various festivals, events and booklets. Here, apart from introducing Diaz, Guarneri introduces the non-Filipino reader to certain dangerous geographies, the histories and geopolitics not only of the Philippines but also of regions ('region-nations' should be more apt with these places housing communist and Islamist guerilla/secessionist forces) such as Maguindanao, where Diaz spent his cinephilic childhood. Then Guarneri's chapter makes a sudden departure from that rootedness to the rootlessness of the digital revolution, situating Diaz's cinema firmly within the latter.

The second section, 'From Death to the Gods: The Resurrection of the National?', features a chapter from an 'insider' (from the Philippines) and an 'outsider', with specific themes in Diaz's films under scrutiny. Some of the concerns in the first section are reiterated here, the likes of a sustained engagement with Dostoyevsky, Catholicism and an idiosyncratic temporality, even if from different perspectives. But specific elements and seemingly independent units in Lav Diaz films reappear in very different conditions. Here the contributors try to locate these elements within the context of the Filipino nation, national history and space. Invoking spatiality in an auteur whose temporal explorations continue to overshadow many other points of concern is something new, and it leads to the inevitable, the aesthetic (or the lack thereof) of Lav Diaz that will form the section that follows.

Marco Grosoli uses a distinctive way of opening his chapter by referring to an inherently visual mode of analysis that he is not interested in and focuses instead on the narrative but not on the redundant reproduction of a narrative. His choice of texts, *Notre, Hangganan ng Kasaysayan (Norte, the End of History)* (Diaz 2013) and *Florentina Hubaldo, CTE* (Diaz 2012) in this case, leads to his consideration of 'the narrative arcs of two characters'. One of them is 'striving to be saved', while the other is '"already saved" and "utterly unsaveable" at the same time'. Dostoyevsky returns with Diaz's obsession for and unending engagement with *Crime and Punishment*, and the conceptual apparatus of the messianic is re-invoked. Diaz's exploration of a precolonial temporality also returns, but Grosoli's analysis is mostly complemented by two largely uncharted territories. The first is theology as he refers to soteriology and eschatology, their association with temporality/end of time and redemption/salvation; the other is philosophical explorations into the messianic *à la* Walter Benjamin and Giorgio Agamben to notice Diaz's 'subversive reinvention', his 'postcolonially informed' intervention into the notion of redemption in a 'traumatized eternal present' marked by historical traumas.

In Katrina Macapagal's reading of Lav Diaz's *Melancholia* (2008), she applies Mikhail Bakhtin's theory of the 'chronotope' (literally, 'time-space'), which is initially used to study the novel form, to explore the key spatio-temporal configurations of the film. Based on *Melancholia*'s novelistic characteristics, Macapagal examines how the idyllic chronotope is manifested in Diaz's choice of location or space for his characters and analyses how their movements accentuate the themes of grief and memory in the film. *Melancholia*'s narrative is also hinged on the characters' search for their loved ones declared as desaparecidos. It is in this context that Macapagal argues how the film's discursive value is embodied in its ability to reveal imaginaries of spatial justice and how this also contributes to the idyllic chronotope, while set against the backdrop of enforced disappearances in Philippine history.

The third section, 'No Cinema, No Art Either', is concerned with the aesthetic of the auteur or the lack of it. It looks more like a round-table with three participants discussing the aesthetic issues with the fourth joining in with his experiences in and information on Lav Diaz's distribution, acceptability and the politics of exhibition in his native industry.

Adrian Martin, a known detractor and trenchant critic of Diaz's style of film-making, makes a significant intervention at this stage into the book. A reworked and more informed version of an earlier review of *Norte* that he did for *Sight and Sound*, Martin's chapter unhesitatingly critiques the Lav Diaz fanboyism and its possible consequences for the film-maker. It should also be read as a review of Diaz criticism in contemporary cinephilia, with some of his former 'fans' expressing their displeasure with his seemingly transitional phase where the running time of films is gradually being reduced and an apparent yet unwelcoming change in style can perhaps be observed. Here Martin refers to something more ambiguous – a Barthean '"degree zero" of artlessness' that, for him, can be located almost everywhere in Diaz's canon.

Perhaps what is 'artlessness' for Martin becomes 'non-cinema' for William Brown and decidedly not in a pejorative sense. Brown designs his often deliberately polemical criticism along two axes: on one hand, he places the celluloid, modernity, capitalism and the nation state and contrasts that with the digital non-cinema, anti-capitalism and the postnational on the other. Diaz and his digital, incredibly long, anti-capital cinema is obviously placed in the latter as Brown moves between cinema and national histories.

An earlier version of Parichay Patra's chapter was presented at the 2017 *Lav Diaz: Journeys* symposium at the University of Westminster. Patra further elaborates on the 'artlessness', with deliberately digressive passages comprising of biblical and cinematic sources, of Dostoyevsky and Rizal. With an array of textual and extra-textual references, the chapter moves through the Diaz canon and attempts to find out the source of the 'artlessness' in the (epic) novel form, arguing that many of the known elements in film aesthetics cannot be used in Diaz criticism primarily because of his investment in 'empty' shots that form the novelistic in the days of the digital.

Michael Kho Lim's chapter looks into the marketing and distribution aspects of some of Lav Diaz's more recent films such as *Norte, Hele sa Hiwagang Hapis (A Lullaby to the Sorrowful Mystery)* (2016) and *Ang Babaeng Humayo (The Woman Who Left)* (2016), which have had commercial theatrical releases around the world. He examines the different promotional strategies utilized by the films such as eventization and banking on Diaz's reputational capital, the idea of endurance viewing and the power of a 'distributor's cut'. Lim also discusses how all these strategies have contributed to the audience development of Diaz's films and concludes that no film can be deemed undistributable.

The interview with Lav Diaz concentrates on his memories, his portrait of the artist as a young film-maker, his formative years, his engagement with different, now-obsolete cinematic forms and technologies such as Super 8, and his politics and aspirations with greater detail. The interview is effortlessly personal as he speaks mostly in his vernacular (it has been transcribed and translated later), recounts his days as a trainee in workshops and expresses his helplessness as a 'cultural worker' in the face of an imminent political crisis in the Philippines that is not immune from the new world order that harbours many fascisms worldwide.

The Alexis Tioseco chapter, reprinted in his memory, was first published in a booklet of the Torino Film Festival and reappeared later in the booklet of the Lav

Diaz retrospective in Brussels. It is a truly introductory essay on (early) Diaz with passionate glimpses into Filipino cine-political histories and Diaz's obsessions and somehow ends abruptly with *Evolution of a Filipino Family* (2005). Tioseco concluded with his 'weight of history' and the responsibility imposed on the contemporary Filipino audience. The abruptness of his ending is not merely symptomatic of not-so-brief essays in festival booklets, it perhaps refers to the abrupt end of Tioseco who did not live to see many of Diaz's later works.

NOTES

1. Diaz won the Golden Leopard at the 2014 Locarno Film Festival for *From What Is Before*, the Alfred Bauer Award (Silver Bear) at the 2016 Berlin Film Festival for *A Lullaby to the Sorrowful Mystery* and the coveted Golden Lion at the 2016 Venice Film Festival for *The Woman Who Left*. His retrospectives include the one at the Australian Cinémathèque in Brisbane at the Eighth Asia-Pacific Triennial of Contemporary Art in 2015, the retros at Jeu de Paume in Paris and the 2015 one in Brussels organized jointly by Cinematek, BOZAR and the Courtisane Festival.

2. *Pinoy* is the colloquial term for Filipino, the official demonym of the people of the Philippines.

3. During the Spanish colonization of the Philippines, the Spaniards used 'Indio' (literally 'Indian') as a derogatory term to refer to the indigenous inhabitants of the archipelago (Owen 2005: xxi).

REFERENCES

Baptista, Tiago, Viegas, Susana, Piçarra, Maria do Carmo, Castro, Teresa and Natálio, Carlos Eduardo (eds) (2017), *Aniki: Revista Portuguesa de Imagem em Movimento*, Dossier on 'A longa duração' ('The Long Duration'), 4:2.

Brown, William (2016), 'Melancholia: The long, slow cinema of Lav Diaz', in T. de Luca and N. B. Jorge (eds), *Slow Cinema*, Edinburgh: Edinburgh University Press, pp. 112–22.

Çağlayan, Emre (2018), *Poetics of Slow Cinema: Nostalgia, Absurdism, Boredom*, Basingstoke: Palgrave Macmillan.

Diaz, Lav (2005), *Evolution of a Filipino Family*, Philippines: Sine Olivia Pilipinas.

Diaz, Lav (2008), *Melancholia*, Philippines: Sine Olivia Pilipinas.

Diaz, Lav (2012), *Florentina Hubaldo, CTE*, Philippines: Sine Olivia Pilipinas.

Diaz, Lav (2013), *Notre, Hangganan ng Kasaysayan (Norte, the End of History)*, Philippines: Sine Olivia Pilipinas.

Diaz, Lav (2014), *From What Is Before*, Philippines: Sine Olivia Pilipinas.

Diaz, Lav (2015), e-mail to Michael Kho Lim, 1 May.

Diaz, Lav (2016), *Hele sa Hiwagang Hapis (A Lullaby to the Sorrowful Mystery)*, Philippines: Sine Olivia Pilipinas.

Diaz, Lav (2016), *Ang Babaeng Humayo (The Woman Who Left)*, Philippines: Sine Olivia Pilipinas.

Ingawanij, May Adadol (2015), 'Long walk to life: The films of Lav Diaz', *Afterall*, 40:1, pp. 102–15.

Jaffe, Ira (2014), *Slow Movies: Countering the Cinema of Action*, New York: Wallflower Press.

Koepnick, Lutz (2017), *The Long Take: Art Cinema and the Wondrous*, Minneapolis: University of Minnesota Press.

Lim, Song Hwee (2014), *Tsai Ming-Liang and a Cinema of Slowness*, Honolulu: University of Hawai'i Press.

Luca, Tiago de and Jorge, Nuno Barradas (eds) (2016), *Slow Cinema*, Edinburgh: Edinburgh University Press.

Mai, Nadin (2015), 'The aesthetics of absence and duration in the post-trauma cinema of Lav Diaz', Ph.D. thesis, Stirling: University of Stirling.

Mazzanti, Nicola, Dujardin, Paul and Mortier, Pieter-Paul (eds) (2015), *Lying Down in a World of Tempest*, Brussels: Cinematek, Courtisane and Bozar.

Owen, Norman G. (2005), 'Changing names', in N. Owen (ed.), *The Emergence of Modern Southeast Asia: A New History*, Honolulu: University of Hawai'i Press, pp. xvii–xxv.

PART 1

LAV DIAZ THROUGH CINEMATIC HISTORIES

1

After Brocka:
Situating Lav Diaz in Philippine Cinema

Clodualdo del Mundo, Jr.

In 2019, the Philippines celebrated the centennial of Filipino cinema. Although motion picture entertainment was introduced in the country towards the end of the Spanish rule in the 1890s and some form of film-making was started by American soldiers and businessmen at the turn of the century, 1919 was the landmark year when Jose Nepomuceno made his film *Dalagang Bukid*. Since then, several generations of Filipino film-makers have contributed towards the formation of a national cinema. Lino Brocka, eminent film-maker in the 1970s, led the third generation of Filipino film-makers to create some sort of renaissance in Philippine cinema. Today, another film-maker is leading his generation towards new heights – Lav Diaz.

Before moving on to the post-Brocka generations, it would be instructive to look at what happened pre-Brocka. The first generation of Filipino film-makers (late 1910s–early 1940s) was active during the pre–Second World War years. It was a period of learning a borrowed medium and adapting or indigenizing film to make it local. The film-makers of this early generation used the entertainment forms that were familiar to them and their audiences, such as the Spanish zarzuela and the comedia which the Filipinos adapted into the indigenized forms called *sarsuwela* and *moro-moro*, respectively. Thus, the first full-length Filipino film, *Dalagang Bukid* (1919), was adapted by Jose Nepomuceno from a popular *sarsuwela*. The *sarsuwela* films of this period show signs of the theatrical form with the stock characters and drama cum music and songs. The *moro-moro* movies, however, are based on the fantasy world of the comedia dealing with the encounter between Christians and Moors. Of course, in the 1930s, local film-makers were also exposed to Hollywood and other foreign movies and were challenged to adapt to the changing times while adhering to the forms that remained ingrained in Filipino film practice. The early beginnings of a film industry happened during this period, but its flowering was interrupted by the Second World War. There are not too many films to judge the quality of the work of the first generation of Filipino film-makers. Only five full-length films are known to be extant – *Zamboanga* (1937), *Giliw Ko* ('My dear', 1939), *Tunay na Ina* ('Real mother', 1939), *Pakiusap* ('Plea', 1940) and *Ibong Adarna* ('Adarna bird', 1941). Very little film-making happened during the Japanese Occupation of the country, and two of the known films during this period were made under strict supervision of the censors.

After the war, film-making resumed to signal a return to normalcy. Film-makers who started making films towards the end of the 1930s and the beginning of the 1940s continued their interrupted careers. This second generation of Filipino film-makers (1940s–60s) developed during the period of the Studio Years. Three major studios (Sampaguita and LVN, established in the late 1930s, and Premiere, established in the mid-1940s) created a little Hollywood. The Big Three Studios had their respective contract stars, directors and production people, their sound stages and their own distribution and exhibition outlets. This second generation saw the flowering of film-making in the country, both commercially and artistically. Three of the major film-makers of the period who went beyond the commercial needs of the industry and made films in the aura of art were Gerardo de Leon, who made a number of films for Premiere, for example, *Sawa sa Lumang Simboryo* ('Python in the old belfry', 1952), *Ifugao* (1954) and *Huwag Mo Akong Limutin* ('Forget me not', 1960); Lamberto Avellana, who did his major films for LVN, for example, *Anak Dalita* ('Child of misery', 1956), *Badjao* (1957) and *Kundiman ng Lahi* ('Song of the race', 1959); and Manuel Conde, who produced his major works himself, for example, *Genghis Khan* (1950) and his satirical takes on the folk character Juan Tamad.

The second generation of Filipino film-makers took Philippine cinema to new heights. Unfortunately, the rise was followed by the inevitable fall. The 1960s sounded the death knell for Philippine cinema. Even though what could be argued as the best films of Lamberto Avellana (*A Portrait of the Artist as Filipino*, 1965) and Gerardo de Leon (*Ang Daigdig ng mga Api* ['The world of the oppressed'], 1965) were made in the mid-1960s for the Manila Film Festival, which was designed to rescue a dying cinema, the depths that commercialism had brought a national cinema had reached the pits. In the 1960s, the Big Three Studios lost their control of the movie industry. Labour issues, big stars building their own production companies, small-time companies getting into the business to get their share of the pie, the changing taste of the audience – in short, a new regime was taking over the industry. Coupled with these developments (or retrogression, to be more exact) was the advent of sex movies that enterprising film distributors imported from Europe and the United States. Finally, in 1970, local movie producers joined the bandwagon in making home-grown sex movies that came to be labelled as *bomba* ('bomb'). It was during this time that a new generation of would-be film-makers was waiting in the wings, armed with the knowledge of art cinema that they had learned in school or in special screenings that the foreign embassies and cultural centres were offering as alternatives to commercial movies. The theatre was set for a new generation of Filipino film-makers, the third in the history of Philippine cinema (1970s–80s).

In the 1970s, there was very little film-making that happened outside the industry. Kidlat Tahimik (*Mababangong Bangungot [Perfumed Nightmare]*, 1977) was one of the very few doing their thing outside the mainstream. Anyone who wanted to make full-length films had to break into the industry. And that was what Brocka and his generation of film-makers did. Brocka established his name doing commercial films that appealed to the popular audience. In 1970 alone, he made *Wanted: Perfect Mother*, *Santiago* and *Tubog sa Ginto* ('Dipped in gold') for Lea Productions. Soon, he was able to make films under his own company, CineManila, starting with *Tinimbang Ka Ngunit Kulang* ('You were weighed but found wanting', 1974) which was a commercial and critical success. Then, he made *Insiang* (1976), the film that would reintroduce foreign audiences to Philippine cinema. A new wave of film-makers would crash the gates of the dead, or dying, industry. The long list of this new wave of film-makers includes Ishmael Bernal, who introduced himself with *Pagdating sa Dulo* ('At the top', 1971) that was bankrolled by his friends. Bernal's later major works include *Manila by Night* (or *City after Dark*, 1980) and *Himala* ('Miracle', 1982). Mike de Leon, who produced *Maynila … Sa mga Kuko ng Liwanag* (*Manila … In the Claws of Light*, 1975), which was directed by Brocka, made his directorial debut with *Itim* (*Rites of May*, 1976). Later, he would do two major films: *Kisapmata* ('In the blink of an eye', 1981) and *Batch '81* (1982). Peque Gallaga, who was known as a production designer, made his magnum opus, *Oro Plata Mata* ('Gold silver death', 1982). Mario O'Hara, who worked as actor and writer for Brocka, made his debut with *Mortal* (1975), followed by *Tatlong Taóng Walang Diyos* ('Three years without God', 1976). Women film-makers of this generation include Lupita Concio, who did *Minsa'y Isang Gamu-Gamo* ('Once there was a moth', 1976); Marilou Diaz-Abaya, who introduced herself with *Tanikala* and *Brutal*, both done in 1980; and Laurice Guillen, actress-turned-director, who made *Salome* (1981). Celso Ad. Castillo (*Asedillo*, 1971), Maryo J. de los Reyes (*High School Circa '65*, 1979), Mel Chionglo (*Playgirl*, 1980) and Gil Portes ('*Merika*, 1984) are other noteworthy film-makers of the third generation. More-over, it should be noted that the wave consisted of other film-makers who were instrumental in the success of this generation. New screenwriters, cinematographers, production designers, music composers, editors and actors contributed to a lively Philippine cinema. Notwithstanding the continuing commercialism and the repressive regime of the Marcos dictatorship in the 1970s, the third generation of Filipino film-makers created a worthy national cinema.

It is ironic that with the newfound freedoms after the fall of the Marcos dictatorship in 1986 Philippine cinema would undergo another cycle of decline. A confluence of reasons, including the conditions of an oppressive commercial system and, more significantly, the disenchantment with the ineffectual Aquino government that was beset with economic problems left by the Marcos regime, was responsible for this slump. Lino Brocka's better films of this period would be funded by foreign sources. He had made a name for himself which enabled him to get foreign funding in the 1980s. Stephan Films, a French company, co-financed *Bayan Ko … Kapit sa Patalim* ('My country … seize the blade', 1984) which dramatizes the urgency of the personal condition that takes precedence over the community action of the labour union. Written by Brocka's close collaborator Jose Lacaba, *Bayan Ko* was chosen as one of the best films of 1984 by the British Film Institute, sharing the honours with Chen Kaige's *Yellow Earth*. Cannon Films produced *Orapronobis* ('Pray for us'/'Fight for us', 1989) in which a man's quest for change through non-violent means is thwarted by the madness of a paramilitary vigilante group. Mike de Leon, however, virtually retired from film-making after 1986. Ishmael Bernal made feature films sporadically and, like Gerardo de Leon of the preceding generation, earned a living by directing advertising commercials. Marilou Diaz-Abaya shifted to directing a public affairs programme and a satiric gag show for television. Laurice Guillen chose to interrupt her film-making to follow the calling of Marian devotion. Others played the game of the commercial industry or remained silent.

Towards the end of the 1980s and until the fatal car accident that claimed his life in 1991, it was Brocka who continued struggling to work within and against the system. *Gumapang Ka Sa Lusak* ('Crawl in the mud'/*Dirty Affair*, 1990), set against the corrupt and immoral world of politics, is a quintessential Brocka commercial movie, a melodrama with a dose of sociopolitical critique. Ishmael Bernal's sporadic feature film-making resulted in *Wating* (1994), another Bernal film that is set in the exploitative world of the city where one has to be cunning and street-smart, a *wating*, in order to survive. It is one of Bernal's more worthwhile projects during this period – and his last. In 1996, he died from an aneurism. The loss of Brocka and Bernal was a big blow to a generation of film-makers that needed to recapture the idealism that energized its takeover of Philippine cinema in the 1970s.

What happened to Philippine cinema after the 1970s and the 1980s when Lino Brocka and his generation of film-makers produced their key works? What happened to Philippine cinema while film-makers from Iran, Taiwan, China and Korea had been winning recognition around the world?

What happened to Philippine cinema in the 1990s during the fourth generation of Filipino film-makers (late 1980s–early 2000s) was a history of footnotes. No film-maker, I dare say, deserves a main entry in this history. In other words, no one is important enough to deserve a treatment in the body of the chapter. Certainly, there were film-makers who attempted to go beyond the commercial, but the contribution of these film-makers after Brocka and his generation was few and far between.

When we talk of Philippine national cinema, it is still the films of Brocka and his generation that we would go to, together with some homage to Lamberto Avellana, Gerardo de Leon and their generation of film-makers in the 1950s. The succeeding fourth generation could not equal the achievement of Brocka's *Insiang*, Bernal's *Manila by Night* (1980), Mike de Leon's *Kisapmata* (1981), Peque Gallaga's *Oro Plata Mata* (1982), Mario O'Hara's *Tatlong Taóng Walang Diyos* (1976), Lupita Concio's *Minsa'y Isang Gamu-Gamo* (1976) and Celso Ad. Castillo's *Burlesk Queen* (1977). In fact, many of the worthy films of the 1990s were done by third-generation film-makers who continued making films into the 1990s and early 2000s, for example, Peque Gallaga's *Gangland* (1998), *Pinoy Blonde* (2005) and *Sonata* (2013); Mike de Leon's *Bayaning 3rd World* (*3rd World Hero*, 2000); Mario O'Hara's *Babae sa Bubungang Lata* ('Woman on a tin roof', 1998) and *Babae sa Breakwater* ('Woman of breakwater', 2003); and Marilou Diaz-Abaya's *Milagros* (1997), *Jose Rizal* (1998) and *Muro-Ami* (1998).

After Brocka, Philippine cinema fell from the pedestal as it were. A few films were able to break into some international film festivals for various reasons, including connections with festival programmers. The only Filipino feature film that was shown in the Cannes Film Festival after the debut of Mike de Leon's two films (*Kisapmata* and *Batch '81*) during the Directors' Fortnight in 1983 was *Babae sa Breakwater* by Mario O'Hara. This happened after a little over two decades; and O'Hara belonged to Brocka's generation.

If we look at the actors today, it would be clear that they are mere footnotes to the major actors during the time of Avellana in the 1950s (e.g. Leopoldo Salcedo, Rogelio de la Rosa, Rosa del Rosario, Anita Linda, Rosa Rosal, Nida Blanca, Lolita Rodriguez, Gloria Romero, Charito Solis, Mario Montenegro and Fernando Poe, Jr.) and to the actors during Brocka's time in the 1970s (e.g. Nora Aunor, Vilma Santos, Hilda Koronel, Gina Alajar, Cherie Gil, Rafael Roco Jr. and Christopher de Leon). Today, there are so many aspiring actors, mostly teen wannabe stars – so many footnotes to the history of film actors in Philippine cinema.

However, it should be noted that the generation of film-makers in the 1990s was faced with daunting production problems. The local movie industry suffered due to the huge competition from high-concept Hollywood movies; for the cash-strapped viewers, television offered an alternative where they could watch their movie idols; cable TV, featuring local and foreign movies, was available; and, of course, at that time, pirated VCDs and DVDs flooded the market. Certainly, the film-makers of the 1970s also faced the issue of commercialism, but they were able to draw a line that they would not cross; there was a limit to compromise. In the 1990s, there were fewer production companies, unlike in the 1970s when new companies with more ambition than producing money-making movies invested in film. In fairness to the generation of film-makers in the 1990s, the economic situation forced them to acquiesce to commercial demands. Soon, the movie industry went through a slump. From an annual output of over 150 movies to as high as 190 movies in the 1990s, production since 2004 had dwindled to a little over 50 movies a year.

However, there were some developments that happened at the turn of the new millennium and continue to happen that are important to write about as main entries in the current history of Philippine cinema. And this is the history that is being charted by independent film-makers, the fifth generation of Filipino film-makers (2000s–present). Towards the end of the 1990s, film-making became more accessible through the advent of mini-DV cameras, and editing became possible through the use of various computer software. Independent film-making became a byword, and indie film-makers did not need to break into the mainstream movie industry to do their thing. During the first decade of the new millennium, film festivals, led by the Cinemalaya Philippine Independent Film Festival in 2005, provided outlets for a new generation of Filipino film-makers. In 1970, it must be remembered that Brocka and his fellow film-makers broke into the scene like a big wave that watered the desert of Philippine cinema of the 1960s. In the second half of the first decade of the new millennium, Filipino indie film-makers created an onrushing wave, crushing against the dilapidated walls of mainstream cinema.

A new generation of Filipino film-makers, the fifth generation, has shown that they have the right to succeed Brocka and his generation. Today, in the age of digital technology, more and more film-makers of the new generation are making their mark in the history of Philippine cinema – and this is happening outside the mainstream of the industry.

The 'young' and 'old' indie film-makers nowadays are too many to enumerate. Many of them have shown promise with their first films, but it remains to be seen what kind of body of work they would produce. Some of these indie film-makers who are consistently creating works outside of the mainstream are: Auraeus Solito, who directed *Ang Pagdadalaga ni Maximo Oliveros* (*The Blossoming of Maximo Oliveros*, 2005), *Tuli* ('Circumcision', 2006), *Pisay* (*Philippine Science High School*, 2007), *Busong* ('Palawan fate', 2011) and *Baybayin* ('The Palawan script', 2012); Mes de Guzman, fiction writer and film-maker, who has made full-length digital videos, notably *Ang Daan Patungong Kalimugtong* (*The Road to*

Kalimugtong, 2005), *Balikbayan Box* (2008), *Sa Kanto ng Ulap at Lupa* (*Of Skies and Earth*, 2011) and *Diablo* (2012); Raya Martin, whose films *Maicling Pelicula nang Ysang Indio Nacional* (*A Short Film about the Indio Nacional*, 2005), *Now Showing* (2008), *Independencia* ('Independence', 2009), *How to Disappear Completely* (2013) and *La Ultima Pelicula* ('The last film', 2013) made waves in some international film festivals; Khavn de la Cruz, one of the most pro-lific Filipino indie film-makers who has made a name with his uncompromising and experimental films such as *Squatterpunk* (2006) and *Mondomanila (or How I Fixed My Hair after a Rather Long Journey*, 2010); Adolfo Alix, Jr., another prolific film-maker who made *Kadin* (2007), *Adela* (2008) and *Circa* (2019); and John Torres, who has done experimentations such as *Todo Todo Teros* ('All, all is terror', 2006), *Taon Noong Ako'y Anak sa Labas* ('Years when I was a child outside', 2008) and *Ang Ninanais* (*Refrains Happen like Revolutions in a Song*, 2010). Some film-makers from southern Philippines in Mindanao have made their presence felt: Gutierrez Mangansakan II, with *House under the Crescent Moon* (2002), *Limbunan* ('The bridal quarter', 2010), *Cartas de la Soledad* (2011) and *Daughters of the Three Tailed Banner* (2016); Arnel Mardoquio, with *Hunghong sa Yuta* (*Earth's Whisper*, 2008), *Sheika* (2010), *Ang Paglalakbay ng mga Bituin sa Gabing Madilim* (*The Journey of Stars into the Dark Night*, 2012) and *Ang mga Tigmo sa Akong Pagpauli* (*Riddles of My Homecoming*, 2013); and Sheron Dayoc, with *Halaw* (*Ways of the Sea*, 2010), *The Crescent Rising* (2015) and *Women of the Weeping River* (2016).

Another film-maker from Mindanao whose thematic concerns are not confined to his land of birth is Lav Diaz. While Diaz tried to break into the mainstream in the late 1990s through the *pito-pito* (moviemaking process developed by Regal Films which limits the production schedule to seven days of pre-production, seven days of shooting and seven days of post-production), he properly belongs to the fifth generation of Filipino film-makers. His attitude, perspective and ambition were counter-mainstream. Indeed, he was able to finish three films under the *pito-pito* system (*Serafin Geronimo, Ang Kriminal ng Barrio Concepcion* ['Serafin Ger-onimo, the criminal of Barrio Concepcion'], 1998; *Burger Boys*, 1999; and *Hubad sa Ilalim ng Buwan [Naked under the Moon]*, 1999), but the whole experience was traumatic for this film-maker. Diaz knew that he would not be able to fulfil his dreams in the mainstream and that he had to do the kind of film-making he wanted somewhere else.

If we plot the various works of Filipino indie film-makers from experimental to more accessible ones that can easily cross over to the mainstream, the films of Lav Diaz would fall near one end that is farthest from the mainstream. Indie film-makers who harbour ambitions of breaking into the mainstream would be very close to the crossover films, for example, Chris Martinez, who made *100*

(2008), his take on a dying character's bucket list, and *Ang Babae sa Septic Tank* (*The Woman in the Septic Tank*, 2011), his reflexive take on indie film-making; and Antoinette Jadaone, with *That Thing Called Tadhana* (2014), a sort of Linklater's *Before Sunrise*, which catapulted her to the mainstream where she has been making successful romcom movies. Somewhere in the middle, but closer to the more accessible films, would be Brillante Mendoza, who started as a production designer in the mid-1980s. Mendoza made his debut indie film *Masahista* ('The masseur') in 2005. His choice of stories borders on the controversial; for example, *Serbis* ('Service', 2008) is set in a sleazy theatre known for pornographic movies and as a place where sexual transactions are made; and *Kinatay* (*The Execution of P*, 2009) is centred on a crime, the abduction of a prostitute who refuses to pay her debt and ends up being raped, killed and chopped to pieces. His other films are based on major news events; for example, *Captive* (2012), which stars popular French actor Isabelle Huppert, takes off with the kidnapping of tourists by armed rebels in a Palawan resort; and *Taklub* (2015), which stars Nora Aunor. is set in Tacloban after the devastation wrought by typhoon Haiyan.

While there may be as many different types of films as there are film-makers in the indie world, these film-makers are one in exercising their freedom to do the films they want; and Lav Diaz exemplifies this film practice. In an interview for a documentary series on Philippine cinema, Diaz enjoins his fellow film-makers: 'Palayain natin ang cinema' (Let us free cinema) (*Habambuhay* 2020). In doing *pito-pito* movies, Diaz realized that he was shackled by conventions in mainstream film practice that constrained his work. Although his *pito-pito* films show glimpses of his future films, he knew that he could do something more. The original cut of *Serafin Geronimo* ran for about three hours. Naturally, he was forced by his producer to cut it down to a length that was acceptable to exhibitors.

Diaz, being at one end of indie film-making that is farthest from the mainstream, looks at film as his art form. There are no conventions, no limits; he gives in to impulse; the act of film creation is organic; there is such a thing as inspiration that can come from odd places. He relates an example: while having coffee in a neighbourhood convenience store, he overhears the exchange between two guys; there is a storm brewing in Nueva Ecija, in Central Luzon, and it is coming the next day. Diaz's film muse creates an image in his mind – a stormy night, a pregnant madwoman on a deserted street, a male artist who is getting out of his mind and the two meet. The image of King Lear comes to his mind. The encounter would form the ending of the film, and he would develop it backwards. Armed with this image and inspiration, Diaz calls two of his trusted actors (Perry Dizon and

Hazel Orencio) and prepares to go up north to face the coming storm and shoot the ending of *Siglo ng Pagluluwal* (*Century of Birthing*, 2011).[1] The example may seem incredible, but that is how Diaz describes his film-making, how far it has gone from his *pito-pito* days.

Since he is not tied to conventions, Diaz eventually developed his film language. *Batang West Side* (*West Side Avenue*, 2001), although its visualization is not radically different yet, has a running time of about five hours. In *Ebolusyon ng Isang Pamilyang Pilipino* (*Evolution of a Filipino Family*, 2004), Diaz has found the style that would characterize his later films – long takes, immobile camera, black-and-white photography – and the running time clocks in at eleven hours. Later, he would use well-known actors (which he had the luxury of doing in *Batang West Side* because of a new and willing producer). In *Norte, Hangganan ng Kasaysayan* (*Norte, the End of History*, 2013), Sid Lucero plays the role of a top-notch law student who gets involved in a crime he refuses to admit. The visual style is now well polished, and Diaz decided to shoot the film in colour when he saw the location in Ilocos Norte. In *Hele sa Hiwagang Hapis* (*A Lullaby to the Sorrowful Mystery*, 2016), two big stars, Piolo Pascual and John Lloyd Cruz, played the major roles based on the Philippine national hero's novel. In *Ang Babaeng Humayo* (*The Woman Who Left*, 2016), Charo Santos agreed to do the role of Horacia who is released from prison and is bent on seeking revenge; John Lloyd Cruz appears as Hollanda, a transvestite prostitute.

Diaz's films have been well received in various international film festivals. And he has reaped some awards not only for himself but for the country as well. His body of work is more than what any film-maker could accomplish in a lifetime. Gil Quito, in his biographical essay on the works of Lav Diaz, concludes:

> Diaz has built a body of work like no other in Philippine cinema, in magnitude and originality of vision. It has its fair share of misses and slip-ups, as is the wont of all human endeavor. But these are wraiths amid some of the most resonant and powerful epiphanies committed to film about his country's arduous struggles, the evil in man's heart, and the abyss of human suffering.
>
> (Quito 2019: 329)

The amazing thing is that Lav Diaz is not resting on his laurels; he continues to be busily engaged in film-making. Nothing can stop him. Not even a pandemic. Film-making is his art. And the pursuit of art is his life.

Lav Diaz is not alone in this pursuit. The fifth generation of Filipino film-makers is one with him in this endeavour. Certainly, they deserve more than a footnote in the history of Philippine cinema.

NOTE

1.   As shown in *Habambuhay* documentary series.

REFERENCE

Habambuhay: Remembering Philippine Cinema (2020), Clodualdo del Mundo Jr. (dir.), Philippines: TBA Studios.

Quito, Gil (2019), 'Lav Diaz: New directions in world cinema, a biographical survey', in C. del Mundo Jr. and S. O. Lua (eds), *Direk: Essays on Filipino Filmmakers*, Manila and Chicago: De La Salla University Publishing House and Sussex Academic Press, pp. 267–332.

2

Homeward Hill:
Messianic Redemption in Diaz
and Dostoyevsky

Tom Paulus

Le temps du monde fini commence.

(Paul Valéry 1931)

The Filipino struggle is similar to the Russian's.
(Teodoro, *Death in the Land of Encantos*, 2007)

A national cinema

In 'La Monnaie de l'absolu' (1998), Episode 3A of *Histoire(s) du cinéma*, Jean-Luc Godard defines what for him constitutes a 'national cinema': linking the concept to the overall argument of his main thesis – the history of cinema is inextricably linked to the Second World War and the Holocaust – he argues that the Italian cinema after the Liberation, in other words neorealism, is the only cinema worthy of the denomination because it resisted the occupation of cinema by the Americans (Rosen 2013: 199–202). Neorealism should not be seen in the traditional way as a direct result of the Resistance, Godard argues. Coming out of a long period of self-doubt, of readjustment to political chaos, economic and social upheaval, post-war Italian cinema embodied the profound need for a national image after a period of fascist dictatorship, German colonization and shifting political and military alliances: 'Italy was the country that fought least, that suffered greatly, but that twice changed sides – and therefore suffered from a loss of identity', the film-maker tells us in a typically choked voice-over. With *Roma, citta aperta* (1945) Italy refound itself as a nation. Focused almost exclusively, in *Histoire(s)*, on European (film) history and its relationship to the two great post-war powers, the Soviet Union and the United States, Godard does not extend his definition of a national cinema as medium of a unified imaginary to the emerging cinemas in the South, which after all were heavily influenced by neorealism and its rough, sketch-like aesthetics of total rediscovery and pressing actuality. More generally, the desire for a cinematic self-image to replace what Fanon (2008) described as an internalized colonial 'Other' has been a central point of attention in postcolonial film studies.

In the light of Godard's oversight, an instructive comparison can be drawn between the modern and contemporary cinemas of Taiwan and the Philippines: both archipelagos suffered long histories of imperialist occupation (both were occupied by Japan) and periods of dictatorship and martial law (Taiwan under the Kuomintang of Chiang Kai-shek, the Philippines under Marcos) and have an ambivalent relationship with the United States (the colonial occupier of the Philippines from the end of the Spanish-American War to the end of the Second World War), where many of their people have sought a better future. Both countries have well-developed film industries (that of the Philippines is the fourth largest in the world) that were at different points in their history geared towards either state-sponsored nationalist propaganda or genre entertainment, and both have produced a strong and heavily political art cinema concerned primarily with recounting untold or censored national history and preserving or restoring native languages and values.[1] Much of the 'New Wave' cinema of both countries can be seen to continue the ethics and aesthetics of neorealism. The 'writing' of unwritten history in the films of Lav Diaz, however, frequently operates according to the more modernist precept of mise en abyme, perhaps most influentially incarnated in *Hiroshima, mon amour* (1959) in which the questioning of historical security happens through the self-referential elaboration of (literary) fiction. Fredric Jameson has extensively studied the use of such modernist devices in Edward Yang's *Terrorizers* (1986) (1992: 114–58), but Diaz's preference for extended long takes and rural settings actually seems closer to Hou Hsiao-hsien.[2] The historical distance between the first (Brocka, de Leon, Bernal, the Hou of *The Boys from Fengkuei* [1983]) and second (Diaz, Martin, Mendoza, Tsai Ming-liang, the Hou of *Millennium Mambo* [2001], the Yang of *A Confucian Confusion* [1994]) New Waves of Taiwan and the Philippines could be framed in terms of modern versus postmodern, but Jameson usefully suggests that in 'Third World Cinema', 'in which neither modernist nor postmodern impulses are internally generated [...] both arrive in the field of production with a certain chronological simultaneity in full postwar modernization' (1992: 151). Our question still is: Can Taiwanese and Philippine art cinema lay claim to the title of 'national' cinema according to Godard's definition of neorealism? The answer is obviously no, since – with the exception of Hou's *A City of Sadness* (1989), the first film after the end of martial law to address the 'White Terror' of the Kuomintang – none of these 'New Wave' films were ever popular with local audiences the way *Roma, città aperta* was. Also, the comparison is ludicrous at the historiographical level, especially in the context of the Jamesonian narrative about increasing globalization, de-territorialization and the borderless free flow of capital.[3] With audiences around the (post)modern world attuned more than ever to Americanized popular entertainment and media and with conglomerates connected to the big television networks controlling movie production and distribution, the power of cinema, taken by Godard in an idealist mode as an art to equal that of Goethe, Balzac and Joyce, or Vélazquez, Goya and Van Gogh, reaching audience numbers undreamt of in the history of art is definitely on the wane. This is precisely Godard's point about cinema's decline under the onslaught of television, a medium incapable of 'projecting' or passing on cultural values. Tellingly, the first sign of decline was signalled by the dismissal, the 'martyrship', of utopian long-form projects by Godard's heroes, Griffith, Stroheim and Gance, those 'Cathedrals of Light' to which Diaz's films (the massive length of which precludes and consciously sabotages fast ticket lay-over) can be seen to belong.[4]

A striking aspect of Godard's account of neorealism is that he attributes a major part of its constitutive value, its role in passing on 'Italian-ness' ('La nostra lingua Italiana', as per the 1980s ballad by Ricardo Cocciante heard on the soundtrack accompanying silent images of neorealist classics), to what at first sight might seem a major technical deficiency: the lack of synchronous sound recording. In an unexpected spin on the Bazinian law of total transparency, Godard argues that the fact that the neorealist masterpieces of Rossellini, Visconti, De Santis and De Sica were recorded silent, while taking nothing away from their power to reflect historical reality, more immediately reveals their kinship with the identity-bestowing power of the classical arts. Pointedly concluding on an image of resurrection from Piero della Francesca's fifteenth-century *Legend of the True Cross*, an emblem of the Italian Renaissance, Episode 3A contends (in a way that approximates André Malraux's concept of 'metamorphosis' or transformation of forms, most elaborately explicated in his massive art history *Les Voix du silence* [1951], from which the episode derives its title) that, by remaining silent, the images speak not only the language of cinema but also the language of Ovid, Virgil, Dante and Leopardi. Godard's argument here is a take on Hegel's observation on Homer that (literary) language is closely related to the culture of a people and expressive of it. That language reflects the deeper spirit of a people is an idea Hegel in turn picked up from Herder, a proponent of *Sturm und Drang* nationalism. Godard's Romantic take on neorealism thus undoes the association of post-war Italy with the internationalism of communism (although at this point Stalin had already dissolved the Comintern) and clouds over the crucial distinction between 'national' and 'nationalism'.[5]

The soundtracks of Lav Diaz's films are completely recorded on location – mostly rain, wind, cicadas, barking dogs, crying roosters, occasionally interrupted by

22

dialogue and poetic monologue – and presented to us scratches and mistakes included. The question therefore becomes – if we want to continue playing our little game – to what extent Diaz's films, characterized by the ambition to tell the story of his people and seemingly gambling on the rhetorical power of the unadorned 'real', are able to reconnect with the culture-defining art of the past, to 'pass on' a tradition that, per the modernist credo, is in danger of being displaced by rampant commercialism? To emphasize once again: the comparison with Italian post-war cinema merely serves a rhetorical end – although only a unified state since 1871, 'Italy' has been synonymous with art and poetry from the time of the Roman Republic, essentially adhering to one Italian language and, since the introduction of Christianity, one religion. The Philippines, on the other hand (like Taiwan), has a folk art tradition that belongs to a Malay or pan-Asian heritage, with a decidedly minor role attributed to artistic painting (imported by the Spaniards in the sixteenth century and mainly serving the spread of Catholicism) or (written) literature. Where the language of Dante became the vernacular lingua franca of the Renaissance, Filipino (or Tagalog) only became a literary language near the end of the Spanish occupation, with the popularity of the epic poem *Florante at Laura* (1838) by Francisco Baltazar (known as Balagtas) and the historical impact of the socialist realist novel *Banaag at Sikat* (*From Early Dawn to Full Light*, 1906) by Lope K. Santos. Moreover, because of centuries-long colonization and a wide variety of indigenous populations of different ethnic backgrounds, Filipino language and culture never congealed into Godard's timeless classicism. This means that the only 'tradition' the (new) Filipino art cinema can pass on is either that of pre-Christian Malay culture or that of modernity itself.[6]

If Filipino modernism can be seen to start with the literary realism of the 'Veronicans' group around H. R. Ocampo or, in painting, with Victorio Edades,[7] modern Philippine literature is usually taken to begin with *Noli Me Tangere* (1887), the great anti-Spanish, anti-Catholic book (written in Spanish) by José Rizal – one of many reformers or '*Ilustrados*' who studied at European universities – that put the match to the powder keg of revolutionary unrest, inspiring the Revolution of 1896–97. Diaz's recent historical epic *A Lullaby to the Sorrowful Mystery* (2016) begins with the execution of Rizal by the Spanish colonial military on 30 December 1896 and features characters drawn from Rizal's political novel *El filibusterismo* (1891). *Lullaby* is as close as Diaz has come to emulating previous adaptations of Rizal by key figures of Philippine cinema: 'National artist for the cinema' Gérardo De Léon adapted *Noli Me Tangere* in 1951, while Eddie Romero, one of the central figures of the political cinema of the late 1970s, adapted the same book as a thirteen-part television series. While Noel Vera has frequently suggested the influence of Rizal's seemingly formless immediacy and political urgency on Diaz – especially in early films such as *Hesus Rebolusyunaryo* (2002) and *Evolution of a Filipino Family* (2004) (Vera 2005) – the question I want to raise, after this long and needlessly essentialist introduction, and still in view of Godard's definition, is why the cinema of Lav Diaz, so focused on Filipino history, breathes the air of the nineteenth-century Russian novel more than that of Rizal? If the epic is going to be your chosen form, why do the Russian epics feel more present in Diaz's cinema than the great Philippine nationalist epic?[8]

Raskolnikov from far-off

Anyone in the least bit familiar with Diaz or his work will have heard of the shaping influence of his parents, his father especially, cultural missionaries and pedagogical idealists in the impoverished and pre-modern area of Maguindanao Province where he grew up. They will also have heard about the moral perspective that the film-maker places highest in his conception of art, whether cinematic or literary, and that it was through being introduced to the great Russians Dostoyevsky and Tolstoy that this moral vision took shape.[9] But is there more to the Russian influence on Diaz's aesthetics, I want to ask, than this anecdotal evidence suggests? More also than Georg Lukács's universalist claim, in his 1949 essay on Dostoyevsky, that 'Raskolnikov came from far-off, unknown, almost legendary Russia to speak for the whole civilized West'? According to Lukács, Dostoyevsky's characters 'stated – imaginatively – all the problems of human culture at its highest point, stirred up ultimate depths, and presented a totality hitherto never achieved and never since surpassed, embracing the spiritual, moral, and philosophical questions of that age' (1962: 146). Is there more also to Dostoyevsky's influence in particular than the proto-existentialist trope of what Lukács calls 'the experiment with oneself' of lonely, God-forsaken men who transgress against conventional morality, which migrated via Sartre's *La Nausée* (1938) and Bresson's *Pickpocket* (1959) to Paul Schrader's script for *Taxi Driver* (1976)? Most of Diaz's characters are the kind of 'monads' Jameson sees peopling the modern/postmodern Taiwan of *Terrorizers*, lonely men and women, either by choice, like Heremias in *Heremias* (*Book One: The Legend of the Lizard Princess*) (2006), or necessity, like Fabian in *Norte, the End of History* (2013), at once tragic and ridiculous. But the question is whether these characters should be read psychologically or sociologically or as sides in a philosophical and theological argument, as in Dostoyevsky. In exploring such questions, I will treat Diaz's films as the creations of a novelist, a poet or a philosopher which, like Godard, he is (and will remain therefore, to my regret, relatively inattentive to the formal particulars of his cinema).

In *Death in the Land of Encantos* (2007), Benjamin (or 'Hamin') Agusan is a poet who lived in Russia, in Kaluga, for seven years on a grant and teaching residency, before returning to the Philippines in the wake of the devastation wrought by Super Typhoon Durian (or 'Reming', as it was locally called). His extended stay in Russia is one of the reason he likes to quote Dostoyevsky. The other is that, like Dostoyevsky, a convict as a young man in a Siberian prison camp, he was a political prisoner who suffered severe trauma at the hands of his Filipino captors. Kaluga, as Nadin Mai points out, used to be a place for exiled politicians and other political prisoners during the period of the Russian Empire (2015: 172). The parallel between the Filipino and the Russian does not end there. 'Russians', Hamin tells his friend Teodoro, 'are a strange race – they're Europeans, and not Europeans'. From the moment Peter the Great decided to institute a bureaucratic oligarchy to govern his country, promising Russian students were sent abroad to study, mostly to France or Germany (after the Revolution of 1789, mostly the latter). The immediate result was that the new Russian intelligentsia imported not only Revolutionary ideas but, after the Revolution of 1848 and the instalment of the Second Republic, a mood of disillusionment with Enlightenment reformist ideals. This led to the first-wave anarchism of Bakunin and Nechaeyev and a political mood of violence and paranoia highly recognizable to Filipino intellectuals like Benjamin. The similarities between cultures that until the mid-1800s were still looking for a national identity, forever torn between East and West, are arguably what first drew Diaz, who emigrated to the United States as a young man and still mainly lives there, to the great Russian novelists. Many of his characters are 'returning' like Benjamin in *Encantos*, or like prominent characters in Filipino literature from Rizal to Juan C. Laya's *His Native Soil* (1940).

There is also the feudal system described and critiqued by the Russians which Diaz may have recognized as close that of the Philippines. Dostoyevsky's novels were written against the background of what his biographer Joseph Frank (1988) has termed 'The Stir of Liberation', the liberation in question being that of the serfs, unfree peasants who, until the abolishment of serfdom by Alexander II in 1861, could be sold together with the land to which they were 'attached'. The Tsar's 'Emancipation Edict' led to the freeing of twenty million serfs, but also to crippling 'redemption' payments on the parts of the farmers, to a rightful clamour for full citizen rights, to mass migration to the cities and increased literacy and embrace of secular values, consequences that would stoke the revolutionary fires (a first assassination attempt on the Tsar occurred a few years later) and ultimately produce a return to reactionary politics. The young Dostoyevsky, like Tolstoy, was fiercely opposed to serfdom and belonged to the group of Mikhail Petrashevsky, a utopian socialist inspired by Fourier and Proudhon and an early reader of Hegel and Marx. It was his membership in the Petrashevsky circle, which was seen as conspiring to overthrow the regime, that got the author facing a firing squad, the death sentence being commuted at the very last minute to four years of hard labour in a Siberian prison camp.

Feudalism, a system inherited from the Spanish occupier, is still in place in the Philippines today, where only a minority of farmers own their land and most work in semi-serfdom for a landlord. These are the characters you see lumbering around Diaz's films that are mostly set in the agricultural parts of the Philippines, like the Bicol region of Luzon (home to Communist guerillas). In *A Lullaby to the Sorrowful Mystery*, the viewer is explicitly invited to discover uninterrupted historical continuity between the feudalism of yesterday and today. Related forms of exploitation can be seen in a film like *Heremias (Book One: The Legend of the Lizard Princess)*: travelling peasants making their painfully slow way through the mountainous province of Rizal, their covered wagons piled high with bits of handicrafts which they sell to the moneyed classes for remarkably low prices. Diaz has also likened his own stint in the Filipino film industry, making exploitation films for the Regal studio, to a kind of feudalist subjection. So is Lav Diaz a revolutionary, a '*rebolusyonaryo*', as the critic Michael Guarneri (2014) suggests? He certainly is, but what kind? What kind was Dostoyevsky, whose deeply felt hate of serfdom only briefly led him to embrace revolutionary politics and did not prevent him from becoming a staunch nationalist and royalist? Diaz has never embraced communism (his father was a socialist, but converted to Catholicism), which, given that in the Philippines the Communist Party and its armed wing, The New People's Army, is still considered a terrorist organization, is not very surprising.[10] But it is striking that only one film, *Melancholia* (2008), explicitly identifies its activist characters as (former) communists: in the haunting third part of the film we witness communist guerilla fighter Renato Munoz and assorted rebels before they are decimated by government soldiers.[11] In the other films, the political prisoners or figures of resistance are most often poets, novelists, rock musicians or film-makers. In *Encantos*, it is a poet who was deemed too dangerous for Philippine society (Diaz does not spare us the details of Benjamin's torture: his hand was crushed, his penis electrocuted, he was sexually abused and he had acid injected into his brain). In *From What Is Before* (2014), communist guerillas[12] are seen only as nameless dead on the road or as shady figures trying to recruit villagers. We are a long way from the heroic resistance fighters of Rossellini's *Roma, città aperta*.

What finally alienated Dostoyevsky from the revolutionaries was their atheism. *Demons* (also known as *The Devils* or *The Possessed*) (1871–72), the novel from which *From What Is Before* took the part of its plot about a far-flung village in the grips of unexplained anomalies,[13] is a scathing indictment of both the revolutionary idealism of the 1840s, with the pathetic Stepan Trofimovich Verkhovensky, a satirical portrait of Alexander Herzen (known as the 'Father of Russian Socialism') and, especially, the anarcho-communism of the so-called nihilist movement. One of the nihilists, Pyotr Verkhovensky, who murders his former comrade Ivan Pavlovich Shatov, is a clear stand-in for Sergey Nechayev, the St Petersburg radical and author of the *Catechism of a Revolutionary* (1869). The most fascinating figures in the novel, however, are the Byronic anti-hero Nikolai Vsevolodich Stavrogin (based on

Petrashevsky cell member Nikolay Alexandrovich Speshnev, influenced by Marx and Max Stirner), the charismatic but self-destructive kingpin of a small revolutionary cell, and Alexei Nilych Kirillov, the engineer under the influence of Bakunin who believes that suicide is the most radical embodiment of free will. These are almost archetypal Dostoyevsky characters, especially if we consider them in the light of Nietzschean or Kierkegaardian existentialism, still the dominant context of the Russian's reception in the West. When we read Stavrogin's confession of having raped and driven to suicide an 11-year-old girl, as told in a chapter that was excised from the original edition of the novel, we are immediately reminded of the desperate '*acte gratuit*' of his author's most famous character, Rodion Raskolnikov from *Crime and Punishment* (1866). Raskolnikov haphazardly kills a pawnbroker to feel that, like his hero Napoleon, he is beyond the pale of the law, not just judicial law but the dictates of conventional morality. It is from these characters that Diaz fashioned Fabian, the unforgettable Satanic anti-hero of *Norte, the End of History*. The great power of Dostoyevsky's art derives from making us feel even for the murderers and child rapists, who act for the sake of immorality, making us accept that even they deserve forgiveness. But Fabian is not just Raskolnikov and Stavrogin, he is also Ferdinand Marcos (the film was shot in the Llocos Norte province where Marcos grew up), who also committed murder as a young man.[14] In the film, Fabian is heard praising the real Marcos's strong will and relentless fight against the communists. Are we supposed to feel sympathy for this character? The film would not have the emotional impact it exerts if we did not feel for the fascist Fabian. But is it Diaz's political message that even Marcos deserves redemption? On Dostoyevsky's pity for the condemned, Georg Lukács gives us one possible perspective, arguing that his characters are 'the most violent protest that could have been made against the organization of life in that time' (1962: 156). What Lukács means is that they are victims of a political and economic system. Marcos a victim?

Another way into this moral conundrum is to see these characters as dialectical foils, Raskolnikov to Svidrigaïlov and Razumikhin, Stavrogin and Kirilov to Shatov, who is the true mouthpiece for Dostoyevsky's politics at the time of *Demons*. Shatov has rejected his former revolutionary beliefs, trading them in for a combination of Eastern Orthodoxy and Slavophile nationalist fervour. He believes that the Second Coming will take place in Russia, an esoteric, millennial attitude that was increasingly that of his author and other figures of the Petrashevsky circle (like the nationalist historian Danilevski, author of *Russia and Europe*) who saw a unified Slavic world as the Messianic answer to the Spenglerian picture of declining nations.[15] In Diaz, the association between Christianity and idealist Hegel-inspired nationalism is almost completely absent: the suffering of the Filipino people, as allegorized in his films, largely exceeds the problems of nationhood and becomes a purely moral problem. But there is in Diaz, as in Dostoyevsky, a strong influence of Christian ideas of salvation and redemption that want to make us believe that the suffering of a Stavrogin, a Raskolnikov, a Fabian serves a higher cause than nihilistic self-punishment.

Radical freedom

Dostoyevsky's existentialist anti-hero, threatened by despair and nihilism, is 'banging at closed doors [...] in an embittered, futile struggle for the meaning of life which is lost or in danger of being lost' (1962: 156). Bitter destitution, (mental) illness and the memory or fear of incarceration ran through Dostoyevsky's life as much as through his fiction. Bitterness and anger produced the 'Underground Man' in *Notes from the Underground* (1864), who tries to elevate sickness and despair into a condition of normalcy and even voluptuous enjoyment, a sorrowful pleasure, like 'melancholia':

> And why are you so soundly, so solemnly convinced that only the normal and the positive – in brief, convinced that prosperity alone is advantageous to man? Can't reason make mistakes about advantages? Perhaps prosperity isn't the only thing that man loves? Perhaps he likes suffering just as much? Perhaps suffering is just as advantageous to him as prosperity? Sometimes man loves suffering intensely, passionately – and that's a fact.
> (Dostoyevsky 2009: 31)

Stavrogin also offers endless suffering as its own masochistic rationale, the final attempt by the subject to affirm his particularity (Kristeva 1987: 15). But like the 'Underground Man' he also lashes out at others – he rapes and murders the innocent, whereas the 'Underground Man' 'merely' takes away their dignity (the young prostitute Liza, who seemed to offer him salvation) as a defence against their own despair. These random and abject acts of cruelty can be given political value in a post-Nietzschean context: Walter Benjamin, for instance, has described Stavrogin as a Surrealist *avant la lettre*:

> No one else understood, as he did, how naïve is the view of the Philistines that goodness [...] is God- inspired; whereas evil stems entirely from our spontaneity, and in it we are independent and self-sufficient beings. No one else saw inspiration, as he did, in even the most ignoble actions, and precisely in them [...] Dostoyevsky's God created not only heaven and earth and man and beast, but also baseness, vengeance, cruelty.
> (1999: 214)

This Nietzschian-Bakunian perspective, however, is completely alien to Dostoyevsky. In *Demons* and elsewhere he shows that the despair that threatens to harm the self and others results from nihilism, which in turn is the result of a crisis of faith. The profound crisis of faith that Dostoyevsky detected in the (political) culture of his time is evoked in his work by Holbein's painting, *The Body of the Dead Christ in the Tomb* (1520–22), which the author saw in Basel and which ended up in the novel he wrote after that European sojourn: it hangs in Rogozhin's house in *The Idiot* (1868–69) and is described by the consumptive Ippolit. The sight of Christ's mortal, grotesquely emaciated body taken down from the cross ('In the painting, the face has been horribly lacerated by blows, swollen, with terrible, swollen and bloody bruises, the eyes open, the pupils narrow; the large, open whites of the eyes gleam with a deathly, glassy sheen') makes Ippolit conclude that such a picture might make people lose their faith (Dostoyevsky 2004: 475–76). In her essay 'On the Melancholic Imaginary', Julia Kristeva reasons that melancholy is especially amenable the Orthodox Christianity or Protestantism and is affirmed in religious doubt ('There is nothing sadder than a dead God') (1987: 5). She cites Dostoyevsky's response to the dead Christ in Holbein's painting as opposed to the 'truth of the resurrection'. Holbein has painted a human and not a mythical Christ, whose suffering must be given a different status from the traditional Pauline notion that Christ's dying on the cross can be given immediate saving significance as atonement for our sins. The suffering of Holbein's Christ appears unredeemed.

The theological problem behind the anarchist-nihilist onslaught on the Christian faith is precisely that of man's freedom and free will: Christ did not come down from the cross because he did not wish to convert through authority or power but through freedom of belief. Revolutionary anarchists like Bakunin reasoned that if God exists, then man is a slave; if man is free, God does not exist. Kirillov's reasoning that if God does not exist, everything is permitted ('I am free, therefore I am God') is a similar attempt to install human liberty as the Absolute. But Kirillov's reasoning is confused: his enactment of freedom and denial is one of self-destruction. Stavrogin also ends up committing suicide, like Fabian or Julian in *Melancholia* (who, like Kirillov, has tried to raise himself to the status of God), but their actions are less confirmations of human freedom than Sadean, blasphemous attempts to force God's hand. By their acts they do no more than confirm the thinking of the 'Grand Inquisitor' of Ivan Karamazov's poem who proposes that humanity cannot handle free will, implying that Christ, in giving humans freedom to choose, has excluded the majority of humanity from redemption and doomed it to suffer. The Inquisitor will devote his life to keeping choice away from humanity.

Ivan Karamazov, a much more worthy opponent for the saintly Alyosha than Shatov was for Stavrogin (to reverse their respective functions), raises a related theological problem in the infamous 'Mutiny' chapter of *The Brothers Karamazov* (1879–80), in which he offers a collection of 'anecdotes' about evil at work (Dostoyevsky 2003: 309–22). The problem is that of theodicy: if there is evil in the world, as Lav Diaz's characters constantly affirm, how then can there be a God? 'Where do you think is God, now that our region is in terrible crisis?' Catalina asks in a Karamazovian register in *Death in the Land of Encantos*. Hamin responds, 'Sometimes it's really hard to understand God's justice.' Unjust suffering is the lot not only of children in Diaz's films (dead children mostly off-screen, as in *Encantos*, or aborted, as in *Century of Birthing*), or of self-chastising 'mutineers' (as Alyosha calls those who, like his brother, question their faith and want to 'return their ticket' [2003: 320]), but of an entire people. Benjamin Agusan in *Encantos* perhaps best embodies this hypostasis of suffering: already a victim of torture and imprisonment and having recently lost a child, he returns to his devastated homeland not only to mourn his beloved, who lies buried under the wreckage, but to confront his guilt over never having visited his mother who was in a mental institution, for his sister committing suicide and for his father dying of loneliness. Suffering is often embodied by characters who remind us of the plight of Job, foremost among them Heremias, clamouring for justice from God, because, as Job says, 'The wicked have taken advantage of the needy and the helpless, who remain in significant hardship, but God does nothing to punish them.' The suffering of these characters, however, does not produce a rebellion or a renunciation, an Apostasis, but a suffering *for* God ('I also want to suffer' is Alyosha's response to Ivan's question if his speech is not overly troubling him [2003: 316]).

Just as Shatov is the true protagonist of *Demons*, the real hero of *Norte* is Joaquin, the character who is imprisoned for the murder committed by Fabian. As Noel Vera (2013) has usefully pointed out, Joaquin can be seen as the film's equivalent of Nikolai Dementiev, a minor character in *Crime and Punishment*, a house painter who is working in the apartment building where Raskolnikov murders Alyona Ivanovna and the handicapped Lizaveta Ivanovna and is falsely accused of the crime. Like Joaquin, Dementiev accepts his plight and believes that he suffers for God. But Joaquin is also Ivan Dmitrich Aksionov in Tolstoy's short story 'God Sees the Truth, but Waits' (1872), an Hitchcockian innocent sent away for a murder he did not commit who also inspired the character of Horacia in *The Woman Who Left* (2016). In prison Aksionov dedicates his life to God, and when he meets the actual murderer, he forgives him. In Tolstoy's later novella *The Forged Coupon*, published posthumously in 1911 (the basis for Bresson's 1983 *L'Argent*), the selfless Maria Semenovna with her dying breath forgives even her murderer Stepan (like Aksionov he confesses his sins and begins to preach the faith in prison). All these characters in Tolstoy are, in fact, Dostoyevskian, based, like the storylines themselves, on *The House of the Dead* (1860–62), Dostoyevsky's semi-autobiographical account of his confinement among peasant criminals in the Siberian prison camp, which was Tolstoy's favourite among his eternal competitor's works. As Joseph Frank offers, the crux of that early work is that even amongst the most lowly thieves and murderers, human nature is not incurably corrupt and the possibility of redemption exists even for the most horrendous crimes. Love in man resembles the love of Christ (on a modest scale, this can be seen in the travelling peasants collecting money to help Heremias after he has lost his cow and cart). This is the exact opposite of Ivan Karamazov's conviction that 'the love of Christ is a miracle impossible upon earth' ('And above all, I do not want the mother to embrace the torturer who tore her son to pieces with his dogs! Let her not dare to forgive him!' [Dostoyevsky 2003: 320]). Lav Diaz seems to be on the side of Alyosha, Aksionov and Maria Seminovna:

> I like this story ('God Sees the Truth, But Waits')[16] because it dialectically questions existence in a different way: we need to suffer in order to see the light. It's very human: forgiveness comes with suffering. We still have to forgive people in spite of everything, and we need to do that now.
>
> (Anon. 2016)

The most naturally self-sacrificial, compassionate and forgiving amongst all Dostoyevsky's characters is Prince Myshkin in *The Idiot* (1868–69), with whose characterization the author struggled longest. Myshkin was originally named 'Yurodivi', which literally translates as 'holy fool'.[17] 'Holy fool' was the name for a wandering pilgrim, an innocent who had ascetically renounced all worldly possessions and dedicated his life to Christ. He is often perceived as a simpleton or a mere beggar, who, when he is not silent, utters the truth concealed by normal social relations or social hypocrisy (think the Franciscan monks in Rossellini's *The Flowers of St. Francis* [1950]). In Dostoyevsky this figure was identified with Christ himself – 'a perfectly beautiful man' – and endowed with Messianic qualities. The holy fool also figures quite prominently in the Dostoyevskian work of Andrei Tarkovsky, from Durochka in *Andrei Rublev* (1969) to the Stalker and the characters played by Erland Josephson in *Nostalghia* (1983) and *The Sacrifice* (1986). In Diaz's work the most important incarnation of the type is Heremias, whose name recalls the prophet Jeremiah, author of the Old Testament 'Lamentations', who, like Diaz's character, had a hard time making people listen to him. Heremias is seen struggling in a typhoon to outfit his cow with a makeshift raincoat, a feat to behold in whipping wind and torrential downpour, an incredibly moving gesture of kindness (reminiscent of Myshkin's empathy for the donkey in *The Idiot*) that is so much more than the attempt of a farmer to protect his source of income. Heremias ends up in a web of (moral) corruption trying to do the right thing, like Myshkin in the St Petersburg of Rogozhin, General Epachin and the aristocrat Totsky, trying to save Helena just like Myshkin tried to save Nastasya Filippovna (when they fail, both Myshkin and Heremias go insane). Many examples of the holy fool in Dostoyevsky are young women, including the mentally unstable Marya

Lebyadkina in *Demons* and Sonya in *Crime and Punishment*, and it is fair to say that Diaz's Florentina Hubaldo is their offspring.

Realism and allegory

The title of Dostoyevsky's most-read work, *Crime and Punishment*, is misleading in that it seems to offer a worldly, 'legal' solution to spiritual problems, while for its author 'justice' was always secondary to divine Grace and its earthly manifestation in acts of limitless compassion and forgiveness. Despite the novel's procedural or detective-novel aspects, Dostoyevsky is simply not interested in the realist detail of the workings of the law, which made it easy enough for Diaz to excise the character of the investigator Porfiri Petrovich without making *Norte* any less faithful an adaptation of Dostoyevsky's novel. My point here is that, just as Dostoyevsky should not be studied as a realist but as a 'deep realist', Diaz's cinema differs completely from the highly admired Lino Brocka's 'socialist realism', his naturalist interest in poverty-stricken locations and the struggle of the underclass. Michael Sicinski has argued that the style of what he calls Diaz's middle period (starting with the so-called trauma trilogy of *Death in the Land of Encantos, Melancholia* and *Florentina Hubaldo, CTE* [2012] and ending with *From What Is Before*) examines Filipino social and political history 'from a worm's-eye view, employing what we could think of as a cinematic version of anthropologist Clifford Geertz's morphological "thick description"' (Sicinski 2017: 67). I do not agree: setting and characterization in Diaz is almost always theatrical, as it is in Dostoyevsky, the stage for metaphysical as much as political struggle, an ideal environment sanctioned by religious and mythic beliefs.

   It is interesting, in light of this argument, to trace the literary genealogy of the allegorical scenes in *Florentina Hubaldo, CTE* of a young, beautiful woman, shackled to a rickety bed by her perpetually drunk, exploitative father and continuously raped by men as her grandfather is forced to watch.[18] The immediate association seems to be with the lurid detail of Zola's *L'Assommoir* (1877), in which 'Little Lalie', the oldest daughter of Gervaise Macquart's next-door neighbour Bijard, tries to keep their hovel clean and watch over the two younger children while her father goes out drinking. Just like Florentina, Lalie lost her mother at an early age and now receives her father's beatings in her stead. Several times Gervaise had found Lalie tied to the foot of the bedstead ('An idea that had entered her father's brain, no one knew why, a whim of his disordered brain, disordered by liquor, which probably arose from his wish to tyrannize over the child, even when he was no longer there' (Zola 2009: 330), where she eventually perishes. When Dostoyevsky conceived of *Crime and Punishment* in the summer of 1865, he had been working on another project, 'The Drunkards', which was to deal with 'the present question of drunkenness [...] [in] all its ramifications, especially the picture of a family and the bringing up of children in these circumstances'.[19] What remains of that project in the novel is the character of Semyon Zakharovich Marmeladov, the hopeless drunk who confesses to Raskolnikov how his alcoholism led to the destitution of his wife and children and ultimately to his daughter Sonya being forced into prostitution (a situation highly recognizable to Filipino farmers struggling to survive). Dostoyevsky's treatment of alcoholism, however, was less informed by sociological fact than by Dickens and by the melodramatic repertoire. Specifically, he was influenced by Eugène Sue's serial melodrama *Les Mystères de Paris* (1842–43), intended to crusade on such issues as public health, prostitution, overcrowding and slum housing, in which an episode recounts the misfortunes of the struggling jeweller Morel who goes mad when he discovers that his daughter prostituted herself to bring food to her family. Sue's melodrama, specifically the characterization of the long-suffering heroine Fleur de Marie, also influenced the creation of Victor Hugo's Fantine and her abject treatment by the Thénardiers in *Les Misérables* (1862), a book that directly inspired *Florentina Hubaldo, CTE*.[20] In Hugo and Sue, the beleaguered women are saved by the philanthropy of the wealthy heroes, Count Rodolphe and Jean Valjean. In *Crime and Punishment* it is the destitute Raskolnikov who gives his last roubles to Marmeladov's consumptive widow, a deed of kindness that begins his redemption. At the point that Raskolnikov falls in love with Marmeladov's daughter, Sonya, who is sustained by her faith in God and reads him the story of Lazarus from the Bible, the story turns from melodrama into a tale of moral regeneration.

Where Sue's, Hugo's and Zola's variations on the slum story are morality tales about the need for rationalist, liberal social reform (the ideal of Herzen that Walter Benjamin referred to as the 'sclerotic liberal-moral-humanistic ideal of freedom' [1999: 215]), Dostoyevsky's novel is about freedom through belief in the possibility of redemption.[21] Like *Crime and Punishment*, *Florentina Hubaldo, CTE* is allegorical rather than naturalistic or realistic: her violation is that of her nation, her loss of dignity is that of her people under colonialism. The striking tableau shots of Florentina and her family in the river, grouped as a pietà, as in the scene with Hamin's mother in *Death in the Land of Encantos*, lift the films to which they belong to the realm of allegory.[22] Unlike in *Crime and Punishment*, however, there is no redemption at the end, suggesting that the cycle of violence will continue: at the end of *Florentina Hubaldo*, the title character speaks straight to the camera: 'My head hurts. My head never stops hurting. It never stops.' In an interview with Michael Guarneri (2017), Diaz talked about the bleak ending to *The Woman Who Left*, which like Bresson's version, failed to match the optimistic ending of Tolstoy's *The Forged Coupon*:

The film ends with Horacia walking in circles, looking for her missing son, just like Gregoria de Jesús had been walking in circles in the forest of *Lullaby*, searching for the corpse of her *desaparecido* husband Andrés Bonifacio [...] It's the vicious circle, this circular, cyclic perspective suggesting that it will happen again and again. If we really want the happy ending, we need to destroy the system – this system based on corruption and oppression.

Here is Diaz '*rebolusyonaryo*' again. But what can be done when the system has proven so resilient, when electoral democracy is still threatened by military coups, various secessionist movements or a general lack of democratic culture?[23] When the question was raised in another interview, the director did not point to the constitutional reforms instigated by more enlightened Philippine governments, such as that of Corazon Aquino. He simply replied, 'I don't know' (Mai 2016: n.pag.). The cyclical nature of the violence in Diaz is not just an effect of trauma (as Nadin Mai and others have argued) but adheres to the Hegelian conception of the end of history, as pronounced by *Norte*. Hegel's notion, that the end of history occurs when thought and action have exhausted their possibilities and all that remains is repetition, explains why Diaz's two science-fiction narratives, *Hesus, Rebolusyonaryo* (2002) (set in 2011) and *The Day Before the End* (2016) (set in 2050), show a reality in which nothing has changed: militias terrorize and tropical storms rage. Hegel's idea of finality has been hitched to the conservative ideology of a Fukuyama, who sees in the triumph and universalization of Western democracy an end point of mankind's ideological evolution (a position which indeed accords with Hegel's idealization of the Prussian nation state but which he has recently had to re-evaluate). According to the Hegelian logic, suffering has a positive aspect of being a necessary step to absolute freedom. Dostoyevsky – a close reader of Hegel – and Diaz believe as little in such logical resolution of history as in the possibility of democratic social reform. As Marx has shown, Hegelian history was written by the victors and has left the victims behind. In his *Critique of Hegel's* Philosophy of Right (1843–44), Marx concluded that the German proletariat would never free itself from its exploitation and suffering without emancipating the whole of society. It could 'redeem itself only through the *total* redemption of humanity' (cited in Löwy 2017: 88). This is where the Messianic aspect of Marx's thinking shines through.

Messianism and redemption

If we look further than their stereotypical characterization as a historical materialist opposed to any kind of religious thinking and an Orthodox Christian mystic alienated from the libertarianism of his youth, we can see how Marx and Dostoyevsky, who were exact contemporaries and wrote their most important works in roughly the same period, both established true affinities between material want and religious faith (Marx's famous quote: 'Religious distress is at the same time the expression of real distress and the protest against real distress. Religion is the sigh of the oppressed creature, the heart of a heartless world, just as it is the spirit of an unspiritual situation' [1982: 7]). The difference is, of course, that where Marx believed in a secular redemption (in the sense of freedom from captivity), reform and the perfectability of man, Dostoyevsky was convinced of man's fallen nature (as Father Zosima's dying brother, Marke, said: 'Each one is guilty before everyone, for everyone and everything' [2003: 374]) and only believed in transcendental redemptive judgement. If Dostoyevsky believes that only Christ can establish a just state, for Marx, the Messiah was the proletariat itself. However, Like Engels in *The Peasant War in Germany* (1950), Marx saw a close parallel between the class struggle of revolutionary socialism and early Christian movements, like those of Thomas Münzer and the Anabaptists, or John Žižka and the Taborites. Dostoyevsky, for his part, was highly inspired by the religious aspects of French utopian socialists like Saint-Simon, Fourier and Cabet or even the irrationalism of Proudhon.

Throughout his work, the Marxist historian Michael Löwy (2001) has tried to establish a genealogical rapprochement between Marxism and what he calls 'Liberation theology', between secular revolutionary thinkers like Marx, Rosa Luxemburg, André Breton or Guy Debord and Christian utopian thinkers or movements. His point of departure is frequently Benjamin's 'Theses on the Philosophy of History' (1940), a seemingly unrealizable attempt to dialectically reconcile historical materialism and Jewish Messianism. Messianism was introduced into Benjamin's thinking by his close friend, the theologian Gershom Scholem, who famously said that in post-war Europe only three grand political options are left: Bolshevism, anarchy and theocracy (see Jacobson 2003: 194). Löwy traces the dialogue between Benjamin and Scholem back to the influence of Messianic thinkers like Franz Rosenzweig and Martin Buber, who all shared the 'end-times' vision of history that questioned the idea of gradual evolution, progress and improvement, and proposed in its stead a redemptive break, a sudden and immense transformation, in other words a revolution, at which point the 'fullness of eternity can be received and a world of peace and harmony will be installed' (Benjamin called it '*Jetztzeit*') (cited in Löwy 2017: 58). We should be careful not to confuse such a conception of revolutionary Messianism with the apocalypticism and millenarianism of doomsday cults, like that of Father Tiburcio's in *Century of Birthing*, who promises spiritual emancipation in time for the end, or that of the Colorum in *A Lullaby to the Sorrowful Mystery*, who want to 'tune out' the Revolution while awaiting the return of their saviour, the mythical folk hero Bernard Carpio, 'the bringer of earthquakes'. For Rosenzweig, Buber, Scholem and Benjamin, the 'Messiah' could not come at a particular point in history but only at the *end of history*: Messianic transformation is at the same time propelled by historic forces (part of the dialectic) and 'outside of history', a unique temporal configuration that is the 'time of the end' (*Et Ketz*), a situation 'so new, so radical as to require a complete reorientation of our consciousness and of the linear metaphors around which we organize our sense of time' (Benjamin called it a 'tiger's leap into the future') (Steiner 1986: 380). End time refuses the continuity or historicism of what Benjamin describes in the 'Theses' as the 'piling of wreckage upon wreckage' (399), a time 'out of joint' that awaits an Absolute world of unity (Levinas 1979: 22).[24] Messianic libertarianism offers a redemptive way out of the dialectical halves of the argument presented in *The Brothers Karamazov* incarnated by Alyosha and Ivan: Ivan wants retribution – 'otherwise I shall destroy myself' – and 'not at some place and time in infinity, but here upon earth, and in such a way that I see it for myself' (Dostoyevsky 2003: 318), while Alyosha believes in transcendental redemptive judgement. George Steiner summarizes the basic opposition in the novel:

> If this Kingdom of God exists beyond mortality, if we believe that there is a redemptive judgment, then we may accept the persistence of evil in this world [...] In this light, evil itself becomes a necessary adjunct of human freedom. But if there is no 'other life' [...] then we must do everything in our power to purge the world of its failings and build Jerusalem of earthly bricks. To accomplish this, we may have to overthrow existing society. Cruelty, intolerance, fanatical rigour then become temporary virtues in the service of the revolutionary ideal.
>
> (1959: 257)

In both cases, the Messianism of Buber and Rosenzweig argues, man is free to act: the order of the profane assists, *prepares* the world for the coming of the Messianic Kingdom.

In Catholic eschatology, before the Last Days, the resurrection of the dead and the beginning of the eternal, universalist kingdom of God, there is the apocalypse. Christ's Second Coming is preceded by a gradual deterioration of human society and the expansion of evil. It is on this millenarist, baroque-allegorical stage (Hell on earth) that Diaz's stories take place. His is an apocalyptic time of cyclical, repetitive manifestations of traumatizing violence and corruption, a time that is given visceral impact by scenes that are stretched beyond endurance, like the 50-minute long take of Heremias, in *Heremias (Book One)*, watching a group of teenagers spitting obscenities, planning the murder of a young girl and listening to eardrum-shattering Filipino death metal (the passage to silence at the end of the silence, to the soothing sounds of wind, leafs, rain, to which the film has accustomed us, almost feels like a liberation in itself) or the similar noise rock dream scene in *Melancholia*. In the Abrahamic tradition the apocalypse concerns the coming of the Messiah but also that of the Anti-Christ, the false Messiah and false prophet; in Diaz's version of the *eschaton* it is pretty clear who this figure is. His 'end of history', in *Norte*, is set in the birth year and region of Marcos. In *From What Is Before*, the apocalyptic undoing of the barrio – the 'fall' of Father Guido, the exploitation of the Joselina (the film's Marya Lebyadkina), the despondency of Hakob and the general feeling of being abandoned by God – coincides with the arrival of Marcos's military thugs and the declaration of Martial Law. This was 1972. *The Woman Who Left* is set a quarter century later, in 1997, a 'very complex, twisted and dark year', according to Diaz (there was the Asian financial crisis and the kidnapping, rape and murder of two nuns, which led to the accomplishment of the death penalty for the perpetrators).

> There was a sense of foreboding: things will go bad, the apocalypse is coming. When I started writing the script of *The Woman Who Left* I decided to set my Tolstoy-inspired story in an epoch of impending doom, in which everything is upside down.
>
> (Guarneri 2017: n.pag.)

Diaz's most recent film, *Season of the Devil* (2019), takes place in 1979, under the dictatorship of the two-faced Chairman Narciso (Marcos with shadings of current president Duterte). The apocalyptic state of alarm created by Marcos is still felt in the Philippines today. A long quotation from Diaz:

> I have more and more the feeling that the so-called 'hell', the so-called 'apocalypse' that we are waiting for has been here with us all along. It happened, it's happening, it will happen. Anytime, anywhere. Besides the so-called 'drug war' initiated by the new President of the Philippines [Duterte] in summer 2016, claiming so far thousands of innocent victims all over the country, there's war now in the Southern part of the Philippines, in Mindanao, the island where I was born. The city of Marawi – this beautiful small city – is under siege because the Philippine army and some islamic groups are fighting. Actually, Duterte has proclaimed Martial Law all over Mindanao and is probably going to bomb Marawi to the ground. He has just given a public speech and said to soldiers that during Martial Law they can rape three women each, they won't be punished. Can you believe it? How can you trust humanity these days? People don't trust humanity anymore and they worry, they have this fear, this feeling of foreboding, they don't know what's going to happen.
>
> (Guarneri 2017: n.pag.)

The apocalyptic mood of Diaz's films is also conveyed by the eternal presence of destructive natural elements reminiscent of the Old Testament sublime of the deluge: tropical storms, typhoons, erupting volcanoes and the destruction they leave in their wake form the natural setting for Diaz's dramas of suffering.[25] *Death in the Land of Encantos* is set in the aftermath of typhoon Reming, which hit the island in autumn 2006. This was only two months after volcano Mayon erupted, wreaking havoc on the Bicol region where *Florentina Hubaldo, CTE* is set. *The Storm Children: Book One* (2014) shares its biblical subtitle with *Heremias* (*Book One*), in which a storm in the province of Rizal has laid most crops to waste and seriously adds to the title character's Job-like ordeal. Where in *Heremias* it is unclear whether the storm in the film's first half was 'staged' or actual, there is no doubting the visceral veracity of *The Storm Children*, a documentary about the impact of typhoon Haida (Yolanda). In the recent and apocalyptically titled science fiction short *The Day Before the End*, the biggest storm in the history of the Philippines has landed as Shakespearian poets are being murdered.

Apocalypticism, however, announces not only the 'end' but the completion of history and a better world to come. In this sense, there is a positive or radically 'optimistic' side to even the most violent catastrophes (whether the natural disasters or the bombings of Muslim fundamentalists). As Steiner writes: 'History may have to pass through Armageddon or decades of political terror. But in the end the state shall wither away and man shall awake once again in the first garden' (1959: 257). Diaz explains (in another long quotation) his optimistic interpretation of the '*tabula rasa*' that the typhoons leave in their wake:

> We are the storm people. The storm could be the Filipino's original Anito (God); we had so many gods before Christ and Allah came to our endless shores. On the average, the Philippines is battered by 28 storms every year, but that doesn't make us a storm-battered race. In fact, we've become this storm-loving people.
>
> (cited in Picard 2012: n.pag.)

And you go back to the pre-Islamic and pre-Catholic Filipino Malay perspective – life is governed by nature. So, yes, the storm gives the Filipino a resiliency that's uniquely Filipino because it has become a metaphor for restarting, rebuilding, reconstruction, relocation, rebirth, recalling, renaming, resurfacing, reissuing, recurrence, reluctance, relapse, return, retain, remain, regain, resurrect, remiss, relief, rogue, rotten, rampant, relax, renegade, rob, run, rush, rip, ripe, rum, rug, rat, rut, retrogression, retro, rope and rock 'n' roll. Amidst a very corporeal history, there is the storm, the Filipino's God of all Gods, which has somehow become the great paradoxical equalizer, giving the Filipino a complex logic/illogic cultural discourse, a philosophy founded on the patterns of nature; the meaning of existence is appropriated by nature's ways. It is so normal to drown in a flood, be buried by a landslide, be sliced by debris from a billboard and be twisted by 21 years of Marcos's brutality (Picard 2012).

The only 're-' missing from Diaz's improvised Beat poem is redemption. Redemption can be, in Christian theology and in Dostoyevsky, the repurchase of man's crimes or sins through love (both divine love and earthly love), which Ivan Karamazov calls a 'childish belief' (some crimes, some forms of suffering are irredeemable). The possibility of redemption, for Dostoyevsky, as argued before, can therefore prove a way out of the problem of theodicy. In the Judaic tradition, redemption is given a more world-historical significance as it refers to the end of the exile of a people. In the Messianic thinking of Buber, Rosenzweig and Scholem, however, the idea of redemption is what is proposed as an argument against relentless progression and teleology. This type of redemption ('Tikkun', 'rectification' in terms of the Kabbalah) is what Walter Benjamin's famous 'Angel of History' – in the most oft-quoted of the 'Theses on the Philosophy of History', inspired by Klee's painting *Angelus Novus* (1920) – aspires to: as he is blown ever forward by the storm of progress, he struggles to awaken the dead of the past. At the moment of redemption – the day of judgement – the dead are resurrected, and this for Benjamin constitutes the only acceptable historical logic: the future is an affair of the past as of the present. True liberation theology, therefore, is restorative: the revolution of the future can only be successful if it incorporates the dead of previous struggles – whether it is Müntzer's Anabaptists or the French Communards.

Diaz has always stressed the dialectical relation of his films to the past:

> Well, my films are dialectical, so I kind of reenact the traumas to confront the past, to examine it. The narratives revolve around those things – the trauma of my people, the struggle of my people. You cannot escape it. These were big epochs in our history. You dig into the past. You examine the past. You create fictional characters, but at the same time, the narrative is affected by these historical things. It's memory. It's culture. It's history.
>
> (Mai 2016: n.pag.)

Memory is traumatic in *Melancholia, Death in the Land of Encantos* and *Florentina Hubaldo, CTE*, films structured around flashbacks (Bergman-like in *Encantos*), whereas other Diaz films are more linear. Most of his films can also be seen as ghost stories (literally so in the case of *Melancholia* and, you could argue, *Death in the Land of Encantos*), given their preference for nocturnal mood and dark forests, but then most of all in the sense of Marx's famous 'Gothic' remark that 'the past haunts the minds of the living like an "incubus"'. There is the constant search for the 'desparacidos': Alberta's search for Renato's body in *Melancholia*; the exhuming of the slain bodies of revolutionaries in that same film; the anguished search of Gregoria de Jesus, in *A Lullaby to the Sorrowful Mystery*, for her husband, the missing Father of the Revolution, Andres Bonifacio. Diaz's films are also frequently seen as showing the detritus of past conflicts, the fossils of the political past, as sedimented in the soil in a way that recalls both Third Cinema and Walter

Benjamin's concept of 'natural history' (Buck-Morss 1990: 159–205).[26] There is also a more medium-specific, Bazinian redemptive aspect to the role of the past in Diaz's cinema. As Homer proclaims in *Century of Birthing*, in a manner not too distant from the Godard of *Histoire(s) du cinéma*, cinema is uniquely constituted as a mnemonic tool: 'We will remember the world because of cinema. We can recreate or re-enact our memories [...] cinema will go back to the past, the present and the future, now!' (Diaz 2011). And there are the Giants that Florentina Hubaldo remembers, that 'help her'. In another interview, Diaz explains his decision of including the Higantes parade: 'I integrated it [the Giants] with the idea of finding a God to save you, finding somebody to redeem you from all this torture' (cited in Mai 2015: n.pag.).[27]

The restitutive aspects of Messianism also have a utopian side that point to a Paradise regained, a rediscovered 'Golden Age' in which modern alienations did not yet exist. For Georg Lukács, in his 1949 text on Dostoyevsky, the utopian dream of a Golden Age for which the 'spontaneous, wild, and blind revolt of Dostoyevsky's characters comes about' is symbolically represented by archaic Greece, as Claude Lorrain imagined it in his painting *Acis and Galatea* (1657) – characterized by genuine and harmonious between genuine and harmonious men (a vision similarly evoked in pastoral terms in the Tolstoy of *Anna Karenina* and its contrast between the lives of Levin and Kitty in the country and the city) (1962: 158). The immanence of the Golden Age in Diaz is associated with organic forms of social life, the collective imaginary of Malay myths, rituals and folklore from the pre-Christian colonization period that he remembers from his childhood in Maguindanao Province (before they were banned by Muslim radicals after Sharia Law was instated in the south of the Philippines): shaman dancing, mourning songs, the burning of dead bodies. All these are featured in films like *Melancholia* (indigenous tribal men carrying Renato's dead body along with the other soldiers to their village and performing a ritual of dance and chanting) and especially Diaz's most explicitly autobiographical film, *From What Is Before*, a film in which he was trying to 'reclaim the past of the Philippines'. In *From What Is Before* the mourning ritual is central – the singing of a capella songs (presaging Kwentista's songs in *Season of the Devil*) chronicling the dead person's life and the singer's recollections, grieving and pain. The mourning songs – and Diaz's films can be taken as such – again approximate these films to the Jewish Messianic tradition, especially since Heremias, of *Heremias (Book One)*, a crucial character for Diaz, taken either as Jeremiah or Job, is a singer of songs of lamentation. Gerschom Scholem detected in lament a remnant of divine language, a distinct form of language that is opposite to a language solely conceived as a carrier of information because it has no content other than its own expression. As a form of language between what is expressible and what is ineffable, lament is seen by Scholem as a border language between revelation and silence (see Ferber 2013: 161–86; Jacobson 2003). His conception of lament as a way to make the unsayable sayable also results from the logic of apophasis or what Benjamin called 'negative theology': the impossibility of knowing God is related to His absolute unity, devoid of properties and therefore indescribable. I want to argue that lament in this sense can be considered a fairly adequate description of Diaz's 'poor cinema', based on a negative aesthetics of absence and silence that has been called 'Beckett-like' but is better served by Scholem's theological conception of apostasy.

Beauty of the soul

One final point. The nostalgic recollection of the past is a trope typical of Romanticism and one of the reasons for the dismissal of the movement (especially in its German form) as reactionary and nationalist. Romantic nostalgia, however, as a memory image of pre-capitalist forms of community, can also be used as a weapon in the struggle for the future, as is the case with Diaz and Godard. Michael Löwy has proposed that his alignment of libertarian theology and historical materialism should be done under the heading of a Romantic critique of modernity. Messianic thinkers like Buber, Rosenzweig and even Benjamin were highly influenced by Romantic figures like Novalis and Hölderlin, with whom they share an emphasis on eschatological renewal. As M. H. Abrams elucidates, poets like Novalis and Hölderlin were obsessed with the French Revolution and even after the Reign of Terror and the Directory,

> continued to be almost obsessively concerned with the bringing into being of a 'new world' which will constitute a recovered Golden Age. The vision of the poet-seer, Novalis indicates in his *Fragments*, portends the future experience of all mankind and demonstrates the power of imagination to effect a perceptual apocalypse [...] and redeem the world of standard experience by the triumph of imaginative vision.
>
> (1971: 347)

Diaz's films contain a multitude of romantic tropes – the anti-bourgeois, anti-capitalist stance against the world of business (including the film business) and bureaucratic domination; a belief in correspondences between the human soul and nature; an interest in madness not only as traumatic symptom but as a break with socially instituted 'reason'. As a musician and poet, Diaz certainly sees himself in the tradition of the visionary poet-prophet, the 'bard' of Hölderlin's early odes. In any case, Abrams's characterization of the poetry of Blake, Shelly, Coleridge and Hölderlin also applies to Dostoyevsky's novels and to Diaz's cinema:

> They incorporate the great political events of their age in suitably grandiose literary forms, especially the epic and 'the greater Ode'; they present a panoramic view of

history in a cosmic setting, in which the agents are in part historical and in part allegorical or mythological and the overall design is apocalyptic; they envision a dark past, a violent present, and an immediately impending future which will justify the history of suffering man by its culmination in an absolute good; and they represent the French Revolution (or else a coming revolution which will improve upon the French model) as the critical event which signals the emergence of a regenerate man who will inhabit a new world uniting the features of a restored paradise and a beauty of the soul.

(1971: 329)

'The beauty of the soul', the pursuit of inner perfectability by the means of art, is perhaps the main concern Diaz shares with the Romantics. As he has said, 'Art should be [...] a commitment to aesthetics, to the *beauty of the soul*' (Romney 2017, my emphasis). As for Schiller, Schelling and Schlegel (all major influences on the idealism of Dostoyevsky, and not just on Dostoyevsky but also on Bakunin and Engels [Löwith 1991: 115][28]), art is the only way out of man's unhappy consciousness. In his films, Diaz regularly stages a discussion on the political value of art: in *Death in the Land of Encantos*, the painter Catalina offers that artists are selfish, that they care only about their art and little about the people around them. In *A Lullaby to the Sorrowful Mystery*, the idea that art is selfish is offered again, but this time the answer is resolute: 'The world needs art for its soul!' Schiller once wrote, in the Platonic love poem 'The Secret of Reminiscence' ('Das Geheimniss der Reminiszenz', 1782), about the exile of the soul from the 'homeward hill' (cited in Abrams 1973: 208). If Lav Diaz's films are indeed, like *Noli Me Tangere*, about exile and returning – most literally in *Evolution of a Filipino Family* and *Death in the Land of Encantos*, most symbolically in *Heremias (Book One)* and *The Woman Who Left* – then this should be taken in this sense.

NOTES

1. The peak year of the Filipino 'New Wave' was 1976, with films such as Brocka's *Insiang*, Mike de Leon's *Itim*, Ishmael Bernal's *Ligaw na Bulaklak* and *Nunal sa Tubig*, Eddie Romero's *Ganito Kami Noon ... Paano Kayo Ngayon?*, Lupita Concio's *Minsa'y Isang Gamu Gamo* and so on. The Taiwanese 'New Wave' crested a few years later, with Hou's *A Time to Live, a Time to Die* and *Dust in the Wind*, Edward Yang's *Taipei Story* and *Terrorizers* and Chang Yi's *Kuei-mei, A Woman*, all released in 1985–86.

2. The title of one of Diaz's most 'urban' and metafictional films *Melancholia* (2008) refers to the book the character Julian is writing in the film, which raises the question whether the 'historical' flashback episode in the film is an adaptation of Julian's book or 'fact'? Jameson notices a similar mirroring effect in Yang's *Terrorizers* (1986). The parallel is even closer to Hou's *Good Men, Good Women* (1995), in which the action switches between the frame story of actors performing a play as rehearsal for the filming of the historical drama 'Good

Men, Good Women' and the historical events being fictionalized. *Good Men, Good Women* is only the most explicit example among the films of the 'Taiwan Trilogy' to raise doubt about the absolute veracity of re-enacted history.

3. To the argument of Jameson (1992: 117) on *The Terrorizers* that '[p]erhaps what is being objected to in the film by Edward Yang is not so much its failure to be Chinese or Taiwanese as the relative absence from it of any ostensible worry about the nature of Taiwanese identity, or any rehearsal of its very possibility notions of national and ethnic identity', you could add the increasing importance of what is often referred to as the 'hybridized map' of festival culture.

4. Suchenski (2016) is most eloquent on the long-form tradition.

5. On Godard's Euro-scepticism and the alternative of the national, James S. Williams (2000: 113–41) provides interesting reading.

6. The idea of cultural transference and artistic tradition, in the context of the Philippines, is even more incapacitated by the fact that most of Philippine cinema of the pre-war years is considered lost.

7. Beller (2006) elaborates on Filipino modernism.

8. I use the term 'epic' in the sense that George Steiner (1980) uses it to qualify not only temporal spaciousness or breath of ambition but Tolstoy's 'organic' qualities – a term favoured also by Diaz to indicate the integration of life in art and even, as we shall see, the centrality of a journey towards resurrection. Tolstoy's novels are taken by Steiner as restoring to literature a 'wholeness of conception' that had passed from it with the decline of epic poetry. Although Steiner differentiates, for his purposes, between the epic poetry of Tolstoy and the tragic drama of Dostoyevsky, I will follow Georg Lukács's (1962) characterization of the latter as an epic poet. Not wanting to take anything away from Nadin Mai's reading of the epic length of Diaz's films as a psychometric expression of trauma, my own take on the temporality of Diaz's films – despite the film-maker's frequent reference to the experience of 'Malay time' (or the lack of an experience of time) – will therefore be less phenomenological than historical.

9. Probing for deep moral issues and spiritual essence is what Isaiah Berlin (2013: 147–48) considers the 'Russian' perspective on literature.

10. Still, there is Bayan, the Marxist-Leninist-Maoist umbrella party established in 1985 as part of the struggle against Marcos, an above-ground democratic party that recently became part of Makabayan, the Patriotic Coalition of the People.

11. In 2002, Bayan claimed that soldiers murdered at least thirteen of its members under the Gloria Macapagal-Aroyo presidency.

12. The Philippine Communist Party, a Maoist splinter group of the Stalinist Partido Komunista that had led peasant rebellions against the Japanese and the United States, was established in 1968 and immediately outlawed under Marcos. Communist guerillas started bombing offices and department stores in Manila in 1972.

13. Although the film was also based on actual 'mysterious' occurrences in the barrio where Diaz lived as a child, the doings of undercover military agents creating confusion and conditioning people through fear.

14. The 21-year-old Marcos murdered one of his father's political rivals and received the death penalty but was acquitted by the Supreme Court.

15. The Slavophile excitement aroused by the Serbian Revolution of 1807 is criticized by Tolstoy in the final chapters of *Anna Karenina*.

16. Tolstoy's story is also told as a Job-like parable attributed to an Orthodox priest in *Death in the Land of Encantos*.

17. This is one amongst several examples of paronamasia – 'nomen est omen' – in Dostoyevsky's work, like Razumikhin, Raskolnikov's loyal friend in *Crime and Punishment*, calling himself 'Vrazumikhin', the one who 'brings someone to their senses'; Taga Timog, the 'Southerner', in *Batang West Side* (2001), author also of the epigraph to *Heremias*, is a similar case in Diaz's work, amongst many others.

18. Rape, the corruption of female innocence, is a motif in Diaz as much as it is in Dostoyevsky; Mouchette's rape in Bresson's Dostoyevskyan adaptation of Bernanos was also an acknowledged influence on *Florentina Hubaldo, CTE*.

19. Fangar (2006: 17) cites Fyodor Dostoyevsky's letter to A. A. Kraevsky from June 1865.

20. Florentina's daughter Loleng was raised by Hector, just as Fantine's daughter Cosette was raised by Jean Valjean.

21. Compare Tolstoy's similar distrust of liberal reform; Tolstoy, however, believed in transforming God into 'Good', in brotherly love amongst men in a form of pre-Marxist utopian socialism also embraced by Vissarion Belinsky and (at one point) Dostoyevsky.

22. As Beatrice Hanssen (2000: 75–76) reminds us, Walter Benjamin maintained that baroque allegory often staged a cultural confrontation between Christian medieval practices and Hellenistic tradition. The baroque allegory that Benjamin was interested in, although threatening to take over in many a Diaz film, is most forcibly present in the Janus-faced figure of Chairman Narciso in *Season of the Devil*.

23. The harrowing lack of insight into historical processes was shown recently by the election as president in 2001 of Gloria Macapagal-Arroyo, former vice president to the corrupt Joseph Estrada. Arroyo was in turn imprisoned for corruption.

24. In *Totality and Infinity* (1961), Emmanuel Levinas (1979: 22) enlists such extra-historical Messianic logic for a Post-Structuralist project that envisions 'new relationships with being' beyond any conception of totality: 'a subjective and arbitrary divination of the future is the result of a revelation without evidences, tributary of faith'. Such a view of history as 'infinity' follows no teleology and exceeds representation ('Of peace there can only be an eschatology, no representation').

25. Diaz's return to the barrio where he had shot scenes for *Evolution of a Filipino Family* is highly reminiscent of Abbas Kiarostami's relationship to the Koker region. Diaz seemed to realize this, since the inquiry into the actions of the photographer, who uses his camera

irresponsibly and ends up destroying his subjects in *Century of Birthing*, seems to mirror Kiarostami's concerns in the 'Koker Trilogy' and elsewhere. The interview sequences in *Death in the Land of Encantos* also mirror the confusion between film-maker and film-maker-character that Kiarostami has exploited to the fullest.

26. Susan Buck-Morss (1990: 159–205) has argued that the Baroque allegorists conceived of nature as transitory, as history; they merged nature and history.

27. Interviewed by Nadin Mai, Locarno Film Festival, Locarno, 10 August.

28. Karl Löwith famously pointed out that Engels and Bakunin attended Schelling's lectures in Berlin in 1841.

REFERENCES

Abrams, M. H. (1973), *Natural Supernaturalism: Tradition and Revolution in Romantic Literature*, New York and London: W. W. Norton and Company.

Anon. (2016) 'Future of cinema if you to know – interview with Lav Diaz', *film parlato*, 17 November, http://filmparlato.com/index.php/numeri/6/item/144-future-of-cinema-if-you-want-to-know-interview-with-lav-diaz. Accessed 10 May 2021.

Aumont, Jaques (1999), *Amnésies: fictions du cinéma d'après Jean-Luc Godard*, Paris: P.O.L.

Beller, Jonathan (2006), *Acquiring Eyes: Philippine Visuality, Nationalist Struggle, and the World-Media System*, Manila: Ateneo de Manila University Press.

Benjamin, Walter (1999), 'Surrealism: The last snapshot of the European intelligentsia', in M. W. Jennings, H. Eiland and G. Smith (eds), *Walter Benjamin: Selected Writings, Vol. 2, Part 1, 1927–1930* (trans. E. Jephcott), Cambridge, MA: Harvard University Press.

Benjamin, Walter (2006), 'On the concept of history', in H. Eiland and M. W. Jennings (eds), *Selected Writings Volume 4 (1938–1940)* (trans. E. Jephcott and others), Cambridge, MA, and London, UK: The Belknap Press of Harvard University Press.

Berlin, Isaiah (2013), *Russian Thinkers*, 2nd ed. (ed. H. Hardy and A. Kelly), London: Penguin, pp. 147–48.

Buck-Morss, Susan (1990), *The Dialectics of Seeing: Walter Benjamin and the Arcades Project*, Cambridge, MA, and London, UK: MIT Press, pp. 159–205.

Danilevski, Nikolai Iakovlevich (2013), *Russia and Europe: The Slavic World's Political and Cultural Relations with the Germanic-Roman West* (trans. S. M. Woodburn), Bloomington, IN: Slavica Publishers.

Diaz, Lav (dir.) (2007), *Death in the Land of Encantos*, Philippines: Sine Olivia and Hubert Bals Fund.

Diaz, Lav (dir.) (2011), *Siglo ng pagluluwal (Century of Birthing)*, Philippines: Sine Olivia.

Dostoyevsky, Fyodor (2003), *Crime and Punishment* (trans. and intro. D. McDuff), London: Penguin.

Dostoyevsky, Fyodor (2003), *The Brothers Karamazov: A Novel in Four Parts and an Epilogue* (trans. and intro. D. McDuff), London: Penguin.

Dostoyevsky, Fyodor (2004), *The Idiot* (trans. D. McDuff, intro. W. M. Todd III), London: Penguin.

Dostoyevsky, Fyodor (2009), *Notes from the Underground and the Double* (trans. R. Wilks, intro. R. L. Jackson), London: Penguin.

Fangar, Donald (2006), 'Apogee: *Crime and Punishment*', in R. Peace (ed.), *Fyodor Dostoevsky's 'Crime and Punishment': A Casebook*, Oxford: Oxford University Press, p. 17.

Fanon, Frantz (2008), *Black Skin, White Masks* (trans. C. L. Markmann), London: Pluto Press.

Ferber, Ilit (2013), 'A language of the border: On Scholem's theory of lament', *Journal of Jewish Thought & Philosophy*, 21, pp. 161–86.

Frank, Joseph (1988), *Dostoevsky: The Stir of Liberation, 1860–1865*, Princeton, NJ: Princeton University Press.

Guarneri, Michael (2014), 'Everyday struggle, struggle every day: Lav Diaz rebolusyonaryo', *Photogénie*, 28 July, https://cinea.be/everyday-struggle-struggle-every-day-lav-diaz-rebolusyonaryo/. Accessed 10 May 2021.

Guarneri, Michael (2017), 'No forgiveness without justice', *Débordements*, 23 July, http://www.debordements.fr/Lav-Diaz-2017. Accessed 10 May 2021.

Hanssen, Beatrice (2000), *Walter Benjamin's Other History: Of Stones, Animals, Human Beings, and Angels*, Oakland, CA: University of California Press.

Hugo, Victor (1982), *Les Misérables* (trans. and intro. N. Denny), London: Penguin.

Jacobson, Eric (2003), *Metaphysics of the Profane: The Political Theology of Walter Benjamin and Gershom Scholem*, New York: Columbia University Press.

Jameson, Fredric (1992), *The Geopolitical Aesthetic: Cinema and Space in the World System*, Bloomington, Indianapolis and London: Indiana University Press and The British Film Institute, pp. 114–58.

Kristeva, Julia (1987), 'On the melancholic imaginary', *New Formations*, 3 (Winter), p. 15.

Levinas, Emmanuel (1979), *Totality and Infinity: An Essay on Exteriority* (trans. A. Lingis), The Hague, Boston and London: Martinus Nijhoff Publisher.

Löwith, Karl (1991), *From Hegel to Nietzsche: The Revolution in Nineteenth-Century Thought*, New York: Columbia University Press.

Löwy, Michael (2001), *Romanticism against the Tide of Modernity* (with R. Sayre), Durham, NC: Duke University Press.

Löwy, Michael (2017), *Redemption and Utopia: Jewish Libertarian Thought in Central Europe* (trans. H. Heaney), London and New York: Verso.

Lukács, Georg (1962), 'Dostoevsky', in R. Wellek (ed.), *Dostoevsky: A Collection of Critical Essays*, Englewood Cliffs, NJ: Prentice-Hall, pp. 146–59.

Mai, Nadin (2015), 'The aesthetics of absence and duration in the post-trauma cinema of Lav Diaz', Ph.D. thesis, July, Stirling: University of Stirling.

Mai, Nadin (2016), 'Lav Diaz: Slow burn', *Guernica*, 15 January, https://www.guernicamag.com/slow-burn/. Accessed 10 May 2021.

Marx, Karl (1982), *Critique of Hegel's 'Philosophy of Right'* (ed. and intro. J. O'Malley, trans. J. O'Malley and A. Jolin), Cambridge: Cambridge University Press.

Picard, Andrea (2012), 'Film/Art – Beware of the Jollibee: A correspondence with Lav Diaz', *Cinema Scope*, 51 (Summer), https://cinema-scope.com/columns/filmart-beware-jollibee-a-correspondence-lav-diaz/. Accessed 10 May 2021.

Romney, Jonathan (2017), 'Lav Diaz: Art is a commitment to the beauty of the soul', *Sight and Sound*, 18 May, https://www.bfi.org.uk/news-opinion/sight-sound-magazine/interviews/lav-diaz-art-commitment-beauty-soul. Accessed 10 May 2021.

Rosen, Daniel (2013), *Late Godard and the Possibilities of Cinema*, Berkeley, LA and London: University of California Press.

Sicinski, Michael (2016), 'El Filibustero: Lav Diaz's *A Lullaby to the Sorrowful Mystery*', *Cinema Scope*, 67 (Summer), https://cinema-scope.com/features/el-filibustero-lav-diazs-lullaby-sorrowful-mystery/. Accessed 10 May 2021.

Steiner, George (1959), *Tolstoy or Dostoevsky: An Essay in the Old Criticism*, New York: Alfred A. Knopf.

Steiner, George (1980), *Tolstoy or Dostoevsky: An Essay in Contrast*, London and Boston: Faber and Faber.

Steiner, George (1986), *Language and Silence: Essays on Language, Literature and the Inhuman*, New York: Atheneum.

Suchenski, Richard (2016), *Projections of Memory: Romanticism, Modernism, and the Aesthetics of Film*, Oxford: Oxford University Press.

Sue, Eugène (2015), *The Mysteries of Paris* (trans. C. Betensky and J. Loesberg, intro. P. Brooks), London: Penguin.

Tolstoy, Leo (2001), *Collected Shorter Fiction (2 Volumes)* (trans. A. Maude, L. Maude and N. J. Cooper; intro. J. Bayley), London: Everyman's Library.

Tolstoy, Leo (2008), *The Death of Ivan Ilyich and Other Stories* (trans. R. Wilks, A. Briggs and D. McDuff; intro. A. Briggs), London: Penguin.

Valéry, Paul ([1931] 1988), *Regards sur le monde actuel*, Cambridge, MA: Schoenhofs Foreign Books.

Vera, Noel (2005), *Critic after Dark: A Review of Philippine Cinema*, Singapore: BigO Books.

Vera, Noel (2013), 'Dostoevsky variations', *Film Comment*, September/October, https://www.filmcomment.com/article/lav-diaz-norte-the-end-of-history/. Accessed 22 June 2021.

Williams, James S. (2000), 'European culture and artistic resistance in *Histoire(s) du cinéma* Chapter 3a, La monnaie de l'absolu', in M. Temple and J. S. Williams (eds), *The Cinema Alone: Essays on the Work of Jean-Luc Godard, 1985–2000*, Amsterdam: Amsterdam University Press, pp. 113–41.

Zola, Emile (2009), *L'Assommoir* (trans. M. Mauldon, intro. R. Lethbridge), Oxford: Oxford University Press.

Figure 2.1: The two sisters in front of the raging sea with their back against the mountains in *From What Is Before*, 2014. Film still. Courtesy of Lav Diaz.

Figure 2.2: The hilly landscape and the waterfall in *From What Is Before*, 2014. Film still. Courtesy of Lav Diaz.

Figure 2.3: The melancholic woman on the boat in *From What Is Before*, 2014. Film still. Courtesy of Lav Diaz.

Figure 2.4: The mad and occasionally possessed woman in her hut in *From What Is Before*, 2014. Film still. Courtesy of Lav Diaz.

Figure 2.5: The banana-seller in *From What Is Before*, 2014. Film still. Courtesy of Lav Diaz.

3
Long Walk to Life:
The Films of Lav Diaz
— May Adadol Ingawanij

Lav Diaz describes himself as a storyteller who makes films about the struggles of his people.[1] In the past two decades, the Filipino film-maker has been fashioning a distinctive mode of epic melodrama. His films tell quiet tales of the sorrow and resilience of a people betrayed by the postcolonial nation state. Extreme in duration, Diaz's epics reference the Philippine state as a force of death – a state that has, since its independence in 1946, consistently turned against its own people despite the promise of collective emancipation that drove the country's national liberation movement against Spanish, then US colonial rule. At a time when people are being abandoned and oppressed by their own nation state, Diaz's films attempt to bring the collective body back to life by embodying the utopian spirit of the nation. To borrow the conceptual language of the political philosopher Pheng Cheah, the nation in its ontological form

May Adadol Ingawanij examines the dialectic between idealist projections of the postcolonial nation and its present aberrations in Lav Diaz's epic tales of endurance.

differs from the historical actuality of the nation state. The ontological form of the

nation, or its national-popular spirit, haunts the empirical nation state as a horizon of possibility: in this sense, the nation is, for Cheah, the most potent modern form for the actualisation of the human ideal of culture characterised by freedom and self-renewal.[2] As Diaz often says, his artistic process involves the search for truth and the struggle for existential redemption.[3] In other words, to make films for Diaz is to incarnate the national-popular spirit of self-renewal and freedom, even if the films themselves narrate the Philippine nation state's betrayal of its own people.

Persisting in making films under this national-popular paradigm situates Diaz within an international genealogy of Third World revolutionary art. This lineage connects the film-maker's work with that of such predecessors as the Indonesian Nobel Prize-winning author Pramoedya Ananta Toer, the internationalist Third Cinema movement and, of course, the Cold War generation of radical Filipino film-makers, especially Lino Brocka, whom Diaz cites as an inspiration.

Physical Realism

Born in 1958 and raised on the southern island of Mindanao, Diaz belongs to the generation of Filipinos that came into political awareness during the martial law period of President Ferdinand Marcos's dictatorship, from 1972 to 1981. Growing up on an island

---

1. See Alexis A. Tioseco's interview with the film-maker: 'A Conversation with Lav Diaz', *Criticine* [online journal], 30 January 2006, available at http://www.criticine.com/interview_article.php?id=21 (last accessed on 22 June 2015).
2. *See Pheng Cheah, Spectral Nationality: Passages of Freedom from Kant to Postcolonial Literatures of Liberation, New York: Columbia University Press, 2003, especially part 2.*
3. See 'A Conversation with Lav Diaz', *op. cit.*

territory that had been autonomous from Manila until Philippine independence had a formative influence over the mode of address and aesthetics of Diaz's films. In the 1990s, he worked as a director and script-writer in the Manila-based film industry while searching for a way to be free to realise his artistic vocation. He began making *Ebolusyon Ng Isang Pamilyang Pilipino* (*Evolution of a Filipino Family*) in the mid-90s, a tortuously extended project that would not be completed until 2004.

To date, Diaz has completed nearly ten films of epic duration (each is between five and eleven hours long). In them, men and women, young and old, take long walks across a rain-soaked land gone to ruin. Male intellectuals and artists slide into degeneracy as they wander, having been broken down by the secret service and their own sense of pol-itical defeat. Mothers, grandmothers, wives and sisters search for loved ones as they push on along never-ending roads. Children are helpless seers who creep up to silently wit-ness the atrocities and sadness of adults.

Diaz's aesthetics blend the national-popular praxis of the Bandung era with the realist film ethics of French theorist André Bazin. An archetypal scene is one framed as a long shot and lasting the duration of a long take. Diaz's *mise en scène* displays the materiality of the physical environ-ment; he stages movement as powerless human bodies traversing through immense space. Land, forest, water, rain and volcanic clouds simultaneously engulf all matter and figure historic destruction. Detritus of past conflicts sediment in soil layers; forest vegetation grows rampant over anonymous, slain bodies from past strug-gles; the cone-shaped Mount Mayon is a mass murderer. A shot may begin with a panoramic view of a paddy field, a forest, a shoreline or a hill. The recorded pro-filmic

space seems depopulated at first, until we catch a glimpse of a tiny figure moving on the furthest plane. The duration of the shot corresponds to the length of time it takes that person to walk into the fore-ground and out of the frame. Diaz often uses the long take to mark the duration of the hard yet purposive labour of peasant and underclass characters. Activities such as farmers planting, miners digging or vendors pushing a cart shape the tempo of scenes and sequences. Further, the extended duration of each shot gives time for bodies to pause from physical activities and to accrue gestural intensity. This staging of gesturing bodies in desolate landscapes is one example of the ways in which Diaz's aesthetics blend the theatrical mode of per-formance with realist filmic space.

Film theorist Lúcia Nagib has recently proposed the concept of physical realism in order to frame realist film-making as an ethical endeavour.[4] Reflecting on long scenes showing the act of running in such films as Glauber Rocha's *Deus e o Diabo na Terra do Sol* (*Black God, White Devil*, 1964), Nagib identifies realism with the physicality of engagement on the part of the film cast and crew with the material envir-onment. A realist presentation is one that conceives of the film as an event shaped by the contingencies of the situation of filming. The film-maker produces pro-filmic space in response to the surroundings; the actors enact their exertion. This concept of phys-ical realism acknowledges the inevitable gap between reality and filmic representa-tion while at the same time emphasising the moving image's indexical connection to the physical world. In other words, it stays true not so much to reality itself as to the process by which the film acquires material life.

This notion of realism resonates well with Diaz's film-making. He has repeatedly

---

4.   See Lúcia Nagib, *World Cinema and the Ethics of Realism*, New York: Continuum, 2011.

Figure 2.6: Young Benjamin and Young Theresa in *Death in the Land of Encantos*, 2007. Film still. Courtesy of Lav Diaz.

Figure 2.7: Benjamin/Hamin in the forest in *Death in the Land of Encantos*, 2007. Film still. Courtesy of Lav Diaz.

Figure 2.8: Fabian and his friends celebrate in *Norte, the End of History*, 2013. Film still. Courtesy of Lav Diaz.

Figure 2.9: Eliza and her children walking in *Norte, the End of History*, 2013. Film still. Courtesy of Lav Diaz.

Figure 2.10: Fabian breaks down and his friends comfort him in *Norte, the End of History*, 2013. Film still. Courtesy of Lav Diaz.

described his practice as an organic process characterised by itinerancy and immediacy of response – at the levels of both scripting and shooting – to the locations in which pro-filmic space will be constructed. He often writes the script only shortly before the shoot and directs his actors to, above all, embody the tempo of a scene. At the stage of editing, Diaz is steadfast in his willingness to turn the engagement with a site and its material properties into the principle of duration for each film. His method is also one that demonstrates an important affinity between the ethics of physical realism and faith in the potentiality of art to incarnate the national-popular spirit. In this context, acts of physical exertion – their duration, spatiality and intensity – become the analogous means by which a film maps a territory and defines a people. Moreover, as a variant of physical realism, Diaz's films address spectators as a people in the making. The framework of physical realism usefully suggests that the basis for valuing the experience of viewing Diaz's films is less about contemplating and bearing witness to the suffering of others than physically incarnating a collective act of faith. To gift the time of viewing, and to be moved by the intensity of the melodrama played out over such durational extremities, evokes the possibility of collectively incarnating the renewal of the nation-form.

Cartography of a Nation

Within the context of English-language criticism, Diaz's films are being framed under the sign of slow cinema. This nomenclature is useful to the extent that it situates his practice and aesthetics within the conceptual parameter of the contemporary realist film.[5] But the discourse of slow cinema tends to end up gesturing rather unproductively towards the idea of contemplative spectatorship as the basis of endowing artistic value. A critical language of realism attentive to the different modes, tempos and directionality of bodies moving in space would seem more suited to assessing the significance of Diaz's aesthetics. Such a reading would take a close look at the physicality of wandering, voyaging, searching, trudging or toiling as enacted by Diaz's characters, and the way in which their journeys construct a symbolic map of the Philippine archipelago, one that is nonetheless connected with territories beyond or anterior to the nation state's boundaries. The world in *Kagadanan Sa Banwaan Ning Mga Engkanto* (*Death in the Land of Encantos*, 2007) is one mapped by the characters' movement across the typhoon-destroyed regions of Bicol, Manila, Mindanao and Russia. *Evolution of a Filipino Family* connects a village, farm and mine with forest spaces concealing separatist rebels as well as with the underworld in Manila. Long, recurring scenes of the families of farmers and miners listening together to radio broadcasts of a soap opera situate their everyday quest for survival within the overarching nation state, as do scenes of radio and TV broadcasts of national political events.

From What Is Before turns the experience of military terrorisation in Mindanao into an emblem of the neglect of the people by the nation-state apparatus.

Rather than championing Diaz's oeuvre in the language of auteurist slow cinema,

---

5. See, for example, Matthew Flanagan, '"Slow Cinema": Temporality and Style in Contemporary Art and Experimental Film', unpublished doctoral thesis, Exeter: Exeter University, 2012. Diaz's films were also included in the AV Festival 'As Slow as Possible' (1–31 March 2012) in a focus section curated by George Clark in Newcastle.

Figure 2.11: The wide expanse of water and the reflection of the sky in *Norte, the End of History,* 2013. Film still. Courtesy of Lav Diaz.

Figure 2.12: The boatmen pass as the sky is reflected into the river in *Norte, the End of History*, 2013. Film still. Courtesy of Lav Diaz.

then, a more fruitful way to discuss his body of work as an interconnected whole might be to take his films as cartographic acts. Mindanoa – the artist's 'paradise, lost'[6] – figures in several of his works. *Melancholia* (2008) is shot in the northern town of Sagada. The plot links this mountain town with both Manila and a forest territory into which political activists have fled. Like *Death in the Land of Encantos*, this portrayal of the suffering of loved ones left behind references the disappearance of dissenters through government agents during the presidency of Gloria Macapagal-Arroyo (2001–10). *Norte, Hangganan Ng Kasaysayan* (*Norte, the End of History*, 2014), Diaz's tale of the totalitarian mentality, partly takes place in President Marcos's hometown in the northern Ilocos region. Loosely adapted from Dostoevsky's *Crime and Punishment* (1866), the film portrays a brilliant yet nihilistic law student in his quest for pure deliverance from the evils of the world, addressing the contemporary Philippines with a reminder of the seductive power of charismatic figures who promise to arrest history with total change.

The cartographic acts of Diaz's films mesh the world of the living with the spaces and temporalities of those who have died but whose presence endures. Voyagers walking in a land of death touch wandering, undead figures. Within the same frame, a son lies down on the lap of the spectre of his mother, who reciprocates his gesture by gently touching him. Diaz's editing of shot sequences intensifies the sense of temporal indeterminacy, a method most strikingly realised in *Death in the Land of Encantos*. In this tale of the descent into madness and suicide of the writer and public intellectual Hamin after being tortured by the secret police, narrative events are portrayed in non-chronological order. Sequences of the protagonist's subjective memories and dreams are contiguous with chronologically unmoored events.

Mula Sa Kung Ano Ang Noon (*From What Is Before*, 2014) opens with a voice-over from an indeterminate source. Harking back to the oral root of storytelling, the voice says that this is a story that comes from memory. Shortly after the opening sequence, a landscape appears with a solitary hut in a paddy field dwarfed by a mountain range enveloped in clouds. The static long shot carries a short caption situating the story in 'Pilipinas 1970'; the film ends when Marcos declares martial law in 1972. Unlike previous films, in which the journeying of characters links far-flung places, the diegetic space of *From What Is Before* remains in and around a single village. One by one, strangers turn up to this remote place: an indigenous healer who seems to have come out of the pre-national time of the Malay archipelago, a Catholic priest, a poet, a vendor with a secret. Cows disappear; villagers die. We hear a scream but don't see the body. Off-screen space evokes the presence of clandestine forces in territories beyond the village border. Halfway through the film's running time, uniformed soldiers appear. One by one, the villagers leave.

From What Is Before is based on Diaz's childhood memories of Mindanao during Marcos's reign of terror.[7] Hakob, a foundling child seer embodying the film-maker's

---

6. 'An Interview With the Great Lav Diaz', pepediokno.com [blog], 8 September 2014, available at http://pepediokno.com/post/96943248395/an-interview-with-the-great-lav-diaz (last accessed on 29 July 2015).
7. 'The Burden of History: A Conversation with Lav Diaz' (the film-maker interviewed by Michael Guarneri), *La Furia Umana* [online journal], no.21, August 2014, available at http://www.lafuriaumana.it/?id=243 (last accessed on 22 July 2015).

generation, perceives but can't comprehend the confusion and terror. The village is subject to clandestine military operations and falls within the zone of Muslim secessionist and communist revolts. The film references the violent post-independence history of an island territory that, in the precolonial period, had been a port state within the maritime network of Southeast Asia.[8] Yet the fabled name of the diegetic space of the film is Pilipinas, and Diaz actually shot this film on the northern tip of the island of Luzon, in a village whose remote setting and atmosphere of abandonment reminded him of the Mindanao of his childhood. This process of translating pro-filmic space into the fable's diegetic space implies a different cartographic construction of post-independence Mindanao. Rather than reproduce the nationalist narrative of Mindanao's assimilation into the nation state or the communal narrative of the islanders' ethno-religious difference as a Muslim Moro people, the film-maker's fictionalisation of *From What Is Before* turns the experience of military terrorisation in Mindanao into an emblem of the neglect of the people by the apparatus of the nation state.

Stories of Mothers

Biological families are destroyed or degenerate in Diaz's tales, gruesomely so in the case of *Norte*. Adoptive families live on, provisionally forming themselves in the face of adverse circumstances. Necessity and ethics come together here. Via melodramatic plot turns, adults who are existentially tortured or lead otherwise precarious lives nevertheless take up responsibility for the care of foundlings and traumatised children. Often it is the female characters – those whose circumstances are extremely vulnerable – who become figures of ethical endurance. Alberta, the wife of the disappeared intellectual in *Melancholia*, brings up the 'rain child' whose parents have met the same fate as her husband. *Norte* ends shortly after the death of Eliza, the wife of the wrongly convicted labourer jailed for life. The ending implies that it is her simple younger sister who will continue to care for the couple's children.

Diaz's films aren't exactly feminist. Their insistence on the motif of rape to symbolise the victimisation of the nation-body leaves a disquieting feeling. But the mothers, grandmothers, sisters and aunts are the ones who go on, and who, for better or for worse, take decisive action. Such figures call to mind a layer of the premodern past ripe for mobilisation in the present. The unusually autonomous place of women in precolonial Southeast Asia signals the importance of assessing the significance of Diaz's work within a regional as well as national parameter. As historian Anthony Reid recently proposed, the premodern agency of the region's women via their monetary control over trade and their participation in various areas of productive labour, notably agriculture, is one important reason for turning to Southeast Asia to think about issues of global importance.[9]

The charismatic farmer-grandmother in *Evolution of a Filipino Family* is reminiscent in this sense of the region's ancestral matriarchal

---

8. See Patricio Abinales, *Making Mindanao: Cotabato and Davao in the Formation of the Philippine Nation-State*, Manila: Ateneo de Manila University Press, 2000.
9. See Anthony Reid, *A History of Southeast Asia: Critical Crossroads*, Oxford: Wiley Blackwell, 2015.

Figure 2.13: The prostitute and her man in *Melancholia*, 2008. Film still. Courtesy of Lav Diaz.

Figure 2.14: Huling, Martina, and Ana in *Evolution of a Filipino Family,* 2004. Film still. Courtesy of Lav Diaz.

Figure 2.15: Grandma Puring with Huling in *Evolution of a Filipino Family,* 2004. Film still. Courtesy of Lav Diaz.

figures. More striking still is the untimely figure of the healer Bai Rahmah in *From What Is Before*. An extended scene towards the beginning of the film shows her performing a dance ritual in the rain to channel the originary power of animistic spirits, with villagers gathering around her in the hope of having that potent power transmitted to them. Shortly after, she reappears singing a long, hypnotic ritual chant to lament the unaccountable murder of her son. In all the scenes in which she features, the imparting of plot information matters much less than experiencing the affective power of the performer's face and voice in intensified duration. Bai Rahmah is a figure from a primordial archipelagic world of animistic gods and rituals, matriarchs, seafarers and the Malay lingua franca, yet she lives on in the film's diegetic time; indeed, the possibility remains that her presence persists beyond it. 'Is' — not 'Was' — precedes 'Before' in the film's English-language title, enunciating a vanishing point beyond the arrival of the Spanish and the Americans; beyond independence and the rise of organised religion; and beyond the systematisation of a state apparatus tasked with conquering peripheral territories, and thus with killing its own people.

Acts of physical exertion — their duration, spatiality and intensity — become the means by which a film maps a territory and defines a people.

As a figure of anterior power, the indigenous healer is an intriguing departure from the trope of the messianic male figure that embodies the force and temporality of self-renewal in the historical canon of Third Cinema (take, for example, Sebastião in *Black God, White Devil*). Rather than bearing the prophecy of cosmic rebirth, once the apparatus of collective death begins to violently dominate, Bai Rahmah becomes a spectral force. As the chronological time of the diegesis ticks toward the declaration of Marcos's martial law, she moves off-screen. The voice-over says she does not come back. Yet, by not dying, her presence may well linger on; her future return remains a possibility. To figure the potency of this spectre from a time long, long before in a tale set in the early 1970s is audacious yet truthful. Mothers originate, and they endure.

Acknowledgment

This article was first published in the journal *Afterall* (Chicago University Press, 2015).

4

Freedom Is a Long Shot:
A Chronicle of Lav Diaz's Artistic Struggle

Michael Guarneri

Introduction

Named after Soviet statesman Lavrentiy Beria, Lavrente Indico Diaz was born on 30 December 1958 in the province of Cotabato, Mindanao island, the son of a socialist intellectual from the Ilocos region and a fervently Catholic woman from the Visayan Islands, who devoted their lives to schooling peasants in the poorest villages of Southern Philippines. Given his parents' commitment to social work and faith in education as a key to a better life, Diaz has always had a utilitarian and humanitarian conception of culture. Consequently, to him, art should not be an end to itself, a purely formalist exercise, but – to paraphrase a Shakespearean play extensively quoted in his short film *Ang araw bago ang wakas* (*The Day before the End*) (Diaz 2016b) – it must hold the mirror up to society so that people might learn something about themselves and the world they live in. The specific horizon Diaz evokes when discussing his mission as a socially concerned artist is that of the nation: halfway between historian and physician, he sees himself as investigating the impact of the 1521–1898 Spanish colonization, the 1898–1946 American rule, the 1942–45 Japanese occupation and Ferdinand Marcos's dictatorship during 1972–86 on the Filipino body politic and psyche. By telling stories that directly or indirectly deal with these 'four major cataclysms' (Guarneri 2014: n.pag.), the film-maker hopes that his compatriot spectators would confront their colonial and dictatorial past, break with it and build a better future for the country. This didactic-redemptive power of cinema is illustrated in the ending of *Batang West Side* ('West Side kid') (Diaz 2001), where the viewing of a documentary about the plight of an overseas Filipino worker moves troubled Filipino American Juan Mijares, a policeman in 2000 Jersey City, to carry out an 'active introspection' (a work of self-analysis that the psychiatrist character in the film compares to 'an

63

exorcism') and confess to the extrajudicial killings he committed 30 years earlier while working for the Marcos administration. To make his intentions even clearer, in a December 2002 manifesto, Diaz presented *Batang West Side*, his first independently produced feature to be released, as follows:

> In Hollywood culture, entertainment and profit are the larger purpose of cinema. Entertainment for the audience; profit for the many producers, directors, actors, film workers and movie theater owners. The same holds true in the Philippines. That is why the Filipinos' appreciation of cinema is shallow and base. In their eyes, cinema is no different from a carnival. It will take a long and involved process to change this perception, especially with Hollywood films still dominating Filipino theaters. [...] We need to begin developing a National Cinema, a cinema that will help create a responsible Filipino people.
>
> (Diaz 2015: 39)

These are the words of a man who, as we shall see in the next section, spent the previous ten-plus years working in the mainstream of the Filipino film industry, trying to express himself while putting up with 'business and bullshit' (Wee 2005: n.pag.).

Five centuries under the influence

According to a popular Filipino joke, the Philippines spent 350 years in a convent and 50 years in Hollywood. After Portuguese explorer Ferdinand Magellan set foot on the Eastern Visayas in 1521, the archipelago was claimed for Spain, named after King Felipe II, Christianized and Hispanicized. Contextually, the exploitation of the Philippines's natural resources and indigenous population by the Spaniards began. A fierce resistance against the European colonizers immediately came from the areas of the archipelago that had been Islamized in the fourteenth and fifteenth centuries (and especially from Diaz's native province Cotabato), while the Hispanicized-Catholicized Filipinos' major attempt at an anti-Spanish rebellion took place in the second half of the 1890s. In 1898, at the end of the Spanish-American War, Spain sold the Philippines to the United States for USD 20 million of the time, and the new owners took it upon themselves to repress anti-colonialist movements in the islands. Once the United States had secured control over the Philippines by force of arms, they 'initiated limited progressive and democratic reforms [...], and included the Filipino elite [...] in the colonial government', with the aim of 'instructing Filipinos in self-rule' and assimilating them 'into a new international order that reflected US ideals of democracy, republican government and free-market economics' (Hawley 2002: 392). Within this paternalistic framework (the Filipinos were called the United States' 'little brown brothers' by William Howard Taft, the 1901–04 governor general of the Philippines), the 1934 Tydings-McDuffie Act established that the Philippines was to be an independent nation by 1946 (Hawley 2002: 393–94). The nation-building process was interrupted during Second World War, when Japan invaded the archipelago and established the Second Philippine Republic, a puppet state whose name paid lip service to the ideals of freedom that had animated the short-lived Philippine Republic proclaimed by Filipino revolutionaries in 1899. With Japan's defeat in the Pacific War, the Philippines returned under US control and, in accordance with the Tydings-McDuffie Act, was granted independence in 1946. Naturally, though, in the post-1945 world divided into a Western and an Eastern bloc, the relations between the United States and the Philippines remained strong: as stated during the 1946 congressional debates over the Philippines Rehabilitation Act by William Howard Taft's son Senator Robert Alphonso Taft: '[C]ertainly [the United States] shall always be a big brother to the Philippines' (Hawley 2002: 409).

Filipino lawyer Ferdinand Marcos took advantage of this history of foreign prevarications and frustrated national pride. Presenting himself as the descendant of an anti-colonialist general of the late nineteenth century and as a war hero who had bravely fought Japanese invaders during the Second World War (Spence 1964: 20–21; Mijares [1976] 2016: 203–14), Marcos quickly rose to political prominence in the post-war period with slogans like 'This Nation Can Be Great Again'. Elected president of the republic in 1965 and again in 1969, he spent his second mandate executing his master plan for staying in power beyond the eight-year constitutional limit. Citing both the endemic Muslim secessionist guerilla in Mindanao and the rise of the armed wing of the Filipino Communist Party as threats to democracy, on 21 September 1972 Marcos put the country under martial law and, with the blessing of the United States, instituted a military-backed dictatorship. Having seized absolute power, Marcos and his clan were free to implement a mix of crony capitalism and kleptocracy that manifested 'the nature of the Philippines as a postcolonial subject [...], a historical entity constructed in the imperial rape and exchange of the colony, and the continuing pillage by its own elite' (Tolentino 2003: 81).

Upon the proclamation of martial law, 13-year-old Diaz and his family found themselves in one of the most dangerous areas of the country, the Maguindanao and Cotabato provinces, caught in the crossfire between Muslim secessionists, communists and the Philippine Army. With violence all around, Diaz managed to finish high school and enroll in university, where he divided his time between economics textbooks and rock-and-roll jams. Importantly, it is in this period that Diaz – a film buff since childhood, when his father would take him to see all kinds of commercial movies from Hollywood, Hong Kong and the Philippines – first realized the power of cinema as a tool to publicly denounce socio-economic and political ills:

> [*Maynila sa mga kuko ng liwanag* (*Manila: In the Claws of Light*) (Brocka 1975)] was such a huge influence on me. I saw that in 1975. [...] Cinema was just entertainment to me back then, no aesthetic issues yet. [...] I was in first year college. [...] I saw [the film] and something woke up in me. It was the height of the Marcos regime then, he was controlling everything. And [*Maynila sa mga kuko ng liwanag*] was liberating, in a sense that you can use this medium to fuck this regime. [...] [*Insiang* (Brocka 1976)] was also very influential. Freshman college, that was the first time I learned about it. Not just the film but the filmmaker, this Lino Brocka. *Insiang* was the bar for social realist cinema. [...] *Insiang* was [...] about what poverty can do to you and your psyche. A poverty born of neglect. Of a system that doesn't work for the masses but maintains the status quo. Very feudal.
>
> (Dayao and Alagbate 2015: 65–66)

Martial law was formally lifted in January 1981 during a papal visit to the Philippines. However, the Marcos regime ended only in 1986 with the People Power Revolution, a series of massive demonstrations that took place in the streets of Manila against extrajudicial killings and electoral frauds. As shown in the documentary *Revolutions Happen Like Refrains in a Song* (Deocampo 1987), a popular slogan from the rallies was 'If Reagan wants Marcos, he can have him', and indeed, as the protesters set out to storm the presidential palace in February 1986, Marcos was flown on a US aircraft to Hawaii, where he enjoyed his last years undisturbed with his family and the wealth he amassed during his kleptocrat reign: the United States did not forget the strategic help Marcos's right-wing dictatorship gave them in the Cold War scenario of South East Asia. The presidency of the republic went to Corazon Aquino, the widow of anti-Marcos senator Benigno Aquino Jr, assassinated under mysterious circumstances in 1983, but many key figures of the Marcos administration remained in their place (following Marcos's death, in 1991, the wife and children of the dictator were allowed to return to the Philippines and immediately re-entered the business and political scene, where they currently occupy prominent positions).

In the last years of the regime and in the democratic Philippines of the late 1980s and early 1990s, Diaz was taking on all sorts of odd jobs in Manila in order to support his wife and children, while at the same time cultivating his artistic dreams of becoming a musician and a film-maker. As for the music, he toured for two years with his band Cotabato (Garcia 2000: 54), whose sound was inspired by Filipino punk-rock legends The Jerks, founded in 1979 and active even today. As for cinema, in 1985, Diaz began to attend a series of workshops at the Movie

Workers Welfare Foundation with mentors like Nick Deocampo, Mac Alejandre, Raymond Red, Christoph Janetzko, Ricky Lee, Peque Gallaga and Lamberto Avellana, and shot his first short movies on 16mm, super 8 and videotape. The experience was a crash course in pragmatism for young idealist Diaz:

> During my early years of struggling to break into cinema, because there was no digital yet, and there was such a dearth of cameras especially the 16mm [...], and even super 8 rolls were kind of expensive, to thrive as a filmmaker meant to go mainstream, the so-called industry. And you know, the industry is the status quo and [...] is very feudal. They protect their turf, they are wary of newcomers [...]. To break in was hardcore. [...] More often, it's more of swallowing your pride and accepting compromise as a norm.
>
> (Tioseco 2006a: n.pag.)

Using the workshops as an occasion for networking, Diaz entered the show business as a screenwriter for Lamberto Avellana, for the television series *Balintataw* ('Pupil') (PTV, 1986–93), for action star Fernando Poe Jr and for Regal, one of the major film studios in the late 1980s and early 1990s Philippines together with Viva and Seiko. In particular, for Fernando Poe Jr, Diaz co-wrote *Mabuting kaibigan masamang kaaway* ('Good friend, bad enemy') (Salvador 1991) about an innocent man breaking out of prison to take revenge on those who framed him; while for Regal, Diaz co-wrote the Eddie Garcia vehicle *Galvez: Hanggang sa dulo ng mundo hahanapin kita* ('Galvez: I'll hunt you down until the end of the world') (Cinco 1993) in which a righteous attorney and a psychopathic drug lord lock horns. Evidently, at the beginning of his career, Diaz was following Lino Brocka's advice about the need to compromise 'to be able to survive in the Philippine movie industry, [...] mak[ing] five or ten movies for the producer to be able to make one good film for himself' (Tioseco 2006a: n.pag.).

Diaz's 'good film for himself' was a screenplay provisionally titled *Ebolusyon ni Ray Gallardo* ('Evolution of Ray Gallardo'). It told the story of a Filipino sailor who jumps ship and starts living illegally in the United States haunted by the ghosts of his past and was meant to be a fresco of Philippine history from the proclamation of martial law to the Aquino presidency. The independently financed 16mm shooting (on black-and-white Kodak 7222 stock costing around USD 80 per roll) started in March 1994 in and around New York, where Diaz had migrated in 1992 in order to support his wife and children by working for a Filipino American newspaper, and it proceeded between the United States and the Philippines in fits and starts due to lack of funds and all sorts of contretemps (Tioseco 2006b). In 1997, with *Ebolusyon ni Ray Gallardo* still nowhere near completion, Diaz had an unexpected breakthrough as a director: while shooting some scenes of his pet project in Luzon island, he was told by cinematographer Larry Manda that Regal had begun producing debut features by young directors through its subsidiary Good Harvest. Diaz, who had already co-written *Galvez: Hanggang sa dulo ng mundo hahanapin kita* for Regal a few years earlier, submitted to the studio his unfilmed screenplays *Ang kriminal ng Baryo Concepcion* ('The criminal of Barrio Concepcion') and *Larong krimen* ('Crime play') and was hired. For Regal, Diaz directed four movies: *Serafin Geronimo: Ang kriminal ng Baryo Concepcion* (*The Criminal of Barrio Concepcion*) (Diaz 1998), *Hubad sa ilalim ng buwan* (*Naked under the Moon*) (Diaz 1999a), *Burger Boys* (Diaz 1999b) and *Hesus, rebolusyonaryo* ('Jesus, the revolutionary') (Diaz 2002), all written by him and shot on 35mm colour film. The experience, whose keyword was once again compromise, was a real eye-opener for Diaz, showing him all the downsides of working in the mainstream of the Filipino film industry.

Diaz was hired as part of the *pito-pito* ('seven-seven') scheme developed by Regal in the aftermath of the 1997 Asian financial crisis. The studio required cast and crew to churn out a 90- to 120-minute feature film on a seven-day pre-production, seven-day shooting and seven-day post-production schedule, on a maximum budget of PHP 2.5 million,[1] which was nothing compared to the average Filipino movie cost of PHP 12 million (Garcia 2000: 54). In Diaz's own words, this was 'one of the most exploitative and brutal schemes ever done in film production', with 'production people collapsing from fatigue' while being paid 'very, very low salaries' (Guarneri 2011).[2] Moreover, the economic imperatives described earlier led to an assembly-line standardization that stifled creativity in Filipino cinema, making conformist and impersonal work proliferate:

> [A] lot of filmmakers practice the 'full coverage' directing – shooting a scene in all angles [from extreme long shot to extreme close-up]. [...] They call it the *sigurista* [('safe')] directing; you have everything; let the editor suffer the pointlessness of it all. The usual practitioners of this kind of filmmaking are movie industry people. And oftentimes, to be able to achieve this, people would shoot for 36 hours straight killing themselves to exhaustion. [...] I am not saying that [full coverage] is not valid [...]. It is still filmmaking indeed. But talk about impatience, man. This is fucking film school. This is a fucking television commercial shoot.
>
> (Tioseco 2006a: n.pag.)

Even more importantly, when the studio owns the financial capital and the means of production, the director basically has no creative control over the finished product, as Diaz found out when Regal 're-cut [*Hubad sa ilalim ng buwan*] with additional sex scenes (shot without Diaz)' (Tioseco 2005: 169) to make the family melodrama about a guilt-ridden ex-priest, his sexually unsatisfied wife and his daughter sleepwalking in the nude more sensational.

The digital (r)evolution

As shown earlier, until the early 2000s the Filipinos seeking to express themselves by making feature films in the country generally had to pitch their ideas to the local film studios, since it was mostly companies like Regal, Viva and Seiko that owned the financial capital and professional equipment needed to bring stories from the page to the silver screen. This condition of near monopoly allowed Filipino film studios to act as the rulers and enforcers of a 'very irresponsible and dishonest' system in which exploited workers are demanded to produce low-cost exploitation movies in the belief that the paying audience is nothing but a bunch of 'morons' hungry for sensational, escapist entertainment and 'undeserving of serious works' (Wee 2005). Even Diaz's *Batang West Side* – independently produced and shot on 35mm colour film in 2000–01 and considered by its author as the first step towards a liberated and liberating Filipino national cinema – prompted 'many [...] heated arguments' between the film-maker and his financiers, as the latter (among whom were young actor Yul Servo's wealthy sponsor Antonio Veloria and Regal's supervising producer Joey Gosiengfiao) feared that the film would not be picked up for distribution due to its 315-minute runtime and therefore urged Diaz 'to follow the dictates of the industry' and cut his work down to a maximum of two hours (Diaz 2015: 38).

The experience at Regal and the struggle to make *Ebolusyon ni Ray Gallardo* and *Batang West Side* independently convinced Diaz that the key to developing an engaged cinema in the Philippines was economic, namely the socially concerned film-makers' ownership of the means of production. The occasion to emancipate from the studios' clutches came in the early 2000s as digital video equipment and editing softwares were becoming increasingly available in South East Asia at a lower cost than 35mm, 16mm and super8 cameras, film stock and post-production facilities. Satisfied with the first tests of the new technology, Diaz reworked the narrative structure of *Ebolusyon ni Ray Gallardo* and, from March 2003 to November 2004, shot plenty of additional Philippines-set scenes on digital with a few professional actors and a small crew of close friends (Tioseco 2006b), transforming the original film about a Filipino sailor lost in New York into what today is known as *Ebolusyon ng isang pamilyang Pilipino* (*Evolution of a Filipino Family*) (Diaz 2004) – a history of 1971–87 Philippines as seen through the eyes of the Gallardo and the Santelmo families, 'apolitical barrio folk' (Tioseco 2006a) trying to make ends meet between the Luzon countryside and Manila.

Synthesizing his father's socialism and his mother's Catholicism, Diaz thus hailed the coming of digital technology that allowed him to finish his ten-year-in-the-making project and to shoot his following three features – *Heremias: Unang aklat – Ang alamat ng prinsesang bayawak* (*Heremias: Book One – The Legend of the Lizard Princess*) (Diaz 2006), *Kagadanan sa banwaan ning mga engkanto* (*Death in the Land of Encantos*) (Diaz 2007) and *Melancholia* (Diaz 2008) – on budgets as low as PHP 160,000[3]:

> You own the brush now, you own the gun, unlike before, whe[n] it was all owned by the studio. Now it is all yours. It is so free now. I can finish one whole film inside this room. [...] We do not depend on film studios and capitalists anymore. This is liberation cinema now. [...] Digital is liberation theology. Now we can have our own media. [...] The issue is not anymore that you cannot shoot.
>
> (Baumgärtel 2007: n.pag.)

As a proof of the newly conquered freedom from 'film studios and capitalists', not only did Diaz release *Ebolusyon ng isang pamilyang Pilipino* in an unmarketable eleven-hour cut, but he also embedded a scathing critique of the Filipino entertainment industry into the plot. The 654 minutes of *Ebolusyon ng isang pamilyang Pilipino* are in fact punctuated with lengthy, static shots showing the Gallardos and the Santelmos sitting still, listening attentively to radio soap opera *Ang lahat ay may pag-asa* ('Hope awaits everyone'). Together with agricultural and mining work, the programme regulates the rhythm of the two families' everyday life as they never miss an episode. Moreover, the radio drama appears to be the favourite talking point of the Gallardos and the Santelmos, as they prefer to discuss its plot rather than their own present and future under the Marcos regime. The Filipino entertainment industry is therefore revealed to be an ally of the powers that be, in that its output distracts common people's attention from their miserable working and living conditions and keeps them in a state of depoliticized passivity. In particular, Diaz indicts *Ang lahat ay may pag-asa* as an extremely effective tool to instil into the Filipino lower classes the fatalism that has been keeping them slaves for centuries: just like '[t]he various rituals of Holy Week [...] were used by the Spanish colonizers to inculcate among the *Indios* [...] resignation to things as they were and [...] preoccupation with [...] the afterlife rather than with conditions in this world' (Ileto 1989: 12), the soap opera bombards the audience ever since its title with the mantra that suffering is inevitable and poor people must endure because they will get their reward someday, in the hereafter if not in the earthly existence.

The very way in which *Ebolusyon ng isang pamilyang Pilipino* was made between 2003 and 2004 manifests Diaz's scorn for the entertainment industry.

Here, the specific target of his iconoclastic furore obviously is the modus operandi of the Filipino studio system, which he followed *obtorto collo* from the late 1980s to the early 2000s. Talking about the digital shooting of *Ebolusyon ng isang pamilyang Pilipino*, which ended up constituting 60 per cent of the finished film, Diaz stated:

> Everything was open – [...] I had a premise, that of capturing the struggles of invisible Filipinos in this very dysfunctional, feudal and corrupt system; [...] but there wasn't a story yet. [...] My process by then would be to write the daily struggles of my characters. I w[ould] just follow them, and oftentimes I would actually write the script, the dialogues a day before the shoot or during the shoot, oftentimes as instinct and common sense would suggest.
>
> (Tioseco 2006a: n.pag.)

In other words, after becoming his own man by trading analog film-making for digital video, Diaz continued his struggle to develop a personal, liberated and liberating national cinema by radically rethinking the function of the screenplay: from a control instrument that studios use to draw up an assembly-line-like production plan, thereby rationalizing and quickening the film's manufacturing, the script becomes just a general guideline for the shooting, one that can be modified at any time under the pressure of new ideas. Fed up with Regal's daily call sheets and tight working schedules, Diaz decided to try out a different way of working, based on taking one's time, moving to the filming location for a while with a small team of friends multitasking as cast and crew and letting the weather, the landscape, the locals and even chance influence the mood of the movie and the events portrayed therein. Diaz dubbed this more relaxed and more open film-making process first adopted in 2003–04 as 'organic' (Tioseco 2006a), and it has been the staple of his independent career up to now, as testified by the following anecdotes about the making of *Kagadanan sa banwaan ning mga engkanto, Siglo ng pagluluwal* (*Century of Birthing*) (Diaz 2011) and *Ang babaeng humayo* (*The Woman Who Left*) (Diaz 2016c):

> In 2006, typhoon Reming destroyed the [Luzon area where I had spent months shooting *Ebolusyon ng isang pamilyang Pilipino* and *Heremias: Unang aklat – Ang alamat ng prinsesang bayawak*, so] I wanted to go [there]. I went there a week after the typhoon struck [...]. Originally, the idea was just to shoot some footage of the destruction. After a few days of shooting, I returned to Manila, and watched what I had shot. I started to come up with some stories, and I decided to do a combination of documentary and fiction [...]. So I invited three theater actors from Manila and started improvising on some ideas and some characters. Every night I would

write the script, and the next morning we discussed it and then we shot in the areas where there was a lot of devastation. I had a vision of where the film was going, but I developed it day by day.

(Baumgärtel 2007: n.pag.)

I actually chose [the ending of *Siglo ng pagluluwal*] because of the storm [...]. I was in Marikina, the town where I live [...], and it was very early [...], like 6am. [...] So while I was having coffee, I heard two guys saying 'Hey, there's a storm coming in Central Luzon!'. Suddenly, [...] I had this image in mind: the Mad Woman [(Hazel Orencio)] and the Artist [(Perry Dizon)] meeting in the storm. I called the actors at once, 'Please, come, let's shoot!'. [...] So we met at 7am and we went to Nueva Ecija, in the area where the storm was going to hit: there we stayed, waiting for the storm – I was ready to shoot, with my camera and an umbrella.

(Guarneri 2013: n.pag.)

I actually wrote [the] ending [of *Ang babaeng humayo*] on the very last days of the shoot. The whole cast and crew was very surprised [...], almost shocked, when I presented them with the material. They were reading it and there was a big silence ... Then John Lloyd [Cruz], who played Hollanda, said something like 'Oh shit, it's me [who kills protagonist Horacia's nemesis, villain Rodrigo Trinidad]!'. You know, in the original plot outline, Hollanda was just a lost soul whom Horacia meets by chance in the streets of Calapan.

(Guarneri 2017: n.pag.)

Combined with the mammoth runtime of Diaz's 2004–18 output (approximately 76 hours across twelve fictional features), the style the film-maker began employing from *Ebolusyon ng isang pamilyang Pilipino* onwards also speaks volumes about rejecting the modus operandi of the Filipino studio system. His recording of pro-filmic action through extremely lengthy shots generally taken from a single camera position and angle is in fact a blatant refusal to adopt the 'full coverage' approach prevalent among 'movie industry people' (Tioseco 2006a: n.pag.).[4] At the same time, this reaction against the dominant film industry conventions goes hand in hand with the desire to fight the anaesthesia of escapist entertainment and use cinema to hold the mirror up to Filipino society, as Diaz's extremely lengthy shots adding up to enormous running times are meant to physically confront the audience with the burden of centuries of suffering endured by the Filipino people. As the film-maker said about *Ebolusyon ng isang pamilyang Pilipino*, and about the four-shot, 21-minute sequence of poor man Ricardo Gallardo's bleeding to death in a deserted Manila alley in particular:

I am capturing real time. I am trying to experience what these people are experiencing. They walk. I must experience their walk. I must experience their boredom and sorrows. [...] In the film's central death scene, I want the audience to experience the afflictions of my people who have been agonising for so long – under the Spaniards [...], under the Americans [...], under the Japanese [...], and then under Marcos [...]. I want people to experience our agony. [Ricardo's death] is the death scene of the Filipinos. I wanted it longer, believe me. It could have been longer if not for a kid with a bicycle who [...] interrupted the shot.

(Wee 2005: n.pag.)

Conclusion

During his stint at Regal, Diaz did his best to address issues he considered important for his fellow countrymen to reflect upon. *Burger Boys* denounces the governmental neglect of the poor through a plot line about an all-talk-and-no-action Secretary for the Unfortunate and by including in the soundtrack the song 'Rage' by The Jerks ('Children begging in the streets at night / Knocking on cars till the morning light / People standing in line for a kilo of rice / Welcome to the dark ages, the era of lies / [...] And the names and faces of the tyrants change / But poverty, pain and murder remains'). *Serafin Geronimo: Ang kriminal ng Baryo Concepcion* shows that the politically motivated murders of journalists and the corruption in the armed forces typical of the Marcos administration continued after the People Power Revolution, while *Hesus, rebolusyonaryo* – whose soundtrack once again features The Jerks singing about seemingly never-ending dark times – imagines a dystopian future in which a Marcos imitator carries out a military coup as Muslim secessionists and communist revolutionaries run riot. Finally, *Hubad sa ilalim ng buwan* inaugurates Diaz's use of the character of the violated young woman wandering around in shock in the vastness of the Filipino landscape as a metaphor for a society that is lost, numb, unable to come to terms with the horrors of its past – an analogy that would later return in *Melancholia, Siglo ng pagluluwal, Florentina Hubaldo, CTE* (Diaz 2012), *Hele sa hiwagang hapis* (*A Lullaby to the Sorrowful Mystery*) (Diaz 2016a) and *Ang babaeng humayo*. However, the constraints imposed on Diaz by Regal prevented him from fully realizing his vision of 'a National Cinema [...] that will help create a responsible Filipino people' (Diaz 2015: 39).

It is only after the introduction of digital video in the country around the turn of the millennium that Diaz became his own man and abandoned the mainstream to pursue a liberated and liberating personal film-making practice. He has been using the 'organic' modus operandi described in the previous subsection to this very day and – together with the critical acclaim he has been receiving at European film festivals since the early 2000s – it is the main reason why studio producers and stars in the Philippines are becoming more and more curious to collaborate with him. In recent years, Diaz has in fact been able to involve in the production of his anti-escapist films not only a number of commercially minded Filipino independent producers like Paul Soriano but also ABS-CBN, one of the biggest media conglomerates in the Philippines, which granted Diaz the use of its contracted stars Piolo Pascual, John Lloyd Cruz and Shaina Magdayao and contributed to the PHP 4 million[5] budget of *Ang babaeng humayo* via its television channel Cinema One. Whilst the film-maker's non-Regal body of work remains very little seen in the Philippines, confined as it is in the alternative circuit of (mostly Manila-based) film festivals, cultural institutions and art galleries,[6] it is undeniable that, from the production side, Diaz is slowly yet effectively working in his home country 'to destroy this classical divide – the indie and the mainstream. There should be no divide: cinema is one, cinema is [...] art' (Guarneri 2016: n.pag.) and, as stated in *Hele sa hiwagang hapis*, 'Art expresses only one thing: freedom'.

NOTES

1. Between USD 60,000 and 80,000 in the late 1990s.
2. Since Diaz went beyond schedule for *Burger Boys* (shooting started in late 1997 based on the screenplay *Larong krimen*) and *Serafin Geronimo: Ang kriminal ng Baryo Concepcion* (shooting started in mid-1998 based on the screenplay *Ang kriminal ng Baryo Concepcion*), Regal halted both films before completion: the latter Diaz managed to finish because he renounced his salary, while the former was completed only after *Serafin Geronimo: Ang kriminal ng Baryo Concepcion* made some money through a brief theatrical run.
3. Between USD 2,800 and 3,800 in the 2005–08 period.
4. There occasionally are very lengthy shots in Diaz's studio films and in independent effort *Batang West Side* too. However, it is only when the film-maker embraced digital technology that the duration of almost every shot within the films became massive, with peaks of 61 minutes – an entire MiniDV cassette – in *Heremias: Unang aklat – Ang alamat ng prinsesang bayawak*.
5. Around USD 85,000 in March 2016, when pre-production started.
6. Broadcast by ABS-CBN on 11 June 2017 as part of Cinema One's primetime series 'Blockbuster Sundays', *Ang babaeng humayo* is the exception that confirms the rule.

REFERENCES

Balintataw ('Pupil') (1986–93, Philippines: PTV).

Baumgärtel, Tilman (2007), 'Lav Diaz: Digital is liberation theology', *GreenCine*, 7 September, http://web.archive.org/web/20150608031447/http://www.greencine.com/central/lavdiaz. Accessed March 2019.

Brocka, Lino (1975), *Maynila sa mga kuko ng liwanag* (*Manila: In the Claws of Light*), Philippines: CineManila.

Brocka, Lino (1976), *Insiang*, Philippines: Cinema Artists.

Cinco, Manuel (1993), *Galvez: Hanggang sa dulo ng mundo hahanapin kita* ('Galvez: I'll hunt you down until the end of the world'), Philippines: Regal.

Dayao, Dodo and Alagbate, Mabie (2015), 'Beer and Brocka', in S. Debuysere (ed.), *Lav Diaz: Laying down in a World of Tempest*, Brussels: Cinematek, pp. 61–68.

Deocampo, Nick (1987), *Revolutions Happen Like Refrains in a Song*, Philippines: n.p.

Diaz, Lav (dir.) (1998), *Serafin Geronimo: Ang kriminal ng Baryo Concepcion* (*The Criminal of Barrio Concepcion*), Philippines: Good Harvest.

Diaz, Lav (dir.) (1999a), *Hubad sa ilalim ng buwan* (*Naked under the Moon*), Philippines: Good Harvest.

Diaz, Lav (dir.) (1999b), *Burger Boys*, Philippines: Good Harvest.

Diaz, Lav (dir.) (2001), *Batang West Side* (*West Side Kid*), Philippines: JMCN, Hinabing Pangarap.

Diaz, Lav (dir.) (2002), *Hesus, rebolusyonaryo* (*Jesus, the Revolutionary*), Philippines: Regal.

Diaz, Lav (dir.) (2004), *Ebolusyon ng isang pamilyang Pilipino* (*Evolution of a Filipino Family*), Philippines: Sine Olivia, Paul Tañedo and Ebolusyon Productions.

Diaz, Lav (dir.) (2006), *Heremias: Unang aklat – Ang alamat ng prinsesang bayawak* (*Heremias: Book One – The Legend of the Lizard Princess*), Philippines, Netherlands and Sweden: Sine Olivia, Hubert Bals Fund and Göteborg Film Fund.

Diaz, Lav (dir.) (2007), *Kagadanan sa banwaan ning mga engkanto* (*Death in the Land of Encantos*), Philippines and Netherlands: Sine Olivia and Hubert Bals Fund.

Diaz, Lav (dir.) (2008), *Melancholia*, Philippines: Sine Olivia.

Diaz, Lav (2011), *Siglo ng pagluluwal* (*Century of Birthing*), Philippines: Sine Olivia.

Diaz, Lav (dir.) (2012), *Florentina Hubaldo, CTE*, Philippines: Sine Olivia.

Diaz, Lav (2015), 'The aesthetic challenge of *Batang West Side*', in S. Debuysere (ed.), *Lav Diaz: Laying down in a World of Tempest*, Brussels: Cinematek, pp. 37–40.

Diaz, Lav (dir.) (2016a), *Hele sa hiwagang hapis* (*A Lullaby to the Sorrowful Mystery*), Philippines and Singapore: Ten17P, Epicmedia, Sine Olivia, Potocol and Akanga Film Productions.

Diaz, Lav (dir.) (2016b), *Ang araw bago ang wakas* (*The Day before the End*), Philippines: Sine Olivia.

Diaz, Lav (dir.) (2016c), *Ang babaeng humayo* (*The Woman Who Left*), Philippines: Sine Olivia and Cinema One Originals.

Garcia, Roger (2000), 'The art of pito-pito', *Film Comment*, 36:4, pp. 53–55.

Guarneri, Michael (2011), 'Exploitation is never cool to me: A conversation with Lav Diaz', *Fellinia*, http://www.fellinia.com.ar/entrevistas/explotation-is-never-cool-to-me-the-anti-feudal-cinema. Accessed 1 March 2019.

Guarneri, Michael (2013), 'Militant elegy: A conversation with Lav Diaz', *LFU*, http://www.lafuriaumana.it/index.php/29-issues/numero-17/16-michael-guarneri-militant-elegy-a-conversation-with-lav-diaz. Accessed 1 March 2019.

Guarneri, Michael (2014), 'The burden of history: A conversation with Lav Diaz', *LFU*, http://www.lafuriaumana.it/?id=243. Accessed March 2019.

Guarneri, Michael (2016), 'Philippines year zero: A conversation with Lav Diaz', 2 October, *Débordements*, http://www.debordements.fr/Lav-Diaz. Accessed March 2019.

Guarneri, Michael (2017), 'No forgiveness without justice: A conversation with Lav Diaz', *Débordements*, http://www.debordements.fr/Lav-Diaz-2017. Accessed March 2019.

Hawley, Charles V. (2002), 'You're a better Filipino than I am, John Wayne: World War II, Hollywood, and US-Philippines relations', *Pacific Historical Review*, 17:3, pp. 389–414.

Ileto, Reynaldo C. (1989), *Pasyon and Revolution: Popular Movements in the Philippines, 1840–1910*, Quezon City, Philippines: Ateneo de Manila University Press.

Mijares, Primitivo ([1976] 2016), *The Conjugal Dictatorship of Ferdinand and Imelda Marcos*, Quezon City, Philippines: Rizal Library Digital Collection, https://web.archive.org/web/20180218231827/http://rizalls.lib.admu.edu.ph:8080/ebooks2/Primitivo%20Mijares.pdf. Accessed March 2019.

Salvador, Augusto (1991), *Mabuting kaibigan masamang kaaway* ('Good friend, bad enemy'), Philippines: Tagalog Ilang-Ilang Productions.

Spence, Hartzell (1964), *For Every Tear a Victory: The Story of Ferdinand E. Marcos*, New York: McGraw-Hill.

Tioseco, Alexis (2005), 'Indictment and empowerment of the individual: The modern cinema of Lav Diaz', in R. Manassero (ed.), *23° Torino Film Festival*, Turin: Museo Nazionale del Cinema, pp. 168–71.

Tioseco, Alexis (2006a), 'A conversation with Lav Diaz', *Criticine*, http://criticine.com/interview_article.php?id=21. Accessed March 2019.

Tioseco, Alexis (2006b), 'Brief notes on the long journey of *Ebolusyon*', *Criticine*, http://criticine.com/interview_article.php?id=21&pageid=1139148986. Accessed March 2019.

Tolentino, Rolando B. (2003), 'Postnational family/postfamilial nation: Family, small town and nation talk in Marcos and Brocka', *Inter-Asia Cultural Studies*, 4:1, pp. 77–92.

Wee, Brandon (2005), 'The decade of living dangerously: A chronicle from Lav Diaz', *Senses of Cinema*, http://sensesofcinema.com/2005/filipino-cinema/lav_diaz/. Accessed March 2019.

PART 2

FROM DEATH TO THE GODS: THE RESURRECTION OF THE NATIONAL?

5

Never, Always and Already Saved: A Soteriological Reading of *Norte* and *Florentina Hubaldo, CTE*

Marco Grosoli

In his '*Melancholia*: The long, slow cinema of Lav Diaz', William Brown makes a very important point about temporality in Diaz's cinema. Taking the cue from Jonathan Beller's (2006) concept of heliotropism, Brown (2016: 119) argues that *Melancholia* (Diaz 2008) conflates two modalities of time. One is the abstract time that cinema is bound to by way of its inherently heliotropic character: by writing with light, cinema makes things visible and turns them into a spectacle at the price of imposing abstraction on them. Yet time is, by definition, not something that can be visualized, and indeed the other modality described by Brown stands in relation to the heliotropic one (with which it is inextricably intertwined) as darkness stands to light. The abstraction of time into something like a cinematic action is of course there, yet what is also there is time followed in its invisibility so that the non-abstract side of the world can somehow appear.

> [A]s I watch the jungle sequence with Renato and colleagues, my sense of time and my desire for 'action' begin to change and soon I find myself marvelling at how raindrops make quiver a branch and leaves that extend from off-screen and into the foreground of one of the section's various images. That is, I suddenly find joy in the minutiae of the film because everything is seemingly alive.
>
> (Brown 2016: 121)

What is at stake, in other words, is a worldly thickness of a Kracauerian kind, which exceeds and contrasts the heliotropic abstraction that cinema cannot but perpetrate. Diaz refuses to constrict his films into the abstract time of spectacle-driven cinema, making them rest upon a different kind of time altogether, in order to elicit a fuller perception and a sensual awareness of that thickness. His cinema does not attach any value to slowness per se but embraces a certain kind of contemplative temporality that may be perceived as slow in order to bring to the fore the dark side of time, that is, time qua invisible as opposed to abstracted time.

In this chapter, I set out to explore a similar temporal twofoldness in relation to *Norte, hangganan ng kasaysayan* (*Norte, the End of History*) (Diaz 2013a) and *Florentina Hubaldo, CTE* (Diaz 2012). One of his rare works in colour, the former lends itself particularly well to a similar exploration, in that even a superficial glance at it cannot fail to notice how cinematographer Larry Manda consistently attempted to enhance the blackness of blacks, always very present in the frame, while maintaining throughout a difficult balance between the richness of the palette and the sharpness, blaze and desaturation of digital chromatic textures.

Yet although this photographic style embodies somewhat blatantly the aforementioned interpenetration between cinema's inherent heliotropism and darkness, I will focus not so much on the visuals but rather on narrative. Indeed, while finding Brown's hypothesis fully convincing, I think it would have benefited from greater consideration of narrative as it is by no means a secondary component of Diaz's cinema.

I should add, however, that I will not carry out a full-fledged narrative analysis of the two films at issue here (*Norte* and *Florentina*); rather, my scope will be limited to one single structural aspect shared by both, namely the juxtaposition of the narrative arcs of two characters, one of whom (Fabian, Florentina) is stubbornly striving to be saved, while the other (Joaquin, Lolita) is strangely 'already saved' and 'utterly unsaveable' at the same time. The reference to salvation, here, is not incidental: while Brown rightly links the aesthetic dimension of Diaz's cinema with its political/postcolonial implications, by drawing attention to narrative I would also make *religion* enter the equation. By drawing upon *Norte* and *Florentina*, I will thus articulate together the aesthetic, the political/postcolonial and the religious dimensions of Diaz's cinema.

Norte, the End of History

Fabian, the main character, is unambiguously a twenty-first-century version of Rodiòn Romànovič Raskòl'nikov, the (anti)hero of Fyodor Dostoyevsky's *Crime and Punishment* ([1866] 2014). A former law student imbued with vaguely Nietzschean beliefs of moral superiority, Fabian kills an aged female pawnbroker just like Raskòl'nikov. His goal was not only to prove his philosophies right but also to let penniless Joaquin, along with his wife and their children, find respite from the woman's relentless financial blackmailing. What he gets, however, is irreversible doom for precisely the people that he wanted to save: Joaquin, charged with murder, ends up in prison, and consequently, his family gets poorer and poorer. Accordingly, two narrative threads are intertwined throughout *Norte*. One is the story of Fabian, whose first murder triggers a chain reaction entailing more and more crimes, always with the best of intentions: his is the story of someone who constantly struggles to set things right only to make them more and more wrong instead. The other story is that of Joaquin and his family, extremely poor people whose quiet acceptance and resignation, and whose good-hearted stoicism in the face of almost inhuman adversity, make them look as if they were no less than saints. *Norte* systematically alternates between these two strands, Fabian and Joaquin (and/or his family), never reaching a narrative closure for either of them. Each is trapped in his own dead end, one in jail, the other rejected by everybody, aimlessly wandering around, alone, desperate, half-crazy (he rapes his sister and kills his dog for no apparent reason), without a clue as to what to do with his life.

Those who are familiar with Diaz's films prior to 2013 can hardly be surprised by the *Crime and Punishment* connection. The main character of his debut feature, *Serafin Geronimo: Ang kriminal ng Baryo Concepcion* (*The Criminal of Barrio Conception*) (Diaz 1998), was clearly modelled after Raskòl'nikov and so was the hero of his *Hesus, rebolusyonaryo* (Diaz 2002). Dostoyevskyan themes also appear in *Batang West Side* (*West Side Avenue*) (Diaz 2001), in *Melancholia* and in *Kagadanan sa banwaan ning mga engkanto* (*Death of the Land of Encantos*) (Diaz 2007a). As attested by his anthology *Critic after Dark* (2005), Noel Vera has been diligently following this Dostoyevskyan strand of Diaz's filmography since the very beginning, so when *Norte* came out he was in a good position to deliver a masterful analysis of the 'Dostoyevsky variations' (Vera 2013) in that film.

Vera draws our attention to two elements in particular. The first is that in Diaz's film there is no detective Petrovich any longer. Second, to make up for this substantial lack, the screenwriters have blown up the narrative relevance, the screen-time breadth and the structural importance of another character, namely Joaquin. The latter stands for Nikolai Dementiev, who in Dostoyevsky's novel was a painter whose religious quasi-fanaticism pushed him to agree to pay for somebody else's guilt. In *Crime and Punishment*, Dementiev is but a marginal figure whose story-line does not occupy much of the novel's texture; in a sense, Dementiev is but a symptom of Raskòl'nikov, the main character, in that it fleetingly indicates a path of religious salvation Raskòl'nikov is not quite able to follow. Accordingly, Joaquin too should stand for a religious salvation Fabian is too self-absorbed to be even willing to attain. However, in contrast with Dementiev's, Joaquin's story-line stretches throughout the film and runs parallel to Fabian's, from the beginning to the end.

This is no minor twisting of *Crime and Punishment*'s original structure. In the novel, Petrovich supplied a substantial part not only of the story's dramatic spinal tap (as detections typically do) but also of the psychological analysis of the main character. *Norte*, however, needs neither of them. It relegates both psychology and straightforward, goal-oriented, linearly concatenated action to the background so that religion can occupy a prominent position in the foreground.

What should by no means be overlooked is that both the relative rejection of the former and the emphasis given to the latter have to do with a certain conception of temporality. As is well known, linear teleological time is the bête noire of a lot of postcolonial thinking, and Diaz is no exception as also openly acknowledged in his interviews:

> I am applying the theory that we Malays, we Filipinos, are not governed by the concept of time. We are governed by the concept of space. We don't believe in time. If you live in the country, you see Filipinos hang out. They are not very productive. That is very Malay. It is all about space and nature. If we were governed by time, we would be very progressive and productive. [...] In the Philippine archipelago, nature provided everything, until the concept of property came with the Spanish colonizers. Then the capitalist order took control. I have developed my aesthetic framework around the idea that we Filipinos are governed by nature. The concept of time was introduced to us when the Spaniards came. We had to do oracion at six o'clock, start work at seven. Before it was free, it was Malay.
>
> (Diaz 2007b: n.pag.)

Accordingly, Diaz's aesthetic project can be easily, and correctly, recognized as a politically charged struggle within and against linear time as also hinted by the reference to the two modalities of time (and light) at the beginning of this chapter. And this applies to *Norte* as well. The elimination of Petrovich is a way of getting rid of both the orderly concatenation of dramatic action and the reconstruction of causes and effects through psychological analysis. Thereby, teleology loses ground. But what about religion then? Does not Christian eschatology locate salvation very teleologically in the end of times? And indeed, something like a possible spiritual rebirth for Raskòl'nikov can be glimpsed only at the end of *Crime and Punishment*.

Yet whereas Dementiev is a fleeting symptom of a religious salvation that in Raskòl'nikov's case is lying *ahead*, Joaquin embodies a religious salvation that runs *parallel* to Fabian's gradual descent into damnation. Unlike Raskòl'nikov, the Filipino student never experiences any respite, not even as a mere possibility and not even in the ending; still, that possibility is there *throughout* his closure-less and completely desperate narrative arc, as hinted at through Joaquin. Salvation is not the resolution of damnation ahead of it but rather runs *alongside* it, and *with* it.

As any interview would confirm (including the excerpt given earlier), Diaz knows fully well that the roots of the seemingly never-ending predicament of the

Filipino people must be located, among others, in the violently imposed Christian legacy of the ancient colonizers. It follows that artists who, like Diaz, strive to contribute to the emancipation of the Filipino people should, among others, attempt to break free from that legacy by turning it against itself. *Norte* does not simply negate the Christian paradox of the inextricability between damnation and salvation; rather, it pushes it to its extreme by expunging teleology out of it. Fabian never stops trying to save himself, and all he gets in return is inescapable damnation. Joaquin accepts fully, unresentfully and unreservedly his cursed fate from the very beginning, and although his life in jail is nothing short of hell on earth (because of violence, privations, loneliness etc.), he is the one who is saved, and attains some kind of beatitude, however harsh his earthly condition is, if only in the guise of quiet and self-contented resignation. Joaquin is at one and the same time utterly unsavable and always already saved insofar as he never tries to attain salvation, whereas Fabian is only utterly unsavable because he never gives up trying to save himself. In this regard, Joaquin is again the symptom of Fabian but in an entirely different fashion from Dementiev's. By virtue of the very fact that the two narrative arcs are parallel, and equally immune to change (neither characters ever really incur in any significant transformation), Joaquin appears to be the embodied objection against the teleological principle Fabian never gives up. Thus, the entire structure of the film comes down to a path (Fabian's) that originally seems to be oriented teleologically but ends up in fact getting stuck, along with the negation of that very teleology (Joaquin) running parallel to it. It comes down, in other words, to the *immediate* coincidence between damnation and salvation, without any teleological articulation between the two. Salvation must be looked for *within* damnation – not beyond or ahead of it.

What matters most is that Diaz, of course, does not leave all of these at the stage of abstract religious speculation but translates it in straightforwardly visual terms. The last two scenes sum it all up by showing first Joaquin lying motionless on his back and suddenly levitating upward towards the sky, never breaking the horizontal pose; then Fabian floating on a small boat on stagnant waters more and more slowly until the boat moves no more – and in fact, its motion is so slow that one cannot quite tell when is the exact moment when the boat ceases to move. Fabian constantly moves horizontally (as in he tries to attain an exclusively mundane salvation by acting in this world) but only gets to the point where motion and stillness are indistinguishable; Joaquin gives motion (i.e. action) up until he finds the only possible motion within stillness through vertical ascension – one that never reaches any sky though.

The mundane hell Fabian is a prisoner of is instead the hell of horizontal-only motion in which there can be nothing else than causes and consequences. In one of his last books (*Karman*), Giorgio Agamben shows through thorough philological research that in Roman law, both *causa* ('cause') and *culpa* ('guilt') were origin-ally not so much juridical concepts as marks of 'the point at which a certain act or fact enters into the sphere of the law' (2018: 5), thereby laying the foundations for the edifice of law to exist. What both *causa* and *culpa* share is that they enable the imputability of man's actions to a system of causes and consequences; what is crucial here is that man is not *inherently* imputable to this system but only because of the external existence of this legal mechanism per se.

> [*Causa*] is the 'thing' [*cosa*] of the law, what gives rise to a trial and, in this way, implicates people in the sphere of the Law. The primal cause is the accusation. [...] *Causa* is a certain situation, an 'affair' [*cosa*] – in itself non- juridical – at the moment in which it is included in the sphere of the law [...] [*Culpa*] indicates the threshold across which a certain behavior becomes imputable to the subject, who is consti-tuted as 'culpable' (*in culpa esse*; *obnoxius*, culpable, does not designate the one who has caused the crime but, according to the originarily locative meaning of the preposition *ob*, the one who stands in *culpa*). We are dealing with a fatal threshold, because it leads into a region where our actions and our gestures lose all innocence and are subjected to an alien power: punishment or pain [*pena*], which means both the price to be paid and a suffering for which we cannot give ourselves a reason.
>
> (Agamben 2018: 3–6)

The fact that causes have consequences is, in itself, beyond man's control and does not depend on man *stricto sensu*; hence the whole idea of responsibility, resting upon the link between causes and consequences, cannot but be, to a cer-tain degree, always arbitrary and Kafkaesquely unfounded. Because of this need to attach to somebody's responsibility the (essentially separate) fact that causes have consequences, law projects on man the shadow of imputability, and since as early as Aristotle ethics is first and foremost a product of this projection of respon-sibility. As a result, definite ends start to be attached to human activity, thereby also entering a conundrum that would haunt Western civilization for centuries, namely the insoluble conflict between means and ends. Eventually, Christianity would unsuccessfully attempt to come to terms with that same conundrum by introducing the concept of 'persons' endowed with free will, a conscience, a psy-chological individuality and so on. That is to say, by misleadingly assuming that action is the product of subjects' *voluntary deliberation* (not to be confounded with the *responsibility* of the Greeks, which is mere imputability), Christianity came up with a new criterion whereby to distinguish between legitimate and illegitimate means, as well as legitimate and illegitimate ends. Yet the subordination of means to ends remained untouched and so did the original conundrum of Western ethics itself. The only way out would then be *means without ends*, that is, in the final liberation of means from their purposiveness. The elaboration thereof is, according to Agamben, the task of the coming civilization.

Norte takes one of the novels that went the farthest ever in exploring human psychology and conscience and completely de-psychologizes it. In lieu of ana-lysing Raskòl'nikov psychologically, it adds a parallel character (Joaquin) who is nothing but a man wrongly accused of something he did not do. Fabian, the de-psychologized Raskòl'nikov, is stuck in the hellish and deceptively teleological circle of means and ends: it starts off by murdering a woman to prove that self-appointed ends can justify the means but ends up committing crimes merely for their being ends in themselves without any other purpose (e.g. when he rapes his sister and kills his own dog). Meanwhile, Joaquin, the very embodiment of man's foreignness to law, lives out his life in jail passively, with no goal at all, and every-thing he does (mopping the floor, weaving straw baskets or being violently abused), he does with a sort of blessed and resigned neutrality.

To bring to life his twenty-first-century Raskòl'nikov, Diaz refuses the Chris-tian/Dostoyevskyan mask of psychology, which was meant to replace the void of personhood, itself but a by-product of the juridical apparatus of *causa/culpa*. Instead, he focuses precisely on this Kafkaesque apparatus (into which Joaquin falls in the beginning by being unjustly accused) and pits it against a subversive reinvention of Christian eschatology. There is no way out: the machinery of lan-guage and law has irreversibly contaminated the world, trapping us forever into the hell of means and ends, of causes and consequences, from which we vainly attempt to escape through purposive action, thereby getting more and more entangled in it instead. However, salvation *can* be found *within* this perpetual damnation, because space can be opened up nonetheless for life to be experienced and lived away from the purposiveness that crushes our world. This space is none other than the dark and invisible side of time that was sketched at the beginning of this chapter, the worldly thickness that forms the underside of heliotropism, of instrumentality, of abstraction. Diaz does not give up cinematic action altogether: he just refuses to elevate it into the guiding principle of pacing and makes it be entangled instead in the physiological rhythms of beings and of their environments. Ultimately, the attention to them is so great that the purpose itself of actions is, as it were, liquefied in this contemplative underside of the world in which motion is followed closely and carefully, so as to let it find a shape of its own. In this way, motion seemingly belongs no more to the orderly, mechanic concatenation of causes and effects that we usually call 'action' or to the conscious responsibility of a definite agent but is displayed in all its innocence, in a quasi-nirvana-esque state, well within the hell that world is, away from the juridical machinery (of which psychology is but a by-product) that brings action forth by allocating to it consequences, some pur-pose and some titularity.

Joaquin's wife dies right before the levitation scene, in a bus accident – but not incidentally. In a way, her death is required by the logic itself of the story. Throughout *Norte*, she is the only one circulating between Joaquin and Fabian; thus, her death only reinforces the point that there should be no *narrative* mediation between damnation and salvation, between the vain activity of action (Fabian) and the passive endurance of a guilt (Joaquin) that is never the agent's own and never more than a pure and subject-less by-product of action itself, bypassing the fiction of psychology. Because the whole point of the film lies in its inextricability, it also lies in forcing the viewers themselves to discern outside the narrative and away from any teleological articulation, but rather in the carefully composed and colour-graded textures of the images themselves, the interpenetration between darkness and heliotropism, stillness and motion, worldly thickness and abstraction, time qua entropic invisible force and orderly narrative concatenation. Or, as Agamben would put it, the moment when goal-oriented action seems to lose its purposiveness along the way and, thanks to Diaz's highly choreographed and yet so natural direction of actors, becomes pure gesture.

Florentina Hubaldo, CTE

Joaquin, however, is not merely Dementiev's equivalent. In his 'Dostoyevskyan Variations', Vera rightly points out that *Norte*, through Joaquin, incorporates

> a short story by another great Russian writer, namely Tolstoy's 'God Sees the Truth, But Waits', in which a man is wrongly exiled to Siberia for murder. Like Tolstoy's Ivan Dmitrich Aksionov, Joaquin is basically a decent man; like Aksionov he's beaten severely (tellingly Tolstoy emphasizes not the physical but the psychological toll of long internment: the shame, the sense of injustice, the prolonged separation from loved ones).
>
> (Vera 2013: 43)

Tolstoy's tale also inspired *Ang babaeng humayo* (*The Woman Who Left*) (Diaz 2016), a film which also expands upon a few thematic strands coming from *Melancholia* (especially the friendship between Rina and Alberta and the confusion of identities). This is but one example of the fact that Diaz's oeuvre is, among others, a densely interwoven tapestry in which a number of elements recur across different films. The rest of this chapter will thus be dedicated to tracing a few parallels between *Norte* and *Florentina*.

Florentina is a young girl living with her father, a brute who systematically rapes her and obliges her to prostitute herself as well as to undergo an unspecified number of abortions. Her mother obviously ran away, while her daughter Loleng was miraculously rescued from her grandfather's murderous fury and delivered to some neighbours a few years before. There, she leads a relatively decent life, although she suffers from a chronic pneumonia that renders her unable to do anything else but sit on a chair. This is of course nothing compared to the hell on earth Florentina must undergo, and from which she periodically tries to run away, to absolutely no avail, as her father always catches her back. Her multiple traumas arrested her growth, so she now is basically an eternal child, stuck in a never-ending state of mindless and childlike stupor.

Like in *Norte*, two characters are followed more or less in parallel. One is utterly unsavable but nonetheless constantly striving to be saved: Florentina never gives up the hope of running away from her dreadful conditions. The other is at the same time already saved and unsavable: Loleng has virtually been saved by her well-meaning neighbours, but she is nevertheless unable to lead a normal life due to her health conditions. Unlike in *Norte*, though, one of the characters does undergo transformation as Loleng dies of tuberculosis. The point, however, is that she does not disappear from the *fabula* of the film: not long before the ending, but still after Loleng's death, a flashback shows Florentina along with Loleng as a little child. Hence the parallel is maintained for most of the film, if in a slightly different way from *Norte*.

Loleng's death also intersects a third narrative strand: two city dwellers spending several days in the countryside area where Loleng's adoptive family also lives, looking for a treasure they will never find. Meanwhile, they also engage in another pursuit, which turns out to be successful: after having been bothered by a gecko constantly crying nearby and after many failed attempts to catch it, one of them finally manages to do so. Eventually, however, in the wake of the emotions generated by Loleng's death, he sets the animal free. Thus, this third strand consists of the juxtaposition of two different negations of teleology: for one, the end is never to be attained (the treasure can never be found); for the other, even when the end is attained, it is attained *in vain* (the gecko, first caught and then freed). Therefore, this configuration can be regarded as a mise en abyme of the Florentina-Loleng juxtaposition. The film ends with Florentina trying to flee from her father for the umpteenth time, sheltered in a house encountered along the way. While the film remains ambiguous as to whether she finally found salvation, it does show her in a similar situation as the one Loleng has previously been in, thereby further enhancing, even after Loleng's death, the inextricability between the unsaveable-but-striving-towards-salvation and the already-saved-but-still-unsaveable.

Like in *Norte*, this multiple intertwinement between damnation and salvation has distinctly religious undertones. Florentina often dreams of her childhood, when she would attend the Feast of San Clemente (the patron of the fishermen), with giant paper-mache dolls portraying Spanish conquistadores (the *higantes*) parading on the streets. These larger-than-like figures were ostensibly little more than ridiculously big caricatures, but in Florentina's infantile dreams they become something like a celestial, angel-like apparition, embodying an indefinite promise of some sort of redemption. One that is, however, forever out of reach: she recalls/imagines herself stretching her hands towards them without ever managing to touch them. In her mind, constantly going back to them as a way to escape her lifelong sufferings, these big white giants are not just caricatures but also something of *messianic* figures.

To clarify what kind of messianism is at issue here, it is worth referring again to Agamben – perhaps less as a philosopher in his own right than as the exceptionally erudite scholar endowed with an outstanding sense of synthesis, enabling him to summarize century-old patterns of thought in a few, remarkably concise and precise definitions. In *The Time That Remains* (2005), Agamben has showed that a closer look at Saint Paul reveals that according to the original Christian messianism, the end of time does not lie ahead of ordinary linear time. Rather, it lies in the gap between two coexisting temporalities: one constantly approaching its end, the other always already ended.

> In every representation we make of time and in every discourse by means of which we define and represent time, another time is implied that is not entirely consumed by representation. It is as though man, insofar as he is a thinking and speaking being, produced an additional time with regard to chronological time, a time that prevented him from perfectly coinciding with the time out of which he could make images and representations. This ulterior time, nevertheless, is not another time, it is not a supplementary time added on from outside to chronological time. Rather, it is something like a time within time-not ulterior but interior-which only measures my disconnection with regard to it, my being out of synch and in noncoincidence with regard to my representation of time, but precisely because of this, allows for the possibility of my achieving and taking hold of it. We may now propose our first definition of messianic time: messianic time is *the time that time takes to come to an end*, or, more precisely, the time we take to bring to an end, to achieve our representation of time. This is not the line of chronological time (which was representable but unthinkable), nor the instant of its end (which was just as unthinkable); nor is it a segment cut from chronological time; rather, it is operational time pressing within the chronological time, working and transforming it from within; it is the time we need to make time end: *the time that is left us*.
>
> (Agamben 2005: 67–68, original emphases)

Florentina may identify it in those giant caricatures, but the film locates messianic salvation elsewhere, namely in the opening up of a second temporality, freed from purposiveness, while time runs towards its end, as was already described with regard to *Norte*. One example of this twofoldness would be another boat scene, although it is technically not a long take. Loleng is dying, and her adoptive father takes her on a pond, presumably in search of more salubrious air. Eight shots of the seemingly still boat follow (one of them though is a puzzling insert of Florentina and young Loleng standing on the shore). Nothing happens except, literally, time approaching its end: Loleng is dying and spurts blood in the seventh shot – otherwise she lies completely immobile. Yet our attention is caught by a myriad of details: by the way more and more clouds gather in the sky, by the alternation between the adoptive father's moment of desperate stillness and the moments in which he changes his posture, by the murmur of cicadas occasionally interrupted by other sounds, by the reflections on water, by the latter's ripples – and especially by the subtle chore-ography between the movements of the camera and those of the boat, *both* mostly imperceptible, so much so that it is often difficult to figure out which is moving and which is not. Like in that other similar scene in *Norte*, then, stillness and motion are deliberately confounded so as to visualize the interpenetration between time as per-petually reaching its end and time as having already reached it, yet here even more blatantly the form that this interpenetration takes is the sensual texture, the rhythm created by the interaction among all these visual and aural elements. Rhythm, here and elsewhere, is motion 'already ended', in the sense that it comes across as always/already crystallized in a shape, while still running towards its end.

Diaz would call this an 'organic' rhythm – an adjective he uses very often in interviews and elsewhere. Thorsten Botz-Bornstein (2017) has written an illuminating book on the organic in the films by slow cinema master Béla Tarr, and despite a few differences having to do with their respective historical and geo-graphical contexts, the conclusions he draws are very helpful in understanding what is organic in Diaz's cinema too. In essence, 'organic' means that a certain har-mony can be recognized in the moving images, which has not been imposed from without, but rather, and much like living organisms, consists in the way their parts relate to one another regardless of any overarching organizational principle. It is, in other words, a centreless equilibrium, that is, a sense of equilibrium between parts that does not depend on a centre on whose basis every part would find its place and role – which is also why the 'organic' is as far as it can be from the 'geo-metric'. The wholeness between them does not depend on them conforming all to a certain principle, but rather on a dynamic, dispersive and unstable system constantly renovating the terms by which an indefinite and ever-evolving number of parts relate differentially to one another so that harmony emerges from the constantly changing interplay of the relative differences occurring among them and not in relation to any centre. The typical Diazian long take, with people lengthily walking in a landscape and reciprocally interacting, certainly allows for a number of patterns to be individuated in the way walking, gesturing, talking and so on occur, yet they hardly ever are geometrical patterns – and it is precisely the non-geometric way people walk (typically, from the back of the frame toward the foreground, usually not in a straight manner) that helps building the organic continuity between man (or action) and environment that is evidently the main guiding principle of his mise en scene. Aural and visual patterns can also be recognized in the 80-second-long take in which Florentina stands in the middle of a running stream, holding Loleng in her arms: a certain way the two concurringly subdued noises of the wind and the water provide a background against which birds occasionally chirp, the uneven distribution of light (the right side is darker, and with more clouds), the graphic correspondence between the trees in the back of the frame and the two women in the background, and especially the many mutually resonating triangular patterns formed by the posture of the two human figures, by the stream and by both shores. Yet what is crucial is that none of these patterns result in an actual triangle: the landscape lets them be gently bent out of shape so that none of them can be reduced to a geometrical figure. To be sure, some compositional balance is there, but it is far from freezing the entirety of the image into rigidly all-encompassing geometrical patterns.

Figure 3.1: Triangular patterns in *Florentina Hubaldo, CTE* (2012). Film still. Courtesy of Lav Diaz.

Likewise, the eight shots of the aforementioned boat scene do follow a recognizable editing pattern: the first shot is shorter than a minute, the second and third are longer, then again two shorter, one longer and two shorter. And as the relative length of the shot decreases, the camera gets closer and closer to the boat. Yet this arrangement between editing pace and camera distance is not at all the main organizational principle of the scene but rather only one of the visual and aural rhythms displayed in it, along with Loleng's adoptive father changing his posture, the reflections of water and so on. All of these rhythms resonate harmonically with one another without any one harmonic principle taking over centripetally.

This is also why Botz-Bornstein insists that the organic harmonies between these rhythms cannot be analytically broken down into smaller grammatical units. In Diaz as much as in Tarr, the long take (or even the edited scene) is a whole that cannot be reduced to the sum of its components or mathematized by any rigid formula. A formalistic approach trying to pin down exhaustively the way a certain scene works by reconstructing the exact interaction between its elements is destined to fail because the differential interplay between them is virtually limitless.

> [T]ime (cinematic time or just any time) cannot be rendered through mathematically calculated structures even when time is rhythmic. While a formalist will look for the right balance of scenes by applying a mathematically calculated (geometric) model in which movement and time make logical sense, an organic film director will choose another path: she will let one scene (one 'real element') grow out of another element [...]. In other words, the movement creates its own temporal logic that can be called an organic rhythm.
>
> (Botz-Bornstein 2017: 183)

Thus, in spite of their differences, both the boat scenes in *Norte* and *Florentina* exemplify the 'dynamic paralysis' that according to Botz-Bornstein (2017: 29) is key to the concept and practice of the organic. Yet the main difference between the two films is elsewhere. Every now and then, Florentina tries to deliver some autobiographical information ('my name is Florentina Hubaldo, I was born in Antipolo, but when I was almost ten years old I transferred here to Bicol', and so on and so forth), but she never manages to arrange the events in her life into a linear, chronological sequence and unfailingly messes up their order beyond recognition. This is also what happens in the very last scene, when she is sitting in the house of her rescuers, whom we never see. And because its narrative thread is completely jumbled, non-chronological and ultimately cubist, blending actual events, memories and fantasies in no recognizable order, it can be argued that the film ends with a self-referential nod to its own structure – one that is very different from *Norte*'s relentless linearity.

That temporal structures breaking away from linear chronology can be linked to trauma is by now a commonplace of both narratology and trauma studies, so it can safely be claimed that the film's structure sympathetically mirrors Florentina's mental confusion. Because of her multiple traumas, her mind, like the film itself, constantly leaps between different times far removed from one another, as well as between reality and imagination: Florentina is thus unable to put together a proper temporal articulation and is stuck in an eternal present of sorts. By being plunged into the temporal zigzagging of this deranged mind, however, the viewers are not simply meant to sympathize with her unfortunate condition: rather, they are also asked to acknowledge that damnation is also salvation – which means that salvation can be, to a certain degree, found precisely in the eternal present Florentina is hopelessly stuck in.

Diaz looks for redemption not ahead, but in the aesthetically driven sculpting of the present moment. The point is not just that of showing how devastatingly miserable Florentina's life is but also that of seizing the fleeting moments of beauty therein. The timeless present inside which she is stuck is not only the seat of utter hopelessness but also of a precarious childlike bliss. Indeed, an impressive chunk of the film's screen time is dedicated to Florentina doing just nothing, just standing around, playing, dancing, singing and so on. In these quasi-Warholian moments, in which the lead actress visibly takes the reins of the film, captured by the camera with evident fascination, nothing really happens except, as it were, life as such, away from any instrumentality – better still: just some motion *in excess*, on top of a stillness that seems to have taken hold of time. The secret of Diaz's extremely refined mise en scène is to be found precisely in this painstaking orchestration of motion so as to convey the impression that stillness and motion are not really reciprocally incompatible after all because a certain way of pacing strings them together. Incapable of achieving a proper representation of time, Florentina can only live in a sort of eternal present; accordingly, the film's irregular structure mirrors her incapability to adhere to chronology, and very much as in Agamben's quotation given earlier, it is precisely this gap that makes messianic time possible. Because chronology is severely disarticulated, our attention is drawn all the more on the only temporal dimension left, that is, on the present; thereby, the emphasis is enhanced on the messianic possibility of a different use of time taking shape, within the continuous present of the single take (or, more rarely, of the single edited scene), in the guise of an organically rhythmical underside of time.

One should not fail to notice, however, that Florentina's predicament is the predicament of an entire nation. That Diaz in many interviews declares Florentina to be a metaphor of the Philippines should not surprise us; what should, however, retain our attention is the fact that sometimes his descriptions of the 'Malay space-time' (such as the one quoted earlier in the present chapter) make direct references not only to the negation of linear time but also to trauma.

> The waiting is very much related to the fact that the Malay is governed by space, too much space. Our understanding of time is, like, the sun going down, the sun coming up, the storm coming. We have twenty to twenty-eight typhoons every year. We wait for typhoons to arrive and destroy us again, to devastate us once more. And after the typhoons, we regenerate, there is rebirth, we accept this cycle of life.
>
> (Diaz 2014: n.pag.)

Diaz could not be farther from assuming that the historical traumas of colonialism disrupted a quasi-heavenly original Malay condition. Traumas were part and parcel of it already. In the precolonial era, trauma and a non-linear conception of temporality (such as the cyclical one sketched in the typhoon example) were already tied together in a knot of sorts. Yet Diaz's modernist works such as *Florentina Hubaldo, CTE* seem to imply that if a return to that alleged original innocence as if the profound traumas of modernity and colonization never happened is of course impossible, a similar knot persists even now, amidst the perpetual catastrophe triggered by modernity, and should be recognized as such. More precisely, what should be recognized is that the knot is different (in *Florentina*, the modernist disarticulation of chronology in the wake of trauma), but the two threads (trauma and non-linearity) knotted thereby are still the same. *Florentina*'s point is seemingly that to overcome historical trauma does not mean to eradicate it but rather to consciously appropriate it, to regain a close, intimate familiarity with it, because it is only through the irregular temporality that it engenders that the potentialities of the present moment can emerge. Much like Walter Benjamin's revolutionary *Jetztzeit* (the 'now-time' which Agamben and others link to messianic revelation), the potentialities of the present moment freed from the purposiveness of time teleologically and instrumentally oriented seem to be adumbrated somewhere in the eternal present Florentina is stuck in. It is in that traumatized eternal present, so Diaz seems to suggest, that should be sought what could come closest to the original Malay space-time now that, after colonization and other historical traumas of modernity, it must be regarded as irretrievably lost. As damnation and salvation overlap, the Christian eschatology that is commonly and correctly associated with colonial oppression can also be the key to its own subversion. To make Spanish conquistadores into *higantes* may be a submissive form of magnification – but also an ambiguous, ambivalent one to say the least.

Conclusion

On the occasion of the 70th anniversary of the Venice Film Festival, Lav Diaz made *Ang alitaptap* (*The Firefly*) (Diaz 2013b), his shortest film to date. A 100-second single-take short film, shot in Cannes from the window of the director's hotel room, it shows nothing but a stumbling and rickety old man slowly treading on a street. Meanwhile, a voice-over utters: 'The day will come we shall set sail from the mysteries of mythologies. And I shall be singing hymns to set you free' (Diaz 2013b: n.pag.). The political and emancipatory potential of singing will eventually be tackled in *Ang panahon ng halimaw* (*Season of the Devil*) (Diaz 2018), but what is most relevant for the purpose of this chapter is that *Ang alitaptap* simply juxtaposes a straight line (the street) and a trajectory (the old man's) that is too limping to be straight – just like in Diaz's films, as already noted, cinema's inherent heliotropism (the 'mythologies') meets, and mingles with, its dark counterpart. And it is in the gap between these two temporalities (one straight, one not) that the possibility for 'messianic' emancipation can open up, in the form of a shapely, organically paced present time, transfiguring the apparent shapelessness of time into hymns to be sung.

Like many other postcolonially informed film-makers, Diaz is aware that in order to break free from the colonial framework still largely infesting the so-called Third World, it is imperative to break free from linear teleological temporality to regain familiarity with a *spatial* temporality that is also the only way to conceive of original precolonial temporality. In the case of the Philippines, this must also mean to subvert the linear teleological temporality implied in the Christian conception of salvation in favour of a view of salvation and damnation as fully overlapping. This is why the narrative structures of *Norte* and *Florentina* both consist in the arc of a character that is utterly unsavable and always already saved as well as in another parallel arc of a character that is only utterly unsavable because it never gives up trying to be saved. Salvation does not come after damnation: if the damnation of human condition lies in our being stuck in a time that can only run inconclusively towards its end, salvation lies in approaching time-qua-damnation from a different angle, that is, in bestowing a certain kind of organic spatiality on time, wresting it away from its purposiveness and its subordination to end(s). Even in the hell on earth that is Florentina's life, time can be redeemed into the epiphany of some kind of grace.

REFERENCES

Agamben, Giorgio (2005), *The Time That Remains: A Commentary on the Letter to the Romans* (trans. Patricia Daley), Stanford: Stanford University Press.

Agamben, Giorgio (2018), *Karman: A Brief Treatise on Action, Guilt and Gesture* (trans. Adam Kotsko), Stanford: Stanford University Press.

Beller, Jonathan (2006), *Acquiring Eyes: Philippine Visuality, Nationalist Struggle, and the World-Media System*, Manila: Ateneo de Manila University Press.

Botz-Bornstein, Thorsten (2017), *Organic Cinema: Film, Architecture, and the Work of Béla Tarr*, New York: Berghahn Books.

Brown, William (2016), '*Melancholia*: The long, slow cinema of Lav Diaz', in T. de Luca and N. Barradas Jorge (eds), *Slow Cinema*, Edinburgh: Edinburgh University Press, pp. 112–22.

Diaz, Lav (dir.) (1998), *Serafin Geronimo: Ang kriminal ng Baryo Concepcion* (*The Criminal of Barrio Conception*), Philippines: Good Harvest Unlimited.

Diaz, Lav (dir.) (2001), *Batang West Side* (*West Side Avenue*), Philippines and United States: JMCN and Hinabing Pangarap Productions.

Diaz, Lav (dir.) (2002), *Hesus, rebolusyonaryo*, Philippines: Regal Films.

Diaz, Lav (dir.) (2007a), *Kagadanan sa banwaan ning mga engkanto* (*Death in the Land of Encantos*), Philippines and The Netherlands: Sine Olivia and Hubert Bals Fund.

Diaz, Lav (2007b), 'Lav Diaz: Digital is liberation theology', interview with Tilman Baumgärtel, *GreenCine*, 7 September, https://www.greencine.com/central/lavdiaz. Accessed 20 June 2015.

Diaz, Lav (dir.) (2008), *Melancholia*, Philippines: Sine Olivia.

Diaz, Lav (dir.) (2012), *Florentina Hubaldo, CTE*, Philippines: Sine Olivia.

Diaz, Lav (dir.) (2013a), *Norte, hangganan ng kasaysayan* (*Norte, the End of History*), Philippines: Wacky O Productions, Kayan Productions, Origin8 Media.

Diaz, Lav (dir.) (2013b), *Ang alitaptap* (*The Firefly*), Philippines: Sine Olivia.

Diaz, Lav (2014), '*Manila in the Claws of Darkness*: Lav Diaz', interview with Giulio Bursi, *Mousse*, 45, http://moussemagazine.it/lav-diaz-giulio-bursi-2014/. Accessed 30 March 2019.

Diaz, Lav (dir.) (2016), *Ang babaeng humayo* (*The Woman Who Left*), Philippines: Sine Olivia and Cinema One Originals.

Diaz, Lav (dir.) (2018), *Ang panahon ng halimaw* (*Season of the Devil*), Philippines: Epicmedia and Sine Olivia Pilipinas.

Dostoyevsky, Fyodor ([1866] 2014), *Crime and Punishment* (trans. Oliver Ready), London: Penguin.

Vera, Noel (2005), *Critic after Dark*, Singapore: BigO Books.

Vera, Noel (2013), 'Dostoyevsky variations', *Film Comment*, 49:5, pp. 42–47.

6

The Idyllic Chronotope and Spatial Justice in Lav Diaz's *Melancholia*

Katrina Macapagal

> *Nature is a big actor in my cinema.*
>
> (Lav Diaz in MUBI 2017)

The vastness of Lav Diaz's epic melodrama *Melancholia* (2008) can be ascribed to both the duration of time and the expanse of space captured in the film. The 450-minute film traverses rural and urban settings – Sagada, Mindoro and areas of Manila are some of the film's identified locations – providing glimpses into the lives of three characters who have long been searching for their loved ones declared *desaparecidos*, activists and guerrilla fighters presumably abducted and killed by the military. While the duration is, as with most of Diaz's films, the most apparent distinctive element of *Melancholia*, the film's presentation of space undoubtedly enriches its discursive value.

Although filmed in black and white, there is a sense of grandeur in the rural landscapes featured in *Melancholia*, where the film's characters are initially emplaced. The framing of images of the film's rural settings – the mountainous views of Sagada and the dense jungle of Mindoro in the epilogue, views of the sea and the shoreline – are a striking contrast to the tight framing of interiors (offices, cafes, bedrooms, sitting rooms). In the urban setting, scenes with the rural signifier of water are striking, particularly scenes of heavy downpour and the film's final scene by the riverside. These rural images are presented in various ways throughout the film, serving to lay the groundwork for the unfolding of *Melancholia*'s non-linear narrative.

In this chapter I wish to explore *Melancholia* more closely in terms of its chronotopic or key spatio-temporal configurations, exploring how this film, ostensibly about mourning and haunting, is also a film that spatially demonstrates the struggle for living and persisting. I will first lay out the groundwork for chronotopic reading, exploring how *Melancholia* produces a historically grounded melodramatic rendering of the idyllic chronotope which dialogues with character configuration. Through its use of rural chronotopes that enable its particular mode of melodrama, *Melancholia* reveals powerful imaginaries of spatial justice for its lost figures – a concept that pertains to a 'particular emphasis and interpretative perspective' of social justice as 'spatial' (Soja 2010: 13).

The idyllic chronotope in Diaz's epic melodrama

Although *Melancholia* shifts from rural to urban settings, its rural spaces and signifiers are much more pronounced in the film and indeed in many of Diaz's other works. Unlike other film-makers from what is often dubbed the Philippine new wave of digital film-making, such as Cannes Best Director winner Brillante Mendoza, who is known for his gritty films set in the urban spaces of Manila, Diaz sets himself apart through his choice of rural settings – which William Brown (2016) has observed to be a key element of Diaz's long, slow cinema that are specific to Philippine regional localities. *Melancholia*'s rural spaces, however, function not just as mere setting, but chronotopically – they are absolutely crucial to the film's narrative and generic development as a kind of epic melodrama. In other words, *Melancholia*'s unfolding is crucially enabled by its rural chronotopes comprising what I approach as the chronotope of the idyll.

Literally meaning time-space, Russian theorist Mikhail Bakhtin proposed the chronotope as a useful term to refer to the spatio-temporal configurations in the novel that are crucial to narrative unfolding and genre formation. Chronotopes refer to the forms in the novel that show 'the intrinsic connectedness of temporal and spatial relationships that are artistically expressed in literature' (Bakhtin 1981: 84). He develops this theory mostly through example – for instance, he identifies the chronotope of 'adventure time' in the Greek romance novel, referring to the reversibility and the suddenness of events that do not have any bearing on the characters who remain the same from beginning to end. In later examples he identifies particular spatial forms, such as the castle or the road, which are forms of chronotopes that are charged heavily with time and history, bearing utmost significance to narrative development. As Bakhtin explained: 'Thus the chronotope, functioning as the means for materializing time in space, emerges as the center for concretizing representation, as force giving body to the entire novel' (Bakhtin 1981: 250). There has been a long-standing discussion as to whether the chronotope is a device, a function or motif, not least because of Bakhtin's poetic turns of phrase, but my own view is that the term could operate as any or all of those, depending on how these time-spaces are wielded within a narrative.

While chronotopes organize the fictional times and spaces of the artistic work, Bakhtin posits that these artistic forms are imagined from actually existing historical times and spaces, and as such, their meanings inherently have ideological significance and can change over time. It follows the same principle of dialogism, another Bakhtinian theory, which broadly refers to how meanings are constantly conditioned by others. Chronotopes are dialogic, as Bakhtinian scholar Michael Holquist (2002: 138) explains: '[T]he time/space relation of any particular text will always be perceived in the context of a larger set of time/space relations that obtain in the social and historical environment in which it is read.'

Although initially used for the study of the novel form, Robert Stam (1992: 11) has argued that it is 'ideally suited' to the study of cinema where time literally takes place before its viewers. After all, a film can be regarded as a literal encapsulation of the taking place of time, the screening itself an event through which 'spatial and temporal indicators are fused into one carefully thought-out concrete whole' (Stam 1992: 11). Interestingly, in interviews, Diaz has said that the scope and structuring of his films are like novels, which lend them all the more to chronotopic readings (Mai 2016; MUBI 2017). In an interview with Nadin Mai (2016: n.pag.), Diaz explains the influence of classic Russian literature on his film-making:

> Tolstoy, Dostoyevsky – their work has so many gaps, so many spaces that if you were a so-called postmodern editor, you could cut *War and Peace* in half. But for the reader, you cannot erase those gaps because they are important. They contextualize the whole struggle. My cinema is like that. There are so many spaces, but you cannot cut them.

What Diaz meant by these spaces in his cinema, to my mind, are the literal spaces that can be said to materialize time through Diaz's use of space. In *Melancholia*, rural spaces arguably constitute the film's chronotope of the idyll – this refers to the film's 'organizing centres' (Bakhtin 1981: 250) or 'the place where the knots of narrative are tied and untied' (Bakhtin 1981: 250).

Bakhtin spoke of early novelistic typologies enabled by the classic chronotope of the idyll based on notions of love, the family and agricultural labour. He argued that the idyllic chronotope shows a particular unity of space that corresponds to a cyclical, folkloric time, where space takes precedence over time. In narratives constituted by the idyll, time is bound by what Bakhtin called the unity of space: 'an organic fastening-down, a grafting of life and its events to a place, to a familiar territory with all its nooks and crannies, its familiar mountains, valleys, fields, rivers and forests, and one's own home' (Bakhtin 1981: 225). This unity of place gives way to the 'cyclical rythmicalness of time' (Bakhtin 1981: 225) carried over from one generation to the next.

In his study of what he called 'accented cinema' or films made by film-makers in exile, Hamid Naficy (2001) explores the ways in which film-makers use images of nature as chronotopic representations of the homeland. Naficy uses the framework of the idyllic chronotope to show the homeland's 'boundlessness and timelessness by cathecting it to the privileged sites of natural landscape, mountain, monument, and home and the retrospective narratives of longing, nostalgia, fetishism, and return – all of which emphasise continuity and descent' (2001: 187). Similarly, in *Melancholia*, rural images and signifiers can be regarded as the film's privileged sites, constituting a kind of idyllic chronotope specific to the historical times and spaces from which the film's fictional time and spaces were derived and imagined.

May Adadol Ingawanij (2015) suggests that Diaz's films can productively be approached as cartographic acts that map the Philippine nation's postcolonial history. The rural images in *Melancholia* might thus be approached as the forms derived by a localized or culturally specific chronotope of the idyll, grounded in the times and spaces of both Philippine cinematic and postcolonial history. It might be said that *Melancholia*'s initial grounding in Sagada, and the subsequent rural signifiers that dialogue with this preliminary setting, constitute the film's idyllic chronotope, creating a narrative that dialogues powerfully with the theme of haunting that runs through the entire narrative. The images in which *Melancholia* lingers on landscape views of Sagada dialogues with the national traumatic history where the fictional characters are placed.

In terms of its figuration in Philippine cinematic history, *Melancholia* is an example of what Patrick Campos (2016) considers new rural films. These are films that privilege the rural space but depart from traditional and romanticized depictions given their commitment to place-making. Campos (2016: 410) suggests that while pastoral space is still perceived in some rural films as 'the fountain of the Filipino's moral innocence', some films from Philippine contemporary independent cinema are more politically inclined, signalling to the particularities of these places alongside the development of the nation, in the process unsettling the myth of the rural-urban divide. Diaz's films are the flipside of the same coin in the development of Philippine independent cinema, developing alongside the emergence of new urban cinema popularized primarily by the gritty realist films of Brillante Mendoza. In my own research, I have proposed the theory of the 'slum chronotope' as that which operates in Philippine urban cinema, foregrounding the dialogic relationship between the fictional world and the world from which the slum imaginary is created. Here I am proposing that the chronotope of the idyll functions similarly in a rural film like *Melancholia*.

The idyllic chronotope in *Melancholia* emerges out of the particular imaginary of Sagada, a small municipality of around 12,000 residents in the Mountain Province located north of Manila. Today, Sagada is frequented by domestic and international tourists alike as a space to escape the chaos of the city. In Philippine popular imagination, Sagada has featured in dramas and romantic comedies representing some form of escape for its urban-based characters, such as in national blockbusters like *Don't Give Up on Us* (Bernal 2006) and, more recently, the widely popular break-up film *That Thing Called Tadhana* (Jadaone 2014).

On one level, *Melancholia*, an art-house film that was not shown commercially in the Philippines apart from the Manila-based Cinemalaya Film Festival, also taps into this romantic notion of Sagada as a rural space of renewal for the three wandering characters searching for some kind of redemption. Sagada is an idea that conjures an imaginary of the idyllic chronotope, its mountains, cliffs, caves and streams creating a picturesque space providing reprieve from urban life. Sagada stands for a particular cartographic point in Philippine postcolonial history, an area regarded for preserving its indigenous history and traditions in the face of colonial interference through the arrival of American Episcopalian missionaries in 1905. Philippine historians and anthropologists would easily link Sagada with the work of American missionary William Henry Scott (1988), who studied and published writings on the culture and history of Sagada. A journalistic account provides the stereotypical description of Sagada in popular imagination:

> Its center is a portrait of American colonial uprightness: it is anchored by a picturesque Episcopal compound with its church of solid gray stone slabs, a sweet clapboard rectory, a whitewashed hospital named St. Theodore's, a graveyard, and a charming café where one could sample Auntie Josephine's homemade lemon pie, made from homegrown lemons first planted in Sagada by the Episcopal missionaries who had brought with them industriousness as their core value.
>
> (Molintas 2016: n.pag.)

Sagada's history and what it represents in national consciousness is embedded in its built environment, reflective of the coexistence of indigenous and Christian ways of life, which *Melancholia* is able to effectively reveal in its unfolding.

More importantly, the choice of Sagada as setting dialogues powerfully with the theme of haunting that endures in *Melancholia*. As a tourist destination, Sagada is known for its hanging coffins and burial caves, produced by the death rites practiced by Sagada Igorots from 2,000 years ago. The coffins are attached to cliffs and at the entrance of caves, symbolic of the coexistence of the dead and the living. Accounts of burial rites practiced by Sagada Igorots reveal elaborate ways of mourning depending on the age and the manner of death, be it the death of a child, a man or woman or the elderly (Piluden-Omengan 2004; Pacyaya 1961). These physical markers of ancient burial practices, while now only practiced by a small minority, constantly resurface the postcolonial town's past into the present, revealing a constant negotiation between old and new, death and life – a tension that *Melancholia* draws from as its characters traverse the spaces in and around Sagada.

Moreover, to approach *Melancholia* as a film constituted by the idyllic chronotope means to explore the film's broad generic contours and how it enriches narrative meaning – in this case, its obvious dialogue with the mode of melodrama, given its ostensible theme of loss, mourning and trauma. Diaz's privileging of rural chronotopes in his films is a means through which his melodramas engage in the dialectics of pathos and action towards achieving the melodramatic mode's struggle for 'moral legibility' (Brooks 1976; Williams 1998). Like many of Diaz's films, *Melancholia* might be viewed as a radical intervention in the melodramatic mode/genre in Philippine cinema through its grounding on the chronotope of the idyll. Diaz's melodramatic characters correspond to the emergence of a kind of radical 'victimhood' as suggested by Thomas Elsaesser (2014), referring to melodramas of this particularly age that are able to configure the victim as agent, despite and because of his/her suffering. The ways the characters inhabit the rural spaces in *Melancholia* to map their mourning and grief reveal the nature of the loss they have long suffered, their struggle to find justice and, simply, to live.

The chronotope of the idyll, emerging from the imaginary of Sagada and subsequent rural signifiers, organizes time and space in *Melancholia* according to a version of cyclical time/space that implies constant slippage between past and present, death and life, with the film's entire duration permeated by the theme of haunting. This time-space of haunting resonates, for instance, in the images of nature that Diaz reverently presents throughout *Melancholia*, usually in locked frames, simultaneously majestic and foreboding. It is through this constant duality or chronotopic tension that the film reveals imaginaries of spatial justice in the ways the characters literally search for some sense of justice expressed through space – justice for the disappeared, for themselves and on a grander scale – for the nation. The characters are, through the melodramatic mode that I have suggested earlier, 'victims' who in some sense perform their suffering through their movements through space.

Locating spatial justice in Melancholia

Spatial justice is a term I borrow from human geography that suggests that the study and struggle for social justice can benefit from a spatial perspective

(Soja 2010). A spatial justice approach involves examining issues of social justice – such as the struggle against oppression and exploitation – through looking at the ways these are expressed, or even manifested and made real, in and through space. This view is grounded in the principle of the production of space, following Henri Lefebvre (1991), which argues that space is a social product and is therefore always a space of conflict. I understand justice in the broadest sense, linking with egalitarian notions of equality and freedom, principles that find expression spatially, for instance, through literal walls built to separate the rich and the poor. However, in *Melancholia*, the struggle for justice can be linked specifically to the search for the disappeared, expressed through the film's spatio-temporal configurations, especially in terms of how the social agents produce and are produced by space.

The sense of haunting that pervades *Melancholia* is anchored in the film's spectral characters, the desaparecidos for whom Alberta (the prostitute), Julian (the pimp) and Rina (the nun) search for. The disappeared are both the source and object of their melancholy. In some sense, the cyclical time and space of the idyll is comparable to the time and space occupied by desaparecidos in that they are trapped in a memory loop as long as their bodies are never found. The perpetual deferral of justice in the case of desaparecidos is what makes it a kind of suffering different from death – there is no physical body to mourn, only unanswered questions about the fate of the disappeared. Anchoring the narrative of *Melancholia* on the search for desaparecidos adds specificity to the chronotope of the idyll as being in constant dialogue with the history of enforced disappearances in Philippine history. The theme of haunting enabled by the idyllic chronotope in *Melancholia* is thus necessarily political, conversing with the dark history of desaparecidos that casts a long shadow of mourning in the nation's past, present and future. As Avery Gordon (2011: 115) explains, reflecting on Argentina's desaparecidos:

> Disappearance is not only about death. Disappearance is a thing in itself, a state of being repressed. To counter it and its particular mode of operation requires contact with and work on what it is [...] disappearance is a state-sponsored procedure for producing ghosts to harrowingly haunt a population into submission.

Thresholds and landscapes

Melancholia's use of deep-focus framing, long takes and wide shots in the scenes set in Sagada aligns with the chronotope of the idyll that dialogues eloquently with the film's theme of haunting. The cyclical times and spaces that produce the sense of haunting is rendered visually in the film, as laid out poignantly in some of the film's more memorable scenes.

In particular, I highlight the recurring use of framing used multiple times for the character of Alberta/the prostitute, which can be described as a passageway view where something vertically cuts the middle of the screen. This shot is also used once to frame Julian/the pimp, but interestingly, it was not used at all for Rina/the nun. In this scene, the character is framed in the middle of a deep-focus shot, as if one were looking through a doorway. This is the second space we see in *Melancholia* just three minutes into the film, effectively setting the stage for the film's unfolding. In characteristic Diaz style, the presentation of space precedes the entry of the figure. The deep-focus shot arranges a view of the sky and the mountains, contrasted with walls of the cabin-style hotel and balcony railings. An odd figure enters the scene – a woman wearing skimpy clothing and thigh-high heeled boots, making a call and smoking a cigarette. The natural sound that accompanies this opening scene – the faint sound of crickets, the rustle of leaves, a rooster crowing – adds to the seeming disjunct between the space and the figure who just entered.

Nadin Mai (2015) has described these scenes as indicative of the duality of *Melancholia*'s characters, the push and pull of light and darkness, of life and death, which certainly ties into my own reading of haunting in the film. To flesh out this idea further, I approach these scenes as threshold chronotopes enabled by the chronotope of the idyll. Bakhtin described threshold chronotopes as

> the main places of action in his works, places where crisis events occur, the falls, resurrections, renewals, epiphanies, decisions that determine the whole life of a man. In this chronotope, time is essentially instantaneous; it is as if it has no duration and falls out of the normal course of biographical time.
>
> (Bakhtin 1981: 248).

These portal scenes in *Melancholia*, however, while providing space and time for the characters to enter deep introspection, do not function in exactly the same manner that Bakhtin has described in terms of propelling the narrative further, since *Melancholia* does not move along linear time. The power of these scenes lies in their capacity to call attention to the character's suffering. It is in these scenes that Alberta performs her melancholia – prompting us to remember the reason behind this performance in the first place. In these scenes, Diaz's aesthetic preference for darkness and duration serves to enhance the performance of suffering. In some of these scenes, we watch the prostitute Jenine smoke a cigarette in real time (she does not smoke as Alberta), lost in her melancholy against the backdrop of rain. In the scene where Julian/the pimp is framed in the same way, he is hunched over, a bottle of beer in hand, absolutely distraught, enshrouded in darkness, the sound of rain adding to the melancholic mood. The dividing line in this threshold chronotope functions not just to symbolize the thin border that separates life and death, but the line that separates biographical time from historical time. By historical time, I mean the time existing alongside the film from which the fictional suffering characters were imagined and with which the film is continuously in dialogue.

The time in which *Melancholia* was produced saw the intensification of abductions and extrajudicial killings of activists in the Philippines, encouraged by the declaration of 'all-out-war' against the New People's Army (NPA) by then president Gloria Macapagal-Arroyo (Conde 2006). A 2008 report by United Nations special rapporteur Philip Alston confirmed that Arroyo's call emboldened the military to systematically target and execute civil society leaders, journalists and human rights activists who were not members of the NPA (Karapatan 2008). A representative case from that period was the abduction of two University of the Philippines students and community organizers Karen Empeño and Sherlyn Cadapan (*Inquirer News* 2011). A witness testified that the two were tortured by the military, upon the command of General Jovito Palparan – also known as 'the butcher' who is linked to hundreds of enforced disappearances and extrajudicial killings (*Inquirer News* 2011). The mothers of Karen and Sherlyn, until today, are demanding justice for their daughters and have become stalwart figures and organizers for the families of the disappeared in the Philippines (de Leon 2016). This specific historical time is referenced directly in *Melancholia*, for instance, when Alberta begs a former activist to testify against a general who was responsible for the abduction and torture of her husband.

References to how the film's characters were politicized as university students also dialogue with the long history of enforced disappearances and imprisonment of hundreds of student activists from the Martial Law period until today. One particular scene that functions as threshold chronotope shows the bridging of fictional time and historical time through Alberta/the prostitute's interaction with a man who apparently knew her and her husband from university. Presented once again with railings cutting across the middle of the screen, Alberta is on a bench, smoking, seemingly just waiting for something to happen. She flaunts her boots, propped on the railings, and is joined by the man who had previously insisted she looked like Alberta. Alberta insists she is Jenine, the prostitute – she effectively maintains her performance of suffering by inhabiting this fictional role in Sagada. The scene abruptly cuts to a bedroom, where the man ends up talking to Jenine about what happened to Alberta, filling in some of the gaps of the story for the viewers. We find out that Alberta devoted her life to the search for her husband's body. The man reflects: 'Many people are like Alberta. They forever live their lives in purgatory until they find the bodies of their missing loved ones' (Diaz 2008: n.pag.).

These threshold chronotopes – the most inward-looking, introspective moments of suffering in *Melancholia* – traverse biographical time into historical time not just through their framing but also when put into dialogue with views of Sagada's landscapes. After the first time this framing is used, the scene cuts to a tracking shot of Alberta, the camera placed behind her, showing glimpses of the town's natural surroundings. At one point, she stops to peer at the view of trees below. In another scene using the same vertical cut, Alberta is on a bench, seemingly waiting for the rain to stop. She is once again smoking a cigarette which is filmed in real time, hunched over, sometimes looking out into whatever view is in front of her. The scene cuts to a view of Sagada's famous Church of the Virgin Mary, where it lingers for a few minutes before the tiny figure of the nun rapidly walking towards the front of the church is seen. Meanwhile, the scene right after Julian's night-time threshold chronotope is a landscape view of the town during the day, the new day absorbing the suffering of these lost figures who are trapped in the cycle of mourning and searching. These threshold scenes of deep introspection and melancholia that are allowed to unfold in real time are projected onto the spaces of Sagada's built environment – the road, the trees, the church, the landscape – taking in the melancholia of these characters seeking reprieve from suffering. On one hand, we can say that the rural images are illustrative of the characters' emotions; on another level, this dialogue between threshold chronotopes and the rural spaces of Sagada could be read as the characters inscribing their excess emotions onto these spaces, and the time and space granted to the rural spaces that immediately follow these intensely melancholic scenes grant us, the spectators, time to feel and project our own emotions onto the film's spatial environment.

Spectral embodiments, and walking as ritual of mourning

In her chapter about ghost films within the genre of fantastic cinema, Bliss Cua Lim said: 'The ghost film allows characters (and those spectators who identify with them) to experience *time with the ghost*' (Lim 2009: 161). The ghost, through haunting, shores up what Lim has called 'immiscible temporality' or the meeting of irreconcilable times that productively destabilize the dominance of modern, homogenous time. Lim describes ghosts as figures that have allegorical significance in films, especially in relation to national history, if ghosts are viewed as aggrieved figures of the past whose resurfacing in the present calls for this injustice to be addressed.

Melancholia's chronotope of the idyll, heavily laced with the theme of haunting, certainly partakes in this temporal critique. Spectral time exists alongside historical time in the film, given its very grounding in the search for the disappeared and the sudden appearance of a 'real' ghost (Julian's wife) before the film leaves Sagada and transitions into city spaces. More so, it can be argued that *Melancholia* configures Alberta, Julian and Rina as ghosts themselves, figures heavy with the past, bearing with them the memory of the disappeared. *Melancholia*'s presentation of the town of Sagada as almost always empty (at least in the first two hours) makes it seem like a ghost town, this emptiness compounded by darkness, fog, mist and rain. If the space itself is haunted space, it could even be said that the nun, the pimp and the prostitute are spectral embodiments of loss and sorrow, and taking on this perverse role-play becomes the means through which Alberta, Julian and Rina attempt to experience time with their loved ones who have vanished. The ones left behind by the disappeared become spectral embodiments of haunting through their endless search, as articulated by the character of Rina: 'After this, then what? We go back to Manila. We are still the loneliest people. The most wrecked. The living dead.' To which Alberta replied: 'We'll make it work. This is our struggle' (Diaz 2008: n.pag.).

Walking is the form through which the three characters struggle against the melancholia of being left behind. This spatial practice dialogues with the chronotope of the idyll; the rhythm of this spatial act corresponds to the cyclical nature of time and space in the rural space. As Gabrielle Finnane (2016: 125) has remarked, approaching *Melancholia* as a walking film: 'The long scenes of walking and wandering characters of Lav Diaz's epic compose a postcolonial psychogeography in relation to the history of an environment'. They walk the haunted streets of Sagada to perform their suffering, or in more spatial terms, to map their mourning – in the process attempting to lay claim to the production of space that they can inhabit and make their own. It is through this spatial practice of mapping mourning that the spectral figures in *Melancholia* can be viewed as figures seeking spatial justice. The embodied spatial practice of walking, framed in deep focus and the long take that capture the spectral figures entering and disappearing from the expanse of rural spaces, illustrate their struggle to produce space, to invest this chosen space of Sagada with mourning according to their own terms. This struggle for producing and inhabiting space is what the pimp alluded to in a conversation with the prostitute in an encounter where both sought refuge from a heavy downpour. Responding to the prostitute's remark about the town being small enough to explore under an hour, the pimp replies: 'Sagada is vast. There's the forest. There are caves. Ricefields...plains...There's a lake. A great hiking area...the people. This place is vast, baby' (Diaz 2008: n.pag.).

In some ways, the three wandering figures of *Melancholia* are comparable to what Bakhtin identified as typical figures of disruption in the novel – the rogue, the clown and the fool, who 'create around themselves their own special little world, their own chronotope' (Bakhtin 1981: 159). These figures are masks, Bakhtin argued, they are meant to be metaphorical and because of this are given the 'special rights' (Bakhtin 1981: 159) within the narrative to do vulgar acts that their 'real' personas would not have been permitted to do. This, of course, brings to mind the pimp and the prostitute as roles that enabled Alberta and Julian to immerse in their chosen masks. Meanwhile, Rina, acting as nun, had to endure ridicule from the pimp and the prostitute when she told them to repent for their sins. Inhabiting these roles in the idyllic space of Sagada gave them the right to perform their suffering according to what is associated with their masks. Despite the unusual nature of the roles they have chosen, however, the characters do not meet hostility as they walk along the streets of Sagada. Alberta becomes friends with the vendor in the local shop, Rina is greeted by kids on the street as she solicits alms for the poor and even Julian blends in easily with the locals as he hangs around eateries. Even as they map their mourning as they walk along the streets of Sagada, this haunted space reveal signs of life and living at every corner, not just through people, but through the natural sounds that puncture some of the intensely melancholic scenes. The sound of a rooster crowing, a dog barking, children shouting, even the sound of heavy rain – all become part and parcel of the space that cannot fully be inscribed with the characters' melancholia.

This is not to say, of course, that this mapping of mourning proves successful therapy for the three characters, with Rina's suicide foreshadowed by her final walking scenes in Sagada. Her struggle to inhabit rural space on her own terms is visually reflected in the ways her figure inhabits the screen, starkly different from how the prostitute and the pimp are framed. In a number of scenes, the rural space overwhelms her tiny figure, reflective of her character slowly losing faith in the struggle to insist on her place in the world. In her last few sequences about two and a half hours into the film, she ventures outside the city centre and makes her way through rice paddies with the backdrop of mountains in a heavy downpour. She explores and attempts to make connections with some of the local inhabitants but is rendered immobile when she hears a woman singing. This cuts to another wide view that Rina enters. Braving the rain, she makes her way up a street, stopping midway to receive a call from Alberta. Rina smiles, tells Alberta she is okay and exits the frame leaving a lingering shot of the rural space she departed from. Similarly, Julian's character withdraws into himself more and more, his madness reflected in the explosion of noise staged by an imagined band in his house in the city. His descent to madness is imagined through a return to rural space, preceded by another appearance by the ghost of his wife. Julian crawls through mud and leaves, as though swallowed whole by the wilderness around him.

The last person standing at the end of the film is Alberta, although we are left wondering what her expression in the final frame implies. Compared to the other spectral embodiments, however, Alberta's character demonstrates how haunting can also be a source hope. Instead of movement as ritual of remembrance, one particular scene offers stillness. From interior urban spaces, the film shifts to rural space in what can be considered *Melancholia*'s most tender sequence, set in an unidentified beach. The scene dialogues clearly with the threshold chronotopes set in Sagada, once again set up with the shoreline cutting the screen in the middle. Alberta is at the beach with her adoptive child, Hannah, the daughter of another friend from university who disappeared. Although Alberta's relationship with Hannah has been difficult, this scene at the beach invokes the memory of Hannah's mother to bring the two figures of melancholia together. Both are fixed in the frame, foregrounded by sand and a bonfire, as Alberta tells Hannah stories of her mother.

Melancholia's epilogue in the imagined forest of Mindoro is an ode to remembering the disappeared, mirroring the film's opening in the rural space. The film's return to rural space is signalled by Alberta's stillness by an urban riverside, where she surfaces the memory of her husband's death. The epilogue in the forest is grounded on *Melancholia*'s particular idyllic chronotope, in this space signifying the torture of cyclical time in rural space for the insurgents trapped in nature. Here the film projects the individual's melancholia into the space of national melancholia, articulated poignantly by the memory of the ghost of Alberta's husband: 'It is about my sadness. It is about the sorrow of my people. I cannot romanticize the futility of it all. Even the majestic beauty of this island couldn't provide an answer to this hell.' He mirrors Alberta's threshold chronotope, his figure in the middle of the frame divided vertically by rocks along the river, in this way establishing dialogue with the film world's past and present.

Melancholia leaves us with a heavy heart but also with an important question for the present: Where and when is justice to be found? Beyond its fictional world grounded in the chronotope of the idyll, *Melancholia* engages its spectators to endure haunting *with* the film's spectral embodiments. The film itself, eight hours long, endures as a chronotope of haunting, a challenge to remember that we live in spectral times and that the dead walk amongst the living.

REFERENCES

Bakhtin, Mikhail M. (1981), *The Dialogic Imagination: Four Essays* (ed. M. Holquist, trans. C. Emerson), University of Texas Press Slavic Series, no. 1, Austin: University of Texas Press.

Bernal, Joyce (dir.) (2006), *Don't Give Up on Us*, Philippines: ABS-CBN Film Productions and Star Cinema Productions, http://www.imdb.com/title/tt0496693/. Accessed 10 May 2021.

Brooks, Peter (1976), *The Melodramatic Imagination: Balzac, Henry James, Melodrama, and the Mode of Excess*, New Haven, CT: Yale University Press.

Brown, William (2016), '*Melancholia*: The long, slow cinema of Lav Diaz', in T. de Luca and N. Barradas Jorge (eds), *Slow Cinema*, Edinburgh: Edinburgh University Press, pp. 112–22.

Campos, Patrick F. (2016), *The End of National Cinema: Filipino Film at the Turn of the Century*, Quezon City: University of the Philippines Press.

Conde, Carlos (2006), 'Philippines again declares "all-out war" against rebels', *The New York Times*, 19 June, https://www.nytimes.com/2006/06/19/world/asia/19iht-manila.2001486. html. Accessed 10 May 2021.

Diaz, Lav (dir.) (2008), *Melancholia*, Philippines: Sine Olivia, http://www.imdb.com/title/tt1269566/. Accessed 10 May 2021.

Elsaesser, Thomas (2014), 'From dysfunctional families to productive pathologies: Melodrama trauma mind-games', *Journal of the Moving Image*, 12 (December), https://jmionline.org/article/contents_2. Accessed 10 May 2021.

Finnane, Gabrielle (2016), 'Wayfaring in the megacity: Tsai Ming-Liang's *Walker* and Lav Diaz's *Melancholia*', in K. Benesch and F. Specq (eds), *Walking and the Aesthetics of Modernity: Pedestrian Mobility in Literature and the Arts*, New York: Palgrave Macmillan, pp. 115–27.

Gordon, Avery (2011), *Ghostly Matters: Haunting and the Sociological Imagination*, Minneapolis: University of Minnesota Press.

Holquist, Michael (2002), *Dialogism: Bakhtin and His World*, London and New York: Routledge.

Ingawanij, May Adadol (2015), 'Long walk to life: The films of Lav Diaz', *Afterall: A Journal of Art, Context and Enquiry*, 40 (September), pp. 102–15, https://doi.org/10.1086/684220. Accessed 22 June 2021.

Inquirer News (2011), 'WHAT WENT BEFORE: Abduction of UP students Karen Empeño and Sherlyn Cadapan', 17 December, https://newsinfo.inquirer.net/112599/what-went-before-abduction-of-up-students-karen-empeno-and-sherlyn-cadapan. Accessed 10 May 2021. Accessed 22 June 2021.

Jadaone, Antoinette (dir.) (2014), *That Thing Called Tadhana*, Philippines: Cinema One Originals, http://www.imdb.com/title/tt4170436/. Accessed 10 May 2021.

Karapatan (2008), 'MISSION TO PHILIPPINES: Report of the special rapporteur on extrajudicial, summary or arbitrary executions, Philip Alston, *Karapatan*', 30 April, https://www.karapatan.org/AlstonReport. Accessed 22 June 2021.

Lefebvre, Henri (1991), *The Production of Space*, Oxford, UK and Cambridge, MA: Blackwell.

Leon, Dwight Angelo de (2016), 'The battle's not over for mothers of desaparecidos', *Rappler*, 27 June, https://www.rappler.com/moveph/battle-not-over-mothers-desaparecidos. Accessed 22 June 2021.

Lim, Bliss Cua (2009), *Translating Time: Cinema, the Fantastic, and Temporal Critique*, Durham, NC: Duke University Press.

Mai, Nadin (2015), 'The aesthetics of absence and duration in the post-trauma cinema of Lav Diaz', July, http://dspace.stir.ac.uk/handle/1893/22990. Accessed 22 June 2021.

Mai, Nadin (2016), 'Lav Diaz: Slow burn', *Guernica*, 15 January, https://www.guernicamag.com/slow-burn/. Accessed 22 June 2021.

Molintas, Danilova (2016), 'The lost boys of Sagada', 1 March, https://old.pcij.org/stories/the-lost-boys-of-sagada/. Accessed 22 June 2021.

MUBI (2017), 'Emancipated cinema: A conversation with Lav Diaz', YouTube, 20 April, https://www.youtube.com/watch?v=Eyc8nrIOWvE. Accessed 10 May 2021.

Naficy, Hamid (2001), *An Accented Cinema: Exilic and Diasporic Filmmaking*, Princeton, NJ: Princeton University Press.

Pacyaya, Alfredo G. (1961), 'Changing customs of marriage, death and burial among the Sagada', *Practical Anthropology*, 8:3, pp. 125–33, https://doi.org/10.1177/009182966100800305. Accessed 22 June 2021.

Piluden-Omengan, Dinah Elma (2004), *Death and Beyond: Death & Burial Rituals & Other Practices & Beliefs of the Igorots of Sagada, Mountain Province, Philippines*, Quezon City: Giraffe Books.

Scott, William Henry (1988), *A Sagada Reader*, Quezon City: New Day Publishers.

Soja, Edward W. (2010), *Seeking Spatial Justice*, Minneapolis: University of Minnesota Press.

Stam, Robert (1992), *Subversive Pleasures: Bakhtin, Cultural Criticism, and Film*, Baltimore: The Johns Hopkins University Press.

Williams, Linda (1998), 'Melodrama revised', in Nick Browne (ed.), *Refiguring American Film Genres: History and Theory*, Berkeley: University of California Press, pp. 42–88.

PART 3

NO CINEMA, NO ART EITHER

7

How Do You Solve a Problem Like Lav Diaz? Debating *Norte, the End of History*

Adrian Martin

Lav Diaz is a polarizing figure in the landscape of contemporary world cinema. The veritable elder of an experimental movement in Philippine cinema that includes Khavn De La Cruz, Sherad Anthony Sanchez and Raya Martin (all of whom refer back admiringly to the pioneering work of Lino Brocka), Diaz is, for many, a beacon of the slow cinema trend that also includes Lisandro Alonso, Béla Tarr and Albert Serra.

Working with extended running times and long takes, often static and in wide shot, Diaz tends to adopt the form of the social panorama or the family chronicle – a more homely, everyday version of the network, mosaic or prismatic narratives favoured by mainstream cinema in recent years (see Martin 2018). Yet Diaz's vision is harder and bleaker than anything in the networked plots of Paul Thomas Anderson or Alejandro González Iñárritu.

Often using non-professional actors in a blend of half-scripted, half-improvised situations, Diaz draws a painstaking diagram of the social factors that shape the lives of the people he evokes and observes: class, money, religion, law, education. These external, determining factors often give Diaz's films a grim, relentless air of pessimism and inevitability – everybody seems to be trudging towards their particular corner of Hell. But, as in any panorama with Balzacian ambitions, there are also unpredictable, personal factors that can complicate and even reverse the general slide towards doom: random, spontaneous acts of desire or violence, key moments of reflection or compassion, life-altering surprise encounters.

Materialism and humanism in Norte, the End of History

Norte, the End of History (2013, hereby abbreviated to *Norte*), like Diaz's later *The Woman Who Left* (2016), fits the template I have just outlined – indeed, these

films form a kind of diptych. In *Norte*, the character of Fabian (Sid Lucero) is a portrait of the rebel (and would-be artist) as futile philosopher or downright hypocrite,
spouting fancy rhetoric (the film's opening line: 'This is the end of politics'), while
remaining pristinely alienated from anything resembling political activism. Like in
a Leonard Cohen song, Fabian and his friends endlessly, nostalgically evoke 'the
old revolutions' – which are of dubious relevance to their contemporary situation.

Yet Fabian commits himself to a single, impulsive act of anarchistic murder,
in sympathy with the oppressed Eliza (Angeli Bayani). Like a tormented hero
from the novels of Dostoyevksy (who Diaz greatly admires and has often referenced), or from a film by Robert Bresson, Fabian's life is sent into a tailspin by
this one action. He thrusts money at Eliza in the street or behind her vegetable
stall and makes moves to ease or reverse the plight of Eliza's husband, Joaquin
(Archie Alemania), who has been wrongly accused and imprisoned for the crime
that Fabian committed – but without ever going so far as to confess or give himself up. Instead (and this is a typical trajectory in Diaz's cinema), Fabian prefers
to dissolve into anonymity, to become a nowhere man – last glimpsed in a distant
shot, cruising on the water.

Joaquin's years in jail represent the other, contrary side of the Russian literature coin – precisely the side that Bresson, for all the religiosity that some viewers
project onto him, pointedly elided from a film such as *L'argent* (1983). Joaquin
becomes a kind of saint, quietly refusing to perpetuate the cycle of abuse and
exploitation around him. He is the mythic figure of the sacrificial scapegoat – for
Fabian and for his fellow prisoners – who suffers for the sins of others; in turn,
some of those others (such as the sadistic Wakwak, played by Soliman Cruz) come
to their senses and break down in tears, seeking forgiveness and redemption. In
a striking, Apichatpong Weerasethakul–like moment near the film's conclusion,
Fabian is even shown in a dream-vision of angelic levitation.

But it would be wrong to impute a strictly religious viewpoint to Diaz; *Norte*'s
very title alludes to those church cults, rife in the Philippines, that preach the
coming end of the world (just as Fabian preaches a more secular 'end of history'
thesis) – amounting to just another desperate dream of escape from pressing, real-
world problems. Diaz is a humanist with a lucid, materialist view of how society
works – and it is this friction between humanist hope and materialist pessimism
that drives and structures his work. Like Pier Paolo Pasolini or Glauber Rocha
in their respective national-cultural contexts, he reaches into the emotive roots
of religion as a type of empowering populist folklore (rather than as empirical or
spiritual truth), a springboard for anger and action.

It must be said that Diaz's dramatic imagination serves his female characters far
less well than the troubled or abused males with whom (in one aspect or another)
he clearly identifies. Eliza, in her daily struggle for economic survival, is given little

to do by the film other than walk around looking sad for long stretches of screen time. Except for one unforgettable scene, the best and most intense in the entire film, when, atop a cliff, it seems for a moment that Eliza is, in utter despair, about to kill her kids – a gesture, and its renunciation, signalled merely, in a long shot, by her stepping away behind them and then returning to her initial spot. This is a rare instance of what I would call *electricity* in Diaz's cinema: when his way of showing an event fuses perfectly with the dramatic content and his intent as a cruel moralist of our time.

Are we permitted to evaluate Diaz?

Alas, the praise I have just showered upon a single scene cannot be said of much else in *Norte*. Diaz is today championed by many critics – sometimes excessively, in my opinion, without any necessary discrimination between his major and minor works or any assessment of his strengths and weaknesses as a film-maker. He is taken up as a cause by those who nobly carry the torch for challenging, progressive cinema – and we should all recognize the dangers of such projection, identification or investment (in the psychoanalytic sense). As the vernacular expression goes: Is Lav Diaz all he is cracked up to be?

Norte marks an intriguing plateau, and something of a turning point, in Diaz's career. After twelve years of relatively prolific, independent, low-budget production, it was the first of his films to be programmed at the Cannes Film Festival (2013). As a film in colour (as distinct from his frequent use of black and white), and with (for him) the reduced running time of merely four hours, it was even greeted by a few of his acolytes as a little bit of a disappointment, a sell-out to commercial (or at least wider film festival) accessibility.

Such hardcore fans did not need to be overly worried; Diaz's newfound accessibility hardly challenged the fame of Steven Spielberg or even (on the art circuit) Michael Haneke. In fact, while *Norte* does loosen up Diaz's characteristic cinematic style in a number of ways – with a consistent (although not conventionally dramatic) use of slow, gliding camera movements and an almost surreal deployment of aerial landscape footage marking different stages of the narrative – it also holds firm to his standard method.

This method, in my view (and here I depart from the legion of Diaz supporters), approaches what Roland Barthes (1967) might have called a 'degree zero' of artlessness: dialogues in long shot go around and around, scenes drain away, the acting performances are hit-and-miss from one moment to the next, the atmospheric sound is thin and inexpressive (Diaz sticking to his abhorrence for soundtrack music) and many situations (such as characters sitting in coffee shops or ambling down roads) are repeated without significant variation or development, over and over. Diaz fashions a panoramic vision of multiple, interconnected lives, but his ability to signal the passing of time lacks both traditional narrative craft and a more daringly rigorous way with ellipses, in the manner of Maurice Pialat or Pedro Costa.

In some of Diaz's earlier films (such as *Evolution of a Filipino Family*, 2004), this very Warholian air of emptiness and artlessness seemed to justify itself well enough: the space between the daily reality that he was staging, and the means he was using to record it, appeared so thin as to be almost non-existent. There was a certain thrill to this – the kind of thrill that persuades you to endure eight-hour screenings – in search of a new kind of filmic epiphany. But as the years pass by and the Diaz formula hardens from work to work, it becomes harder to recuperate the lack of inventiveness and craft in his work in the name of some spurious neo-neorealism. Diaz's most vocal fans do him no favours in this regard: he might become a better, more self-critical director if people stopped reassuring him that every new film he makes is a deathless masterpiece.

Critique and counter-critique

What you have read so far in this chapter draws upon the text of a review of *Norte* that I wrote for *Sight and Sound* magazine on the film's UK release in June 2014. Resituating and reworking it here, I am all too aware that, within the *dispositif* of this book collection of chapters on Diaz, I am potentially setting myself up as the fall guy, patsy or (like Joaquin!) sacrificial scapegoat of the entire project. I fully expect to be 'made an example of', like those poor kids who get the strap in films about British public school education, by other contributors to the book, as well as by possibly every reviewer of the finished product. Let it be!

The first appearance of my piece, both in print and online, prompted a public string of critical, puzzled and even angry reactions – alongside the many gleeful 'somebody's said it at last!' notes that I privately received. I was accused of failing to consider Diaz in his national production context – which is often merely another, this time nationalistic way of excusing the faults and gaps in his prodigious work – and of being insensitive to developments across his entire corpus (fair go, I had only 1,200 words to deal with one film!). Nadin Mai (2014), in her popular blog 'The art(s) of slow cinema', found my review not only 'rather irritating' but also fundamentally misguided – and, in this regard, exactly like most work on Diaz by (take a breath) 'critics and scholars'!

By far the most considered (while also the most belligerent) response came from the esteemed, veteran Argentinian critic known to the world under the *nom de plume* of Quintín. It was published in the Spanish magazine *Caimán cuadernos de cine* in September 2014, with a response by me. I would like to consider anew Quintín's argument in some detail here so as to extend and further justify my own.

Polemical debate often takes on the trappings of theatrical melodrama: each speaker casts the other in the most negative light possible, usually as the symptom of an abiding social problem or as the representative of a reprehensible social group. Quintín and I actually agree, at the outset, on several points in this argument. First, that it is too easy, as critics, to fall into extreme positions, totally for or totally against any cause or movement in cinema (the concept of slow cinema being itself a prime example of collateral damage in such debates). Second, we concur, alongside André Bazin and François Truffaut, that 'all films are born free and equal' (cited in Holmes and Ingram 1998: 84–85) and that there then can be – must be – discrimination between good and bad examples of any trend. Where Quintín and I came to grief is in our respective estimations of the cinema of Lav Diaz in general and *Norte* in particular.

A very negative image of school and schooling haunts Quintín's intervention (2014: 64). In the roles projected by his scenario, I am cast as the stern and repressive headmaster. He puts these wonderful Spanish words in my mouth: 'Hijo, me tienes que pedir permiso para apartarte de la norma' ('Son, you need to ask my permission to depart from the norm'). In his polemic, Quintín compares me not only to the 'establishment' American critic Roger Ebert (1942–2013), but also to 'the dinosaurs of the Spanish dailies' – an allusion to incrusted, conservative reviewers. The shame of it! On top of all that, I am taken (in an echo of Mai's denigration of 'critics and scholars') as a symptom of the 'academic-festival system' ('el sistema académico-festivalero'), even though I work for neither a university nor a festival, as well as Anglo-Saxon culture in general, whenever it gazes down upon films that arrive 'from the periphery'. This centre/periphery situation is something already diagnosed with acidity by Brazil's Glauber Rocha back in the 1960s – and, indeed, it would be entirely possible to align Diaz's cinema with what Rocha (2018) proposed concerning an 'aesthetic of hunger' (or precarity, to use the more currently fashionable word).

Quintín paints me as the example of a critic who erects a norm and then holds a difficult, adventurous film-maker – in this case, Diaz – to it. Once again, terrible associations are imputed – alongside dreary, teacherly Ebert and some old men of the newspapers, I am also responding just like a philistine Hollywood producer or a hideous scribe for the American trade magazine *Variety*! Mai's critique runs along similar lines: in a general comment on those who criticize Diaz's work, she infers that they are – explicitly or implicitly – asking Diaz to improve his game by stepping up to bigger budgets, more esteemed festival slots, colour, shorter running times and a more extensive narrative component. This happens to be the opposite of my own oft-expressed viewpoint on the matter.

In more general terms, Quintín accuses me of speaking down to Diaz: I am the self-presumed authority and he merely a student. I do not see myself in that way, but this is hardly the central point at stake. Rather, to properly problematize the terms of the debate, I would ask: does not every critic, whenever he or she speaks or writes, run the risk of pronouncing *ex cathedra*? How can this be entirely avoided when we are putting forward not only opinions, or even frameworks for understanding, but also judgements of value? In this context, I would reject Mai's (2014) claim that, when it comes to Diaz (and presumably some similar cases), 'we should not discuss [their] aesthetics' at all. Rocha's position 50 years ago was far more radical and uncompromising: the cultural, social and economic position of underdevelopment must *force* the creation of a new aesthetic, and that aesthetic must swiftly evolve, from one work to the next, to counter the changing times.

I do feel that there is a supportive cult around Diaz that is, and has been, insufficiently critical. I certainly believe that, after so many hours of cinema, Diaz should be better, by now, at what he does. Practice does not necessarily make perfect, but it should at least lead to change, evolution, a refinement and deepening of the artist's own method. But I do not judge that failure or weakness according to a conventional or industrial norm. Rather, I compare Diaz to Pialat, Costa or Alonso: film-makers who *master* their individual, unconventional forms. I see no such mastery, yet, in Diaz. To shelter Diaz from such criticism seems to me simply a different way of patronizing a supposedly 'third world' film-maker and keeping them in their already vulnerable place: poor boy, we should not expect you to improve under the conditions you face; we need to find a safe way to discuss and promote your films…

But Diaz is now (whether he likes it or not!) a citizen of the world and of world cinema. He works in relative autonomy, with a high amount of artistic control, and the fame and notoriety he has so far achieved on the festival and art circuit will lead him further and deeper into international co-production arrangements (as has inevitably happened for other slow-cinema makers). In fact, indications of an evolution in his career are already happening: I take the exploration of musical form in *Season of the Devil* (2018) as an excellent and promising sign. Meanwhile, on the other hand, the critical response to *The Woman Who Left*, as a film retreading old Diaz ground, has occasioned some weary disenchantment even from his most partisan supporters. Scout Tafoya (2017: n.pag.), writing a generally positive notice for the Roger Ebert website, wondered whether its 'wandering focus and rough technical edges', and especially its sound transitions that 'pop loudly', were due to Diaz having to 'rush the film to premiere' – generating a doubt as to whether the director 'knows exactly what he is doing' or his work is more hit-and-miss, 'a product of Diaz shooting, directing, editing and writing the film and just not being able to spread himself equally across all tasks'. Stuart Klawans (2017: n.pag.) in *Film Comment*, less generous and forgiving in his account than Tafoya, diagnosed the film's 'half-sentimental, half-tendentious scheme, which in its diagrammatic clarity forecloses the gradual, unforced revelations that are promised by Diaz's style'. And Nadin Mai (2018: n.pag.), in her blog, has registered acute disappointment that *The Woman Who Left* 'remains at its premise', eschews 'a complex engagement with the actual subject', often fails in its attempt to fit the natural performers into their given fictive roles and in its construction is veritably 'spoon-feeding the audience' by fashioning a predictable narrative that 'washes over' the spectator.

Now we are getting somewhere! Perhaps it is not so shameful to be a scholar – or even a critic – of Lav Diaz, after all.

REFERENCES

Barthes, Roland (1967), *Writing Degree Zero*, New York: Jonathan Cape.

Holmes, Diana and Ingram, Robert (1998), *François Truffaut*, Manchester: Manchester University Press.

Klawans, Stuart (2017), 'Review: *The Woman Who Left*', *Film Comment*, May–June, https://www.filmcomment.com/article/review-the-woman-who-left-lav-diaz/. Accessed 22 June 2021.

Mai, Nadin (2014), 'In defense of a lack of craft', *The Art(s) of Slow Cinema*, 20 July, https://theartsofslowcinema.com/2014/07/20/in-defense-of-a-lack-of-craft/. Accessed 22 June 2021.

Mai, Nadin (2018), '*The Woman Who Left* – Lav Diaz (2016)', *The Art(s) of Slow Cinema*, 2 March, https://theartsofslowcinema.com/2018/03/02/the-woman-who-left-lav-diaz-2016/. Accessed 10 May 2021.

Martin, Adrian (2018), *Mysteries of Cinema*, Amsterdam: Amsterdam University Press.

Quintín (2014), 'El director despreciado', *Caiman cuadernos de cine*, 30:81, https://www.caimanediciones.es/tienda/numero-30-81-septiembre-2014-2/. Accessed 23 June 2021.

Rocha, Glauber (2018), *On Cinema*, London: I. B. Tauris.

Tafoya, Scout (2017), '*The Woman Who Left*', *Roger Ebert*, 19 May, https://www.rogerebert.com/reviews/the-woman-who-left-2017. Accessed 1 April 2019.

8

Evolution of a Filipino Family and/as Non-Cinema

William Brown

Towards the end of *Ebolusyon ng isang pamilyang Pilipino (Evolution of a Filipino Family)* (Diaz 2004), we see a railway track surrounded by countryside as a train hurtles from the background and towards the camera. The train then passes the camera and exits frame left, revealing once again the Philippine landscape beyond. The shot perhaps inevitably recalls one of the earliest films, *L'arrivée d'un train en gare de La Ciotat (The Arrival of a Train at La Ciotat Station)* (Auguste and Louis Lumière, France, 1896), in which a train similarly approaches the camera, before bearing slightly to the left of the frame, stopping and emptying itself of its passengers.

However, while the reference seems unmistakable (to those familiar with the Lumière film), there are important differences between the two shots. The Lumière film, for example, takes place at a station, while the Diaz film is in the middle of the countryside. In *L'arrivée...* the train comes to a halt, while in *Evolution...* the train continues. Furthermore, as the train continues, we see walking along the railway tracks beyond/behind it Raynaldo (Elryan de Vera), one of the film's main protagonists who at this point in the proceedings is crossing the country by foot in order to reach the grave of his dead mother, Hilda (Marife Necesito). The Lumière shot lasts roughly one minute, while the Diaz shot lasts more than twice that long; the train itself takes only fifteen seconds to pass the camera, while we then see Raynaldo walking along the tracks for nigh two minutes.

These differences provide us with much to analyse. For, if the Lumière film suggests the arrival of modernity, both in the sense that it depicts the arrival of a machine as modern as the train and in the sense that the film declares the arrival of a medium as modern as the cinema, the failure of the train to stop in the Diaz film suggests a kind of bypassing of modernity. The modern era might bring with it high technology, but Diaz wants to show us those 'left behind' by modernization, those who do not and cannot take the train, but who like Raynaldo have to cross the country on foot. If historically the train also played a key role in creating a sense of national identity (with train timetables unifying the otherwise diverse times of a nation), then *Evolution…* would seem to suggest a nation without a coherent identity, as it highlights people travelling at a much slower, walking as opposed to locomotive, rhythm. This diversity of rhythms/times in turn suggests a Philippines that is at odds with modernity itself if the latter is defined by the establishment of relatively fixed nation states and national identities and by the rigid imposition of times and locations as measured against the central point of Greenwich in London. Indeed, prior to 2013, when the Philippines experienced the imposition of a single, nation-wide time (known locally as Juan Time), the country did have numerous 'time zones' marginally different from each other. In other words, by holding the shot after the train has passed, Diaz suggests that while there might be such an entity as the Philippines, in that it is recognized internationally as a distinct nation state, in reality what we know of as the Philippines is a heterogeneous mass of different times and rhythms, some of which are slower than modernity, with the lack of unification itself running counter to the unifying project of modernization via the institution of the nation state.

While the contents of the shot from *Evolution…* suggest a diversity of rhythms, the form of the shot also conveys important information. For, in being an unbroken single-take sequence, the shot not only recalls the Lumière image but also 'bypasses' it in some respects. This bypassing is an inversion of the one described earlier, and it is intimately linked to the digital technology used to create the shot, as I shall explain presently. In ending after the arrival of the train, the Lumière film demonstrates how cinema from its outset was designed to conform to (and perhaps to reinforce) the rhythms of modernity; the duration of the film is determined by the amount of film that the camera can hold, while when filming starts and stops is determined by the arrival of the train. While the Lumière film is about a minute long, and thus in some respects constitutes a long take, the conformity of cinematic and locomotive rhythm announces a cinema that will increase in cutting rate over the next 120 years, much as modernity itself will accelerate through, among other things, technologization and the shrinking of distances (the train is faster than walking, but it is slower than the aeroplane and the instant telecommunications technologies that can allow us to see the other side of the world in 'real time'). The Diaz sequence, however, suggests a cinema that does not cut to the beat of modernity, with the shot not ending as the train passes but holding for twice the length of the Lumière film. That is, it cuts to the beat of a pre-modern, pedestrian as opposed to locomotive world.

That said, the ability for Diaz to create this image – and to create a film like *Evolution of a Filipino Family* as a whole – comes about paradoxically as a result not of anything pre-modern but of the *most modern* film-making technology, namely digital cameras (as opposed to traditional analogue ones). Although post-Lumière analogue cameras could record for longer than even the shot from *Evolution...* without having to cut, rarely did they, in part because of the expense of setting up such shots and because of the cost of developing multiple takes of the same shot. It is with the advent of digital cameras, then, that a long-take aesthetic becomes easier to achieve both technologically and in terms of cost-efficiency, even if the earlier sequences of *Evolution...* were shot on 16mm, with the digital being used as the production of the film increasingly wore on. In this way, while the train that is the image's content suggests modernity bypassing a pre-modern Philippines (if there is a unified nation that can be called such), the shot formally suggests the digital bypassing a modern Philippines in order to connect back precisely to that pre-modern world. We might say that if modernity left regular Philippine folk like Raynaldo behind, the 'postmodern' digital world re-establishes the legitimacy of their rhythms.

For, in order to extend the argument a bit further, if modernity as defined by the train leaves Raynaldo behind, and if this modernity is also intimately tied to cinema itself, then the digitally enabled shot from *Evolution...* allows Raynaldo in some senses to catch up in that he now has time to walk through the frame before a cut has to be imposed. That is, if the cinema of modernity would have cut out Raynaldo, rendering him invisible, the digital cinema includes Raynaldo, making him visible once again. If cinema, the train and modernity are coterminous, perhaps even synonymous, then in figuring the pre-modern in addition to the modern (Raynaldo and the train), by including what modernity-cinema-locomotion would have left out, can this shot still be cinema? If for some critics the incorporation of the digital into film production, distribution and exhibition constitutes the end of cinema (it is no longer shot and printed on film stock, no longer shown in theatres), then perhaps we can productively label this moment from *Evolution...*, as well as the film as a whole, as an example not of cinema but positively of non-cinema. Furthermore, if the nation is equally tied to the matrix of modernity-cinema-locomotion, does the move away from cinema and into the realm of non-cinema constitute a dissolution also of the nation?

Finally, if what underwrites modernity-cinema-locomotion-nationality is really the machinations of capital, as made clear by the economic bottom line that determines the rhythms of cinema and modernity, then is *Evolution...*, as an example of non-cinema, also an example of anti-capitalism, not least because it is a film that will struggle to make money as a result of its unwieldy length, its elliptical narration and its slow pace (about which more shortly)? In other words, while digital technology in some senses constitutes the product of capitalism par excellence, do we not also see in *Evolution...* the potential of digital technology more generally to suggest that the very destiny of capitalism (and by extension of cinema, modernity, locomotion and nationality) is its own dissolution, as predicted by Karl Marx and Friedrich Engels some 170 years ago? It is these themes that I wish to explore over the remainder of this chapter.

Philippine revolution

In spite of its title and in spite of an early voice-over from Ana (Sigrid Andrea Bernardo) declaring that the story is about the various members of her family, *Evolution…* in fact follows the plight of (at least) two different families between 1972 and 1987. On the one hand, there are the Gallardos, which include matriarch Purificacion, or Puring (Angie Ferro), her children Hilda and Ricardo, or Kadyo (Pen Medina), his wife Celina, or Ina (Raye Baquirin), and their three daughters Juliana, or Huling (Banaue Miclat), Martina (Lorelie Futol) and Ana. On the other hand, there is the Santelmo family, which consists of Fernando (Ronnie Lazaro), his wife Marya (Lui Manansala) and their two adopted sons Bendo (Roeder) and Carlos (Erwin Gonzales) – respectively the son of one of Fernando's cousins and Marya's nephew.

The link between these two families is Raynaldo, or Ray, the adopted son of Hilda, who leaves the Gallardos after her death in 1980 and ends up being taken in by Fernando and Marya in 1984. While the film focuses alternatively on the Gallardos and Ray's time with the Santelmos, we nonetheless discover towards the end of *Evolution…*, when Kadyo goes in search of Ray in 1987 (at around the time that Ray treks to Hilda's grave), that between 1980 and 1984 Ray lived in Manila with a third family. Furthermore, both at the beginning and at the end of the film, we see Hilda discovering Ray as a baby in a pile of trash and covered in ants – with the ending then showing us Ray's birth mother leaving flowers at the spot where she abandoned him, an act which she tells us in voice-over that she has regretted ever since. In other words, while the film purports to be about one family, it is in fact about several. Or rather, if the film is about one family, then that family is complex in its structure and defined not by blood ties but by a system of care, especially for the foundling Ray.

To suggest that the film is defined uniquely by a system of care would be misleading, however, since it stands in distinct contrast to the repeated tragedies that otherwise structure the film's story. Placing events in chronological order, as opposed to the order in which we see or discover them, Hilda works as a prostitute in Manila, where reportedly she is raped many times. She discovers Ray in 1972, the same year in which President Ferdinand Marcos declared martial law via Proclamation 1081, before at an uncertain point in time leaving Manila to rejoin Puring, Kadyo and his daughters. Hilda's father has at an unknown point in time hanged himself, supposedly out of shame for Hilda, while Kadyo's wife Celina has also died from ulcers.

In 1980, after abuse at the hands of some soldiers who slaughter other locals, Hilda is raped and murdered by three drunks, whom Ray then kills with a gun when they go to move her body for fear of its discovery. While this prompts Ray to move to Manila, the aftermath for the rest of the family is unclear. The next thing we know about Kadyo, for example, is that he is in prison – with Puring on at least two occasions after his release admonishing him for being a thief. Potentially Puring is referring to the guns of some dead soldiers that Kadyo allegedly finds and sells to rebel leader Ka Harim (Rey Ventura). Indeed, theft would seem to fit the amount of time that Kadyo serves in prison (roughly seven years). Nonetheless, Kadyo could be in prison for another, unknown crime; while one would have thought he would receive a tougher sentence for murder, it is also hinted, for example, that Kadyo himself killed the soldiers from whom he took the guns, and while Harim says he will take the rap for Ray's murder of the drunks, whether he does – or whether blame lands on Kadyo – is not clear.

During Kadyo's imprisonment, Puring, Huling, Martina and Ana are forced to travel to various villages in order to work the fields, with Martina at one point living in town, combining school with work for her landlady Violing (Patty Eustaquio). Meanwhile, after the aforementioned period in Manila between 1980 and 1984, Ray joins the Santelmos, who struggle to find wealth by at first panning and then going into a forbidden zone called Doroteo in order to mine (unsuccessfully) for gold. As Marya goes blind, so does Carlos one day go missing, presumably abducted by the henchmen of thuggish rival miner Dakila Lacsamana (Dido Dela Paz). After an unknown period of time looking for Carlos, Bendo and Ray slaughter Dakila and his men with machetes – prompting Ray's decision to return to his mother's grave.

Meanwhile, once out of prison, Kadyo goes fruitlessly in search of Ray, not least because he is not welcome to return to Puring and his daughters, since Puring is, as mentioned, ashamed at his imprisonment. At first scouring the countryside, Kadyo then goes to an address left by Ray in the Rosario district of Quezon City, part of Metro Manila. In Manila, he stays with associates of former prison kingpin Mayor (Joel Torre), who eventually hires Kadyo to help assassinate a very important person, who turns out to be none other than Philippine film-maker Lino Brocka (Gino Dormiendo). However, Kadyo quits the safe house where he is being kept in the build-up to the assassination, only to be stabbed by Mayor in the midst of a crowd during a demonstration. Kadyo dies as does Puring back in the countryside. However, while the film ends with the lament of Ray's birth mother, we nonetheless do see Huling, Martina and Ana finally reunited with Ray and going about menial chores in the family home.

If through the repeated tragedies of *Evolution...* all of the characters both suffer from and commit acts of violence, these do not happen in a bubble. That is, the fictional events that the Gallardos and the Santelmos experience are tied to real events in Philippine history. As mentioned, Ray is abandoned and discovered by Hilda at around the time that Ferdinand Marcos declared martial law, but more specifically Harim is a member of one of several rebel groups (typically referred to collectively as the Bayan, which in Tagalog means 'country' or 'people') taking up arms against the Marcos regime. Kadyo is sympathetic to their cause (selling them arms) not only because of brutality suffered at the hands of government forces but also because he fails to subsist under Marcos, having had to sell his farm. Fernando likewise struggles financially and must turn to dangerous mining instead of farming – the search for gold being sponsored by a city woman who wants him to mine because the Marcoses have allegedly hidden 8,000 tons (twice the amount of gold in Saudi Arabia!) in a secret vault. Finally, Mayor's plot to kill Lino Brocka clearly is part of a pro-Marcos plot, even though the period during which it is supposed to take place, 1987, is after the People Power or EDSA Revolution of 1986 and during the presidency of Corazon Aquino.

If these connections to historical events in the Philippines seem a bit tentative, then the role that such events play in the film is made clearer still by the fact that Diaz interpolates into his film what appears to be television and radio footage of events from the period in question. Not only do we see extensive coverage of the EDSA Revolution of 1986, for example, but we also see images of and the Marcoses' reactions to the earlier assassination of Benigno 'Ninoy' Aquino Jr, an opposition politician (and husband of Corazon Aquino) who returned to the Philippines in 1983 having been in exile in the United States since 1980 – only to be killed at the airport when he landed. In addition, Fernando listens on the radio to reports about Gregorio 'Gringo' Honasan's attempts to overthrow the Corazon Aquino government shortly after her election victory. Finally, the film features a fictional version of real-life film director Lino Brocka. At one point, Kadyo watches the fictional Brocka discussing the real-life institution of Executive Order 868 (in February 1983), whereby Philippine cinema became controlled by the government and thus blunted as a tool for dissent. As part of a fictional documentary, *The Lost Brocka*, which is directed by a character called Taga Timog (Lourd De Vayra), who also appears as a film-maker in Diaz's *Batang West Side/West Side Avenue* (2001), the fictional Brocka even names and brands as a Marcos lapdog real-life censor Manoling Morato. In other words, *Evolution* ... ties its fictional story to real history – with the fact that the period of martial law is roughly equal to Ray's lifespan suggesting that Ray almost embodies (or is a metaphor for) the hope for change in the country during this revolutionary time.

Philippine evolution

However, if the film in some respects charts the road towards revolution in the Philippines, in other respects it takes seriously its claims to be not about revolution, with its rapid turnovers, but evolution, a process that happens at a much slower pace. Since evolution is a process that is slow to the point of being invisible to the human eye, it would be a bit misleading to say that the film's depiction of evolution is 'made clear' by how the film is shot; one cannot 'make clear' the invisible without destroying its very invisibility. Nonetheless, alongside the narrative featuring the successive tragedies outlined earlier, the film is also full of shots that feature characters carrying out mundane tasks, with numerous involving people sitting down and resting. In addition, many shots in the film not only last long enough for the viewer's eye to begin to wander and take in the minutiae of the frame's contents beyond the human elements, but they are also framed in such a way that things like foliage and, in particular, sky take up far more of the frame than the human figures, who otherwise appear in (extreme) long shot. The almost continuous visual and aural presence of animals in the film – dogs, cats, chickens, pigs, carabaos and more – similarly suggests an interest not just in the human but also in the non-human aspects of the Philippine world. Given the predominantly presentational style with which Diaz shows us these non-human phenomena (the use of extreme long shots, often with long takes, the camera regularly static), it is hard to say what the shots specifically 'mean'. Nonetheless, that animals, plants and sky are so prominent in the film does suggest an interest not simply in capturing the human dimension of what we are seeing, including the political situation of the Philippines in the period portrayed, but also the non-human dimension. It is as a result of this interest in the non-human that the film expands from depicting revolution to depicting evolution.

In the synopsis of the film given earlier, I repeatedly use words that connote ambiguity such as 'seemingly' and 'allegedly'. In part this is an inevitable upshot of the film's interest in things beyond the human or what I am terming 'evolution'. Filming in extreme long shot does make it harder to tell apart the characters within the frame since rarely (aside from with repeat viewings) does one get a chance properly to study the faces of, say, Huling, Martina and Ana in order to be able better to individuate them. What is more, many sequences in *Evolution...* take place at night, with darkness also regularly taking up a large percentage of the frame. Not only does an interest in darkness and the non-human arguably help to qualify

Evolution... as an example of non-cinema, in that most mainstream narrative cinema is interested in clarity, light and an anthropocentric vision of the world, but it is also necessarily ambiguous. This ambiguity surely is deliberate (as opposed to arbitrary and meaningless) when we consider the ellipses in the story: we do not know whether Kadyo killed the soldiers, how he ended up in prison and so on. What is more, this interest in evolution, ambiguity, non-anthropocentrism and darkness also ties in with issues of the nation and capital.

Even before Kadyo is tasked with assassinating Lino Brocka, we see the fictional version of the director talking on a radio show, to which Martina is listening. He says:

> I think we have to free ourselves from all our foreign hang-ups, and really determine what is Filipino. You know we have been under Spain for over 400 years. And then the Americans came for another 50 years. And although we have developed some positive traits from these two waves of colonization, we really have to come to terms with our own identity as a people. You know, even in the movies, for example, all these karate movies, they are not doing us any good, they belong to another culture, and these so-called western movies with bourgeois values, they're not doing us any good.
> (Diaz 2004: n.pag.)

The inclusion of this statement suggests several things. First, it expands a contextual understanding of the Philippines from beyond simply the period 1971–87 and into a much longer, 500-year process that includes colonialism and contemporary imperialism. That is, it involves a gesture away from revolution and towards evolution. Second, the statement suggests that the Philippines in its current iteration is an invention of that history of colonialism and imperialism manifested still in a bourgeois cinema that belongs to 'another culture'. In some senses, then, if Brocka asks for a Filipino identity, what he really demands is a non-Filipino identity, if the Philippines itself is an identity imposed from without (as is exemplified by the fact that the Philippines are named after Felipe II of Spain). Exposing the fact that all nations are historically contingent 'imagined communities', the Philippine identity that Brocka asks for in some senses must go against the concept of the nation itself, since not just the Philippines in particular but the system of nations as a whole is part of the project of modernity, which claims to invent the Philippines, and yet which in fact excludes many, including the Gallardos and the Santelmos, who nonetheless remain valid, worthy human beings.

If Brocka's reference to colonialism expands the scope of the film beyond the recent past and into a longer history of modernity, the trope of the mine gives to the film a planetary scale, for the evisceration of the Earth for the purposes of discovering gold (i.e. for making money) speaks about the very reshaping of the planet in the name of capital, the imposition on the world of a(n accelerating) capitalist temporality. The mines are empty, however, and what is left behind is quite literally a black hole, an empty void, bereft of that which Fernando and Dakila seek. Without gold/money/capital, one cannot hope to exist. If the creation of the Philippines was really the colonial business of destroying nature and collecting gold, then 'what is Filipino', as Brocka might term it, is precisely the void that is left behind after the imperialists have gone and after the Marcoses have hidden 8,000 tons of gold for themselves. No wonder Diaz regularly films darkness if darkness is what defines 'what is Filipino' after one removes that which was invented for the purposes of modernity.

More than this, 'what is Filipino' is also not cinema. For if the Marcoses are linked in *Evolution...* to the gold that they have stolen like the colonial and imperial powers before them, then the film also links them to the control of cinema production, distribution and exhibition (references to Executive Order 868), reinforcing the role that cinema plays in the capitalism-modernity-nation-locomotion matrix identified here. Since cinema is interested in reinforcing bourgeois values, then it is outside of cinema that 'what is Filipino' must be found.

Style and self-consciousness

That it is a (fictional version of a) film-maker, Lino Brocka, who demands a discovery of 'what is Filipino' will seem paradoxical if I also am arguing that 'what is Filipino' is not cinema. Indeed, from (the fictional?) Brocka's perspective, cinema might well be one of the 'positive traits' that colonialism and then imperialism brought with it, since Brocka uses it with his films in order to create 'what is Filipino'. However, I would like to emphasize that Brocka himself critiques the 'bourgeois values' of Western cinema (and by implication its imitators). My argument is that cinema is synonymous with bourgeois values and that if one is to challenge those values, then one should create not cinema but non-cinema. This is not to say that non-cinema is not *cinematic*. On the contrary, it can be and perhaps in some senses is more pressingly and politically cinematic than (bourgeois) cinema. For by using long takes, emphasizing darkness and rejecting the rhythms not just of modernity but in some senses also of humanity (an emphasis on nature), *Evolution...* challenges what cinema is rather than accepting a priori a specifically modern definition of what this (modern) invention is or should be.

Perhaps it is partly for this reason that *Evolution...* places so much emphasis on other media aside from film. As mentioned, there are regular sections that feature what appears to be television footage of the recent past. However, the film also regularly features Philippine pop songs and moments in which characters listen to the radio, especially a soap opera the making of which we also see at regular intervals. In effect, Diaz shows that cinema is linked to, as opposed to separate from, these different media, incorporating each of them as and when it can or needs to. Furthermore, in showing us the making of the radio soap opera (that otherwise is perceived as making its listeners lazy, as Fernando says of Ray at one point), Diaz deconstructs the illusion of these media, suggesting that they are not separable from the labour that goes into making them – as opposed to the ready and easy-to-consume appearance that they adopt for regular listeners/viewers, the occultation of labour and exploitation itself being core to the imposition of bourgeois values and the making-invisible of the poor who do the mining, cleaning, farming and other jobs that keep the rich, like the Marcoses, rich.

It is hard to know whether one has seen the 'correct' version of *Evolution*.... The Internet Movie Database (IMDb) suggests that the film lasts 540 minutes, while Wikipedia lists the film as being 593 minutes long. Others list it as being 11 hours long (i.e. 660 minutes). The version that I saw is/was 10 hours, 24 minutes and 51 seconds, including opening and closing credits. Permitting for some human error, this version was comprised of 745 shots, meaning that the film has an overall average shot length (ASL) of 50.32 seconds (without the opening and closing credits included in this run time, the ASL would be slightly shorter). This makes the film resolutely long and slow, but it should be noted that there are some sections with extremely long takes (when Kadyo is stabbed, we follow him stumbling around abandoned Manila architecture for 20 minutes), which in turn means that there are sections with rapid cutting. What should be noted, however, is that the most rapid cutting appears during the television sequences depicting 'official' Philippine history. That is, these faster sections function specifically as interruptions of the rhythms of modernity, bringing with it the fast-cutting news of the nation into what is otherwise a slow film that uses the most contemporary digital technology in order paradoxically to reconnect with that which is not modern, which defies the concept of the nation (the sky belongs to no one) and which is not about the use of the planet's raw materials, including film stock and gold, in order to make money. Moreover, as is widely reported, *Evolution*... was shot over a ten-year period. Not only does one see the actors, especially Elryan de Vera as Ray, physically age, therefore, but this production method is almost unthinkable to commercial cinema. In other words, in the duration of the film's production, in the duration of the film and in the duration of many of the film's shots, we see the film striving towards a deeply cinematic non-cinema that runs counter to the bourgeois values of cinema-as-modernity-as-nation-as-locomotion-as-capital.

In the footage of the EDSA Revolution, and before Kadyo is stabbed by Mayor, we see a prominent poster for *Kapag Lumaban Ang Api (When the Downtrodden Fights Back)* (Ronwaldo Reyes, 1987), an action film starring (and directed under a pseudonym by) Fernando Poe Jr (FPJ). The singular figure of the star in the poster contrasts with the faces of the masses in the streets. Again, we get a sense, then, of Diaz contrasting the bourgeois values of individual heroism, as personified by FPJ, with the collective will of the people. If institutional, state-approved cinema emphasizes the individual (even when carrying a progressive-sounding title like *When the Downtrodden Fights Back*), then that which emphasizes the people might well better be understood as non-cinema (the fact that FPJ went on to attempt a political career himself, losing in the 2004 presidential elections to Gloria Macapagal-Arroyo, equally suggests that national identity and cinema are closely linked). As per the film's insistent long shots in which sometimes it is hard to recognize different characters (thus depriving them of the individuality that is key to bourgeois values), and even if Ray in some senses 'embodies' the nation under martial law, Diaz challenges conventional cinema, in the process producing non-cinema.

The digital technology that came to define the production of *Evolution...* might well be the result of modernity. Nonetheless, since digital technology allows him to film pre-modern rhythms and temporalities, which themselves are linked to an emphasis not just on the human but also on plants, animals and the environment, and which in turn are part of a story that Diaz situates in relation not only to contemporary political events but also to the history of the Philippines, the history of modernity and the history of the planet as a whole, and in helping Diaz thus to depict otherwise invisible darkness, duration, labour and the people, digital technology has an important part to play in the dissolution of the modernity-capital-nation-locomotion-individual-cinema complex and the institution of a new, anti-capitalist, post-national, collective non-cinema of multiple different temporalities. May this digital non-cinema flourish.

REFERENCE

Diaz, Lav (dir.) (2004), *Evolution of a Filipino Family*, Philippines: Sine Olivia, Paul Tañedo and Ebolusyon Productions.

9

Jesus, Magdalene and the Filipino Judas: Lav Diaz and His 'Artless Epics'

Parichay Patra

Prologue

Jesus saith to her, Touch me not; for I am not yet ascended to my Father.

(John 20: 17 1985)

The Russians deny, though weakly and with much hesitancy, that Dostoevsky was outlawed under Stalin.

(Moravia 1989: 619)

I had my first encounter with Lav Diaz back in 2011, at the International Film Festival of Kerala (IFFK), just a few months before I left India for a near-half-a-decade hiatus in the Antipodes. That year IFFK featured a special section devoted to Filipino cinema with the inclusion of *Century of Birthing* (Diaz 2011). Amidst the darkness of the almost empty Kalabhavan theatre, I discovered the violence of the image the way I had rarely done before. The incredible duration of a Lav Diaz film is infamous for provoking a naive fanboyism that rarely contributes to his cinema, and I was not immune to that either. But once the dust settled down on that first experience, his phenomenally static camera and long takes stayed with me, along with the wide expanse of an overcast sky under the canopy of which his man and woman sing the song of the heretic.

Like Manuel Arguilla, Lav Diaz too has a deceptively bucolic charm of the country that will invariably be decimated by a violence that is mostly off-screen. Arguilla, the guerilla-turned-litterateur, was executed by Japanese colonizers, one of the several occupying forces that reshaped Filipino history forever.[1] So far, Diaz has engaged with the Spanish colonization and anti-colonial movements, along with the Marcos dictatorship that ravaged the Philippines in the 1970s. Especially with the latter he has developed a near obsession that often erupts into his frames like a volcano, even in films that begin in a setting far removed from the period.[2] In *Century of Birthing*, the roadside farmers refer to the Marcos era just before that encounter under the overcast sky, and the woman who sings under that sky is one of his innumerable raped women who people the Lav Diaz world and haunt his actors and spectators within and outside the screen illusion, respectively.

So far, the cinema of Diaz has evoked responses that address the obsessive sexual violence, the rise of the matriarchal mythologies in the mythical forms of *Bai Rahamah*,[3] the national artist pondering on the disturbing national history, memories of torture and trauma, Diaz's cinephilic association with a national cinema and its proponents such as Lino Brocka, his engagement with Dostoyevsky and the epic novel, his conceptualization of something as obscure as the 'Asiatic time' that led to an eccentric running time and his wandering figures, the walking dead surrounded by a near darkness and (almost always) accompanied by a tropical downpour. But my interest lies elsewhere, even though I will fall back on the Bible and Dostoyevsky time and again.[4] I am concerned primarily with a history of contestation around Diaz criticism, with the West and the non-West debating over the possible allowance and extent of 'exceptionalism' in his case. From the ashes of a now-dead and occasionally revived auteurism, Diaz evolves as an 'exceptional' representative of the non-West, with several allegations against his 'anemic' cinema that, allegedly, lacks some of the fundamental properties of cinema itself. In defense of Diaz, his supporters rely on the same rationale of exceptionalism and the debate remains at a standstill. Moreover, there have rarely been works that challenge the exceptional status that is demanded for the non-West, for an entire continent, even if Diaz is often (mis)placed within the proverbial slow cinema camp that, by nature, is transnational.[5]

Thus Diaz criticism, so far, has avoided some more fundamental queries regarding film criticism. Given a chance, they will come back to haunt this chapter at a later stage.

Proposition

That the predominantly Eurocentric ways of approaching cinema may not be applicable to cinemas that are geopolitically and ideologically associated with other 'locations' is not a new proposition, something which Solanas and Getino hinted strongly at in their seminally polemical 1969 manifesto that heralded the conceptual initiation of Third Cinema (1970–71: 1–10). The association between

Diaz and Third Cinema is not a new proposition either as May Adadol Ingawanij invokes Glauber Rocha in the context of Diaz (2015: 106). The predominantly 'Western' detractors of Diaz often object to many lacks in his cinema, and his (often 'Western') supporters rise to his defense with their arguments based on the role of the West in the perpetuation of such political conditions in the Philippines that are conducive to his cinema and its lacks (Mai 2014: n.pag.). But this line of defense, associating Diaz with a kind of 'imperfect cinema' as proposed by Espinosa (1979), may not prove very effective against a major aesthetic objection raised against him. In this context I will briefly summarize a Lav Diaz debate between Adrian Martin and Nadin Mai.

Adrian Martin, in his *Sight and Sound* review of *Norte, the End of History* (Diaz 2013), raised the issue of Diaz's evident 'degree zero of artlessness' à la Roland Barthes and also of the 'Warholian emptiness' in his cinema (2014b: n.pag.).[6] His objections included the reiteration of the 'artless' in film after film, Diaz's alleged inability/unwillingness to evolve/change and the fanboyism spoiling him. For Martin, Diaz's apparently unusual engagement with time, despite being non-traditional, lacks the dexterous handling of ellipses that can be located in someone like Pedro Costa or Maurice Pialat (2014b: n.pag.).

Nadin Mai's response was directed mainly at the issue concerning the un-evolving nature of Diaz, as she perceived an unwelcome change in Diaz's cinema since *Norte*, with a brief and occasional return to self with *From What Is Before* (2014), albeit that return was apparently short-lived. Martin, however, has come up with a revised version of his 2013 article for the present volume where he welcomes some of the new directions that Diaz's cinema is heading to and announces that being a (harsh) critic of Diaz is possibly no longer a problem especially since the unsuccessful recycling of the old Diaz materials and style in films such as *The Woman Who Left* (Diaz 2016b) has generated responses of displeasure even from his ardent 'fans'.[7] Martin also refers to the Third Cinema/imperfect cinema mode of argument in the context of Diaz by invoking Glauber Rocha's aesthetics of hunger and offers his rationale for its less applicability in the present context, locating the temporal-spatial-political gulf that lies in between.[8]

Thus Martin separates Diaz and his cinema from the Latin American condition, even though some of Diaz's obsessive concerns have strong resemblances with the situation beyond the Atlantic, some of these being perpetual in the Philippines. The notion of the forced disappearances and the hunt for the remains of the desaparecidos/the disappeared are some of these (Mai 2015).[9] While in such Latin American nations as Argentina and Chile this has been prevalent in the long 1970s under the dictatorships of Videla and Pinochet, respectively, forced disappearance/extrajudicial killing remains a reality in Diaz's archipelago even in the contemporary.[10] In *Melancholia* (2008), the remains of the disappeared guerillas are (to be) found and the hunt is still on. Diaz uses footage of discovering skulls and bones/skeletons of disappeared guerillas in the forest while the armed forces deny their involvement on camera. His protagonists look for the remains of their disappeared whose whereabouts were not unknown even before a decade. Years later, in *A Lullaby to the Sorrowful Mystery* (2016a), Diaz presents the late-nineteenth-century hunt for the remains of Andrés Bonifacio in the ambiguous density of the Filipino forest. The reiteration, as it seems, is beyond the level of the narrative. It is, presumably, historical for a national culture where Manuel Arguilla, with his life, reiterated what happened to José Rizal under the Spaniards.

While both Ingawanij and Martin invoke Rocha for presumably different ends and the Latin American context has been evoked in Diaz's interviews as well, this chapter does not intend to take sides in this debate.[11] Instead, it wants to proceed to an unchartered territory, an intersection of the literary and the cinematic, as both the seemingly exclusive viewpoints help it in its quest.

The quest will begin with a brief response to the predominant modes of film criticism in the West that, as this chapter will argue, may seem futile in the face of the challenges posed by a cinema that we cannot easily grasp.

Film criticism

In a recent virtual class on 'The Practice of Film Criticism' organized by the University of St Andrews, Jean-Michel Frodon, the French film critic, mentioned how his being a critic is inherently associated with his identity as a citizen. Frodon, decidedly, did not add the epithet 'French' to the more general term 'citizen' though. Days before the class, the participants had to watch a film on Vimeo. Titled *Aller-Retour* (*Two Rode Together*, Jacquot and Frodon, 2017), it was a 52-minute filmed conversation on film criticism that took place between Frodon and Benoît Jacquot, the French film-maker. The conversation featured a barrage of references to many, some of them being the Aristarchus of Samothrace, Denis Diderot, Stéphane Mallarmé, Charles Baudelaire, Jean-Luc Godard and Serge Daney.

This 'crit-salad', or 'multitude of references' to (Western) art and culture coupled with 'sequential close reading', is emphasized in contemporary volumes on film criticism, especially when it discusses such past masters as Raymond Durgant or Manny Farber (Clayton and Klevan 2011: 11–12). It goes on to show how someone like Durgnat likes his 'images and ideas to be close, orbiting around each other, forming unexpected associations' (Clayton and Klevan 2011: 12). Film criticism refers inevitably to the close reading and the art of description, and sometimes the critical piece becomes mimetic, mirroring the structure of the film that it critiques, as a mere description/re-narration will always be an ambiguous mode of addressing an ever-present audiovisual medium, consistently running the risk of declining into futility and redundancy.[12] Jonathan Rosenbaum's review of Abbas Kiarostami's *Taste of Cherry* (1997) is an instance of such mimetic criticism (Rosenbaum 2017). The cinephile's obsessive association with certain images will make him extend the power of the image by recontextualizing and reconfiguring it in the digital age, thanks to the advent of the audiovisual/video essay (Keathley 2011). Thus new forms of criticism are emerging, with the essayistic and discursive cinematic work becoming accepted within the university space as academic 'writing'.

Film criticism, more often than not, is dominated by such elusive concepts as *mise-en-scène*, with such classical *mise-en-scène* critics as Bazin indulging in a montage versus *mise-en-scène* debate, followed by his successors having more nuanced discussions on montage/segmentation/decoupage, the social mise-en-scène, the dispositif, its apparent confusion with the apparatus, the way it means the arrangement of the viewing conditions and more (see Martin 2014a). In the post-1968 situation, the ideological implications of these were highlighted mostly by the *Cahiers* critics such as Jean-Louis Comolli who located the existence of mise-en-scène even before the intervention of the camera, citing problems of representation, the problematic of 'the changing, historical, determined relationships of men and things to the visible' and the film image being 'a small part in the multiplicity of the visible' (1988: 139). This advent of ideology criticism coming as a response to the apparently outdated mode of Bazinian criticism that failed to respond to the changing times in the post-1968 era is also a part of decisively French/European history of film theory and criticism with a distinctive spatiality (see Fairfax 2015).

While a detailed discussion on these concepts is beyond the scope and intention of this chapter, it needs to be shown how most of these strategies are unable to cope with certain challenges posed by a specific cinema that adds to the ambiguity of criticism by the means of dissociation. As I would like to propose, the cinema of Lav Diaz dissociates itself from several elements that inform criticism, even from its reliance on the image or the association between specific images and ideas. The *mise-en-scène* criticism may face similar problems here, as the arrangement of the *mise-en-scène* does not determine the properties of the image in a Diaz film. Here the film image decisively takes a 'small part in the multiplicity of the visible', the camera intervenes almost unwillingly and hardly indulges in any movement, the sonic order is equally barren with Diaz's disinterest in soundtrack music and the reliance on the narrative seems somewhat overbearing. Any specific scene analysis or the sequential close reading may not yield effective results here as the scene-units work collectively within the larger spectrum of the epic novel and refuse to offer scope for analysis not through their oft-discussed prolonged temporal absurdity but mostly through the refusal to remain standalone pieces. They are parts of a collective that the Diaz corpus stands for. As Martin has rightly observed in his *Norte* piece, however pejoratively, there are indeed rare instances 'of "electricity"' or 'unforgettable' scenes in Diaz (2014b: n.pag.). I do not disagree with Martin here; instead I would like to argue that this absence/lack/dearth is a carefully made choice on screen that characterizes Diaz's cinema and its decidedly ambiguous response to the standard-received norms of film criticism.

Determining the modes and methods of criticism is not something that this chapter intends to do. Instead, it looks at the specificities of Diaz's cinema that disallow those modes of criticism. The discussion should ideally begin with the notion of reiteration for which we need to rediscover the figures that reappear.

The figures, the cinematic, the performative

The church, in refusing to degrade you, has placed in doubt the crime imputed to you; the Government, in shrouding your cause with mystery and obscurities, creates belief in some error committed in critical moments, and the whole Philippines, in venerating your memory and calling you martyrs, in no way acknowledges your guilt.

(Rizal 2015: n.pag.)[13]

Diaz's cinema does not have characters; instead they have figures that have given this chapter its title.[14] For long he had his own cohort of actors who used to lend their respective bodies to such figures.[15] These figures often initiate a discussion on global cinema history and cine-politics in the nation. The engagement with the histories and politics of cinema manifests through the novelistic and the *performative*. While the former has not gone unnoticed, the latter remains more of a given that is hardly addressed. Together these elements constitute the world of Lav Diaz that denies inroads to the marauding vanguards of standard-received film criticism. Some instances of these figures, their performance and reappearance can be located in what follows.

Somewhere in *Century of Birthing*, the Poet of the Rain (Betty Uy-Regala) indulges in a seemingly endless monologue that features Bonifacio's sacrifice and Emilio Aguinaldo's betrayal years before the making of *A Lullaby to the Sorrowful Mystery*. The monologue is directed at Homer (Perry Dizon), the film-maker, without any response from him. He is trapped into his non-spacious workspace and looks out at the Poet, located outside with an umbrella amidst the tropical rain. In near-darkness, she refers to the way Judas is trapped in his sacrifice, only to celebrate the greatness of a Christ.

Diaz's Jesus, Judas and Magdalene will reappear in film after film. From his 2002 dystopia with Jesus as a nihilist 'revolutionary' to the Christ-like silent sufferer Joaquin (Archie Alemania) in *Norte*, the figures will complicate further and start accommodating more. In *Melancholia* (2008), playing the role of the 'respectable', Magdalene-like prostitute as a therapeutic process will be mandated as immersive for the reluctant Alberta (Angeli Bayani), eager as she is to find the remains of Renato, her partner and former guerilla who disappeared in the Filipino forest. Many of these traits will culminate in *A Lullaby*, even if the eight-hour epic is often dismissed as a non-representative work of Diaz.[16] Rizal's epic tales of deception, betrayal, violence and the futility of revenge in *Noli Me Tángere* (1887) and *El filibusterismo* (1891), adapted by many and accepted as widely read textbooks in the Philippines, have made their way into *A Lullaby*, coupled with the tragedies of Bonifacio and Rizal himself.[17] The title of the former is from the Gospel of St John, where Jesus asks Magdalene not to touch him as he is yet to ascend to his Father, the epigraph with which this chapter began.

The multiple narrative strands in *A Lullaby* follow the hunt for Bonifacio's remains in the forest by his wife Gregoria (Hazel Orencio) and the unsuccessful, occasionally villainous life and the tragic end of Crisóstomo Ibarra aka Simoun (Piolo Pascual), as narrated by José Rizal whose assassination begins the epistolary exposition of the film. Crisóstomo Ibarra aka Simoun, the once-wronged man whose revenge brings down unspeakable colonial misfortune on his nation, is Christ and St Peter/Simoun in the same body, with one self remaining disloyal to the other. Meanwhile the Judases multiply. Caesaria Belarmino (Alessandra de Rossi), the Mary Magdalene, remorsefully harbours a dark secret as her collusion with the Spanish military officers enabled the latter's bloody victory over her fellow villagers in the 1897 massacre of Silang. In her guilt, Caesaria joins Gregoria in the latter's search for Bonifacio's body as the other Judas, Simoun, seeks redemption in a confession beyond death. Unlike in Rizal's novel, the confession is watery here as the body floats over the sea and his plea for forgiveness floats along. On the contrary, in Rizal's *El filibusterismo*, Simoun's 'fabulous fortune' alone makes its way into the tumultuous Pacific where Padre Florentino, the confessor, asks 'the immensity' of the 'eternal seas' to safeguard them from human greed (Rizal 2015: 412–13)

The cinematic engulfs the Diaz universe in myriad ways. In *A Lullaby*, the gathering of the colonial and the comprador elite features screening of early cinema, some of the known responses to the early moving image and references to the experiencing of Lumière films and their exhibition in Paris, something the Europe-touring colonial elite could afford. The offshoots of cinema's association with colonial expansion and movements with the global capital find their way into *Melancholia*, as a discussion on cine-politics in the Philippines leads to the problematic association that existed between popular cinema and populist politics in the islands. Instances of the latter include popular cinema's contribution to Marcos's win and the election of a former actor Joseph Ejercito Estrada as the thirteenth president of the Republic whose policies aroused widespread controversy leading to his impeachment, trial and detention. As a public institution, cinema's political location in the neoliberal Asia has haunted Diaz throughout his career.

But more profound engagement with film aesthetics can be located in *Century of Birthing*. Homer (Perry Dizon), the film-maker with epical associations, puts a poster of *What Time Is It There?* (Tsai Ming-liang, 2001) and sets in a chain of references that comes with it, for who can willingly forget the visual, temporal and tactile insertion of *The 400 Blows* (François Truffaut, 1959) in Tsai's film as many years back *The 400 Blows* itself put up a still from *Summer with Monika* (Ingmar Bergman, 1953)? Here Diaz's referencing goes beyond the cartography of the nation and becomes more of a cinematic discussion of philosophical speculations. The film-maker and the philosopher in the film initiate a discussion on the Bazinian query of what is cinema, shifting to Heidegger's interest in knowing the being and declaring the *unknowable* that is cinema, even though 'we will remember the world because of cinema'. This assertion goes beyond cinema's archival value; it is not merely about the memories of the world preserved in cinematic form. Intensely and affectionately, it hints at cinema's affect, its mode of confession and remembrance and its tactile and affective qualities. Diaz's cinema is a complex repository of memories of cataclysm, self-inflicted violence and confessions to the (absent) inquisitors. It is not a mere database preserving such memories; it is the sole medium through which these can manifest.

From the affective Diaz moves to the performative aspect of his cinema and it abounds. Not only such mythical beings as *Bai Rahamah* in *From What Is Before*, spiristista in *Melancholia* or *Tikbalang* in *A Lullaby* indulge in the performative, it is spread across his cinematic universe. In *Melancholia*, Julian's (Perry Dizon) therapeutic notion of role-playing and coercive make-believe, known as melancholia, drives him to insanity, with others either sacralizing or demonizing his mode of performance. The therapeutic process includes live sex show or the performance of the erotic. The entire process leads to depression and, in case of a vulnerable performer such as Rina Abad (Malaya), suicide.

In *Century of Birthing*, the dangerously insane heretic Father Tiburcio (Joel Torre) is addressed as artist and actor, who, before his violent killing of the self, proclaims loudly about the theatre (of being) that is 'meaningless', 'about to end' and, finally, 'dead'.

The affective-performative in cinema has received considerable theoretical underpinnings in recent years as Elena del Rio charts some of the recent modes of engaging with performativity in cinema studies. Either they are concerned with the denotation of performance in theatre and cinema or their interest in the performative stems from the performance of identity, reductive or exclusionary categories and social constructs (Rio 2008). But then there is a third, exclusive way of understanding the performative as del Rio and a handful of others explore the philosophical in the performative, the affection, the body and the physicality in Deleuzian and other fashions. Rio considers the 'performative dimension of bodies in the cinema' and 'the cinematic image itself as a body' in an ontological sense; bodies become performers 'of sensations and affects that bear no mimetic or analogical ties to an external or transcendental reality' (2008: 4). Lav Diaz and his bodies, figures, eternally walking dead, murderous/suicidal heretics, radical clergymen and fallen nuns, torturers and the tortured, disappeared guerillas, role-players, and the unscrupulous intellectual people his novelistic world and prolong its temporality to the point of the absurd primarily because of the absence of the mimetic tie. A mimetic mode of film criticism will be futile in this case.

Diaz, therefore, is not interested in reconstructing the real or in formulating characters, actions and events. His figures and their performances remained un-exhibited for long, and they have hardly received proper exhibition channel in the Philippines.[18] Regardless of his non-accommodation in a national film culture, the Russophile in Diaz continued with his exploration of the novelistic á la Dostoyevsky.

The Grand Inquisitor

Any acquaintance with the voluminous literature on Dostoevsky leaves the impression that one is dealing not with a single author-artist who wrote novels and stories, but with a number of philosophical statements by several author-thinkers Raskolnikov, Myshkin, Stavrogin, Ivan Karamazov, the Grand Inquisitor, and others.

(Bakhtin 1984: 5)

The epigraph quotes what Bakhtin states at the very beginning of his seminal *Problems of Dostoevsky's Poetics*. Bakhtin's interests have been unimaginably vast, but he concentrates on the polyphony in Dostoyevsky, as opposed to Turgenev or Tolstoy whose novels are 'monologic'. The authorial dominance evaporates in favour of '*a plurality of independent and unmerged voices and consciousnesses*' (Bakhtin 1984: 6, original emphases). What does that signify in the Dostoyevsky-ridden present of Lav Diaz?

My interests do not lie in Diaz's loose adaptations of Dostoyevsky though; those are his minor works and that too from two entirely different phases of his career.[19] Here I am concerned primarily with the novelistic in Diaz, but not in the usual, classical sense of the narrative. Diaz's later works, especially his festival-touring, award-winning works from *Norte* onwards, have often been critiqued for a tectonic shift towards a more classical narrative form, with the inclusion of professional actors/stars from the industry and a perceivable shortening of the infamous duration and average shot lengths. Recently his obsessively satirical engagement with the dictatorial politics in *Ang Hupa* and elsewhere clearly demonstrates an authorial intention, if not the explicit voice/intervention of the auteur, and it is often realized at the cost of his narrative complexity.

What Diaz achieved earlier in the garb of fiction is something that other proponents of digital cinema did in a non-fictional format.[20] His narrative interests have always been deceptive, with ellipses, gaps, chasms, structural complexities and, most importantly, his 'empty' shots. The incredible running time, the unusual average shot length that was not realizable within the confines of celluloid, allowed him to create so many shot-units that do not necessarily contribute to the semblance of a narrative, do not present themselves as representative shots from the films, cannot be analysed in terms of their *mise-en-scène*, decoupage or dispositif. Scene analysis will not be a wise strategy for the critic here, not only because the 'scene' may run for an hour or so, but primarily because the individual scene may not contribute to a discussion on the film. For me, the answer lies in the novelistic in Diaz, especially in his engagement with Dostoyevsky.

Can a more complex association with Dostoyevsky be discernible in Diaz's pre-*Norte* phase? Diaz is a self-proclaimed Russophile, as, apart from explicit adaptations, several other modes of influence of Russian literature abound in his corpus (see Quito 2018).[21] His interviews, including the one in the present volume, often mention his association with nineteenth-century Russian fiction, his protagonist in *Death in the Land of Encantos* (2007) spends his years of exile in Russia and his name is derived from a Russian name.[22] But the advent of the novelistic goes beyond the anecdotal.

Like that of Dostoyevsky, Diaz's world is haunted by nihilism, existential crisis and futility on one hand and the problematic association with theologies and a near-insane drive towards humiliation on the other. This is not unusual from the land of Rizal where the religious establishment, removed as always from the glorious company of the heretics and the excommunicated, has usually been politically, socially and sexually repressive. I do not want to multiply instances from the narratives; the question that arises is whether these elements are accommodated into a polyphonic order and what such an order might implicate for the field of cinema.

It has often been argued that Dostoyevsky, despite his turbulent days with the radical intelligentsia, came back from his Siberian exile as a Christian novelist, especially after his encounter with the folk heritage in rural Russia (Jones 2004). But despite his apparent regaining of faith, Dostoyevsky never declined into a preacher. As E. M. Forster has shown with elaborate passages of the intrusion of the divine leading to something like a confession in George Eliot's *Adam Bede* (1859) and Dostoyevsky's *The Brothers Karamazov* (1880), the former remains a preacher for Forster while the latter becomes a prophet; Dostoyevsky's 'characters and situations always stand for more than themselves; infinity attends them' (Forster 1955: 132), and the affective returns through them:

> They convey to us a sensation that is partly physical – the sensation of sinking into
> a translucent globe and seeing our experience floating far above us on its surface,
> tiny, remote, yet ours. We have not ceased to be people, we have given nothing up,
> but 'the sea is in the fish and the fish is in the sea'.
>
> (Forster 1955: 134)

These eruptions, insertions, interpolations, confessions, the presence and absence of the inquisitors, the violent dislocation of the semblance of a narrative, the nihilistic 'empty' conversations, the affective-performative, the heretic and the excommunicated, the 'correctional' rapes, the resultant insanity, inevitable humiliation and deaths/suicides in Diaz go round and round, without the authorial intervention of the camera. His static and unperturbed camera waits patiently for the physical movements, memories and confessions to happen, and the polyphony in the cinema, unmediated by the omniscient and omnipresent camera/auteur, engages with the cinematic. Meanwhile, Diaz adds to the narratives that seem strategic in order to address the lacunae in the 'original' novels (Quito 2018: 319–20).

On the contrary, in Diaz's more recent films, the overbearing wish for the promotion of his politics becomes the grand inquisitor, the authorial intervention in a formerly polyphonic universe.

A comparison between scenes from early and a recent Diaz film will suffice in this regard. A film such as *Ang Hupa* features several events of apparent brutality, scenes of bizarre conversations and eccentric tea parties with the dictator-president and Diaz's satirical look into it becomes uncharacteristically apparent because of its reduction into character-parodies, with in-your-face scenes contributing to the narrative. A sharp contrast can be located with conversations in *Century of Birthing* or *Melancholia* that do not contribute to the narrative semblances in those films. A scene that is stretched beyond half an hour with philosophical musings on cinema and a non-representative mise-en-scène baffle critics for a reason. The critic is often unable to find a point of entry in the Diaz universe, especially with his European critical arsenal.

Epilogue

The absence of the 'Western-European logic' in Dostoyevsky often led to the rationalist European being 'obdurately prejudiced against' his corpus, as Andre Gide affirms in the context of *The Brothers Karamazov* translations in English (1961: 14). For Gide, it refers to the late arrival of the time of the book. Without drawing any simplified parallels between the two events of late arrival in the cases of Dostoyevsky and Diaz, I would like to ponder momentarily on the aspect of late arrival itself which is not a case of exception.

The idea of the late arrival refers more to the spatiality of the problem and less to its temporality. The geopolitics, the spatial histories of literary and cinematic texts, without claiming any 'exceptional' status for the experience of many colonialisms and a 'late arrival' of modernity, offers insights into the idiosyncrasies of global acceptability. It introduces the problematic 'slow cinema' boom, a category that appropriated various auteurs belonging more to the several national cultures than to their respective national cinemas. It also refers to the politics of the film festival, the site of appropriation, as its mechanism is becoming increasingly visible in Lav Diaz's recent works.

The late arrival, as a phenomenon, should ideally promise more innovative research on Diaz, more repetitions and observations. In the context of his objection to the repetition and artlessness in Diaz, Adrian Martin located Diaz's dissociation from the more classical, standard-received ways of dealing with the temporal as well as from the subtle ellipses as in Pedro Costa. These ellipses or the extremely complex passage of time in Costa, incidentally, often manifest through reiteration. The most memorable instance that I can think of is the deliberately and overwhelmingly repetitive letter of Ventura in *Colossal Youth* (Pedro Costa, 2006), itself lifted from the letter that the surrealist French poet Robert Desnos wrote to Youki, his wife, while in concentration camps, even though that letter never reached its destination. Ventura's letter, as it becomes evident in the film, has not been sent and will never be sent either. In his delirium as a black loner trapped in the Global North, in big, bad Europe, Ventura repetitively and obsessively takes us back to the days of the Carnation Revolution as his is always a late arrival in the contemporary.

I am not interested in comparing Costa and Diaz, two most significant filmmakers of the contemporary who, allegedly, share birthdays. Instead, this chapter merely reminds us of the fact that the repetition, the ellipses, the decentred universe, the strategic-ness of a narrative and many other elements demand a decentred mode of film criticism that is needed for the challenges posed by the digital cinema that lacks a single point of autonomy, a cinema that never settles down, a cinema whose fluidity does not allow us to remain citizens of European schools of criticism.

NOTES

1. Manuel Arguilla (1911–1944), known for his deceptively pastoral short stories as well as for his martyrdom, organized guerilla movement against the Japanese forces and was arrested, tortured and executed by beheading during the Second Great War and the Japanese occupation of the Philippines.

2. The Philippines has encountered several dictatorial regimes even in the post-Marcos era, and several instances of forced disappearances feature in their history even in the 2000s. See Katrina Macapagal's chapter in the present volume for the infamous 2006 disappearance of two University of the Philippines students who were presumably tortured, raped and disappeared by the armed forces.

3. See May Adadol Ingawanij's chapter in this volume for an explanation for the presence of such figures.

4. The idea of the novelistic (and Dostoyevsky/Russian novel) is so prevalent in Diaz criticism that at least three other chapters in the present volume, by Tom Paulus, Marco Grosoli and Katrina Macapagal, resort to this domain.

5. May Adadol Ingawanij, in her article in this volume, asserts that slow cinema is beyond the cartography of the nation and, as it seems, it can be extended beyond the continent as well.

6. A revised and reworked version of Adrian Martin's *Norte* article has been included in this volume.

7. See Martin's chapter in this volume where he refers to Diaz's first musical *Season of the Devil* (2018) as a welcoming move, and Diaz has continued his generic adventures with *Ang Hupa* (*The Halt*, 2019), another sci-fi dystopia after his early work *Hesus, rebolusyunaryo* (*Jesus the Revolutionary*, 2002).

8. Rocha demanded a sort of 'exceptionality' for Brazilian/Latin American cinema in his 1965 polemical essay in terms of different aesthetic and political contexts and parameters, objecting against the ways in which the neocolonial discourse originating in the Global North consistently reduces the Brazilian existence to an object of anthropological interest for the European observer/ethnographer. Whether a similar line of argument can explain the Lav Diaz problematic or not remains a point of concern.

9. Like Nadin Mai, Katrina Macapagal also cites Argentine writings on the desaparecidos in the context of Diaz in her chapter in the present volume .

10. See Katrina Macapagal's chapter in this volume on instances of custodial torture and forced disappearance in contemporary Philippines.

11. Diaz in his interviews has referred to digital cinema as liberation theology, with obvious references to Latin America.

12. Describing/re-narrating the film-text is always a challenging task for the critic as the text is ever-present in its audiovisual form. The mimetic mode of criticism is an interesting and extremely subtle form that has been used by a few.

13. Rizal dedicates *El filibusterismo* to the martyred Catholic priests who were executed at Bagumbayan in February 1872 by the Spanish colonial authorities because of their alleged links with the Cavite Mutiny. The radical, dangerously heretic preachers/priests pervade Diaz's cinema.

14. Figure, figurations and the figurative in cinema may refer to the figuralist school of criticism, a distinctively post-structuralist French theoretical school associated with Nicole Brenez and others. But this chapter is not interested in a figural analysis and abstains from relying on European schools.

15. Some of his ardent admirers did not appreciate him casting major stars of the popular industry in his recent films, a decision that has been made in order to increase the reach of his anti-establishment politics, as Diaz claims in his interview in the present volume. His films are gradually accommodating more stars from an industry that he left long back, even though he is not really hopeful about the efficacy of such a move in a nation that keeps on electing strong men and women who perpetuate dictatorial regimes.

16. Diaz's critics refer to the expressionist cinematography in the film, especially in the halogen-lit forest scenes, and the perpetuation of Weerasethakul-like surrealist insertion of mythological beings such as the *Tikbalang*(s) that do not apparently go well with his cinema.

17. There are innumerable instances of Rizal and/or Bonifacio narratives providing Filipino film-makers with histories to engage with. Films such as *Jose Rizal* (Marilou Diaz-Abaya, 1998), *Bayaning 3rd World* (*3rd World Hero*, Mike de Leon, 2000), *Autohystoria* (Raya Martin, 2007) and *The Trial of Andres Bonifacio* (Mario O'Hara, 2010) can be cited as instances.

18. See Michael Kho Lim's chapter in the present volume on the distribution of some of the recent films of Lav Diaz.

19. Apart from *Norte, the End of History* (2013) that is better known as a loose adaptation of Dostoyevsky's *Crime and Punishment*, Diaz debuted with another very loose adaptation of the same novel, *The Criminal of Barrio Conception* (1998). His adaptations are different from other, more Bressonian adaptations of the novel, the ones by Robert Bresson himself and the more recent one by the Kazakh auteur Darezhan Omirbayev, but that is not my point of concern here.

20. I am thinking of the Chinese film-maker Wang Bing's documentaries here.

21. Gil Quito's article refers to the Dostoyevsky influences and Russophilia, with *The Woman Who Left* also becoming a work betraying Dostoyevsky's influences for him even if it is a Tolstoy adaptation.

22. This is not without its irony as Lavrente Indico Diaz aka Lav Diaz was named after Lavrentiy Beria (1899–1953), the Soviet politician who served as the chief of Stalin's secret police apparatus (NKVD) and was infamous for being a sexual predator. Diaz's parents were left-leaning, his father was associated with the Hukbalahap movement in the Philippines and they, apparently, had little information regarding the nature of the Stalinist administration in the then USSR, as it happened with many leftists in the periphery.

REFERENCES

Bakhtin, Mikhail (1984), *Problems of Dostoevsky's Poetics* (ed. and trans. C. Emerson), Minneapolis: University of Minnesota Press.

Clayton, Alex and Klevan, Andrew (2011), 'Introduction: The language and style of film criticism', in A. Clayton and A. Klevan (eds), *The Language and Style of Film Criticism*, London and New York: Routledge, pp. 1–26.

Comolli, Jean-Louis (1988), 'Machines of the visible', in S. Heath and T. de Lauretis (eds), *The Cinematic Apparatus*, Basingstoke: Macmillan Press, pp. 121–42.

Diaz, Lav (dir.) (1998), *The Criminal of Barrio Conception*, Philippines: Good Harvest Unlimited.

Diaz, Lav (dir.) (2002), *Hesus, rebolusyunaryo (Jesus, the Revolutionary)*, Philippines: Regal Films.

Diaz, Lav (dir.) (2007), *Death in the Land of Encantos*, Philippines: Sine Olivia Pilipinas.

Diaz, Lav (dir.) (2008), *Melancholia*, Philippines: Sine Olivia Pilipinas.

Diaz, Lav (dir.) (2011), *Century of Birthing*, Philippines: Sine Olivia Pilipinas.

Diaz, Lav (dir.) (2013), *Norte, the End of History*, Philippines: Sine Olivia Pilipinas.

Diaz, Lav (dir.) (2014), *From What Is Before*, Philippines: Sine Olivia Pilipinas.

Diaz, Lav (dir.) (2016a), *A Lullaby to the Sorrowful Mystery*, Philippines: Sine Olivia Pilipinas.

Diaz, Lav (dir.) (2016b), *The Woman Who Left*, Philippines: Sine Olivia Pilipinas.

Diaz, Lav (dir.) (2018), *Season of the Devil*, Philippines: Sine Olivia Pilipinas.

Diaz, Lav (dir.) (2019), *Ang Hupa (The Halt)*, Philippines: Sine Olivia Pilipinas.

Espinosa, Julio Garcia (1979), 'For an imperfect cinema', *Jump Cut*, 20, pp. 24–26.

Fairfax, Daniel (2015), 'Introduction', in J. L. Comolli, *Cinema against Spectacle: Technique and Ideology Revisited* (ed. and trans. D. Fairfax), Amsterdam: Amsterdam University Press, pp. 17–45.

Forster, E. M. (1955), *Aspects of the Novel*, San Diego: Harcourt.

Gide, Andre (1961), *Dostoevsky*, New York: New Directions.

Ingawanij, May Adadol (2015), 'Long walk to life: The films of Lav Diaz', *Afterall: A Journal of Art, Context and Enquiry*, 40, pp. 102–15.

John 20: 17 (1985), King James Bible, International ed., Oxford: Oxford University Press.

Jones, Malcolm V. (2004), 'Dostoevskii and religion', in W. J. Leatherbarrow (ed.), *The Cambridge Companion to Dostoevskii*, Cambridge: Cambridge University Press, pp. 148–74.

Keathley, Christian (2011), 'La camera-stylo: Notes on video criticism and cinephilia', in A. Clayton and A. Klevan (eds), *The Language and Style of Film Criticism*, London and New York: Routledge, pp. 176–91.

Mai, Nadin (2014), 'In defense of a lack of craft', *The Art(s) of Slow Cinema*, 20 July, https://theartsofslowcinema.com/2014/07/20/in-defense-of-a-lack-of-craft/. Accessed 11 May 2020.

Mai, Nadin (2015), 'The aesthetic of absence and duration in the post-trauma cinema of Lav Diaz', Ph.D. thesis, Stirling: University of Stirling.

Martin, Adrian (2014a), *Mise en Scène and Film Style: From Classical Hollywood to New Media Art*, Basingstoke: Palgrave Macmillan.

Martin, Adrian (2014b), 'Film of the week: *Norte, the End of History*', *Sight and Sound*, 19 November, https://www.bfi.org.uk/news-opinion/sight-sound-magazine/reviews-recommendations/film-week-norte-end-history. Accessed 11 May 2020.

Moravia, Alberto (1989), 'The Marx-Dostoevsky duel', in G. Gibian (ed.), *Crime and Punishment*, New York: Norton, pp. 619–22.

Quito, Gil (2018), 'Lav Diaz: New directions in world cinema', in C. del Mundo, Jr (ed.), *Direk: Essays on Filipino Filmmakers*, Manila: De La Salle University Publishing House, pp. 267–332.

Rio, Elena del (2008), *Deleuze and the Cinemas of Performance: Powers of Affection*, Edinburgh: Edinburgh University Press.

Rizal, José (2015), *El filibusterismo* (ed. R. L. Locsin and trans. M. S. Lacson-Locsin), Makati City: The Bookmark.

Rosenbaum, Jonathan (2017), 'Fill in the Blanks', jonathanrosenbaum.net, 7 June, https://www.jonathanrosenbaum.net/2017/06/fill-in-the-blanks/#:~:text=The%20hero%20in%20Taste%20of,the%20ground%20if%20he%20fails. Accessed 11 May 2020.

Solanas, Fernando E. and Getino, Octavio (1970–71), 'Toward a Third Cinema', *Cineaste*, Special Issue: 'Latin American Militant Cinema', 4:3, pp. 1–10.

10

Distributing the Cinema of Lav Diaz

Michael Kho Lim

This chapter explores the distribution routes and strategies employed by some of Lav Diaz's films post *Hesus, Rebolusyonaryo* (*Jesus, the Revolutionary*, 2002), the last studio film he made that had a commercial theatrical release (although short-lived) and the time when he started taking the 'independent' path. These films include *Norte, Hangganan ng Kasaysayan* (2013); *Hele sa Hiwagang Hapis* (2016); and *Ang Babaeng Humayo* (2016) among others that have been released outside of the film festival circuit like in commercial theatres, DVDs or online platforms. This chapter also looks into how Diaz's reputational capital as an auteur has worked to his advantage in securing distribution deals for some of his critically acclaimed films and how the effective marketing and distribution strategies have enabled the development of a growing niche market to thrive in the formal film economy.

Background

After doing four films under Good Harvest Unlimited – the indie division of the major Philippine film studio Regal Films – Diaz declares that he could no longer make films under a very confined and limited environment. In a published conversation, he shares that during his time with the studio he has become 'a typewriter not a writer because they dictate what you will do' (Shaw [2002] 2013: n.pag.). Diaz further says in an e-mail interview that his cinema could not breathe at that time.

> I had an illusion that I can create space and articulate my own aesthetics within the overwhelming consumerist perspective of the industry but it was just an illusion. I

understood that it's their game so the only way out was to be able to create cinema on my terms.

(Diaz 2015: n.pag.)

Since Diaz's departure from the studio system of mainstream commercial cinema, his films have been freer and have defined his identity as a film-maker and auteur.

However, being independent also has its challenges. Diaz claims, 'I'm a very poor filmmaker. So to be able to make my cinema, I have to work around such marginalization. I don't complain. I find solutions. I will never be hampered by poverty. My burden is on the truth' (2015: n.pag.). While funding has always been a major concern, Diaz maintains that one needs to be creative or even 'relentless, or scheming, or cruel' in finding the means to fund one's cinema.

> I started really small, so my moneyed friends were the first patrons. I borrowed money. Then I tried the studios. Then I got lucky with some grants, endowments and residencies. Some good souls and philanthropists came along, too, and offered much needed generosity.
>
> (Diaz 2015: n.pag.)

However, some of these local and international grant-giving bodies and institutions that provide subsidies cannot directly fund individuals and require a registered (business) entity that can generally issue receipts to receive funding. Diaz recalls that he had a company registered between 2007 and 2010 so that he could enter into contracts, but this was left neglected because he gave more importance to his cinema. While he acknowledges that he needs to reorient himself in dealing with all the paperwork, he agrees that it is vital to protect the film-maker. Diaz eventually realizes the value and sees the practicality of having a registered film outfit in minimizing deceptive deals after almost signing a bad business contract with a company (2018: n.pag.). Finally on 27 April 2017, Sine Olivia was born under the sole proprietorship of Diaz.

The (slow) cinema of Lav Diaz

The films of Lav Diaz are typically categorized as part of 'slow cinema' (Brown 2016: 112; Çağlayan 2018: x; Schrader 2018: 11). It is a relatively new concept that emerged in the early noughties to refer to a type of art cinema that is characterized by minimal camera movement, long takes, utilizing mostly wide or establishing shots, with limited action and long dialogues, and starkly marked by the film's long running time (Çağlayan 2018: 47; de Luca and Jorge 2016: 3; Schrader 2018: 10). It is important to note however that for Diaz, cinema has no labels: 'There is just cinema' (2015: n.pag.).

According to Russian film-maker Andrei Tarkovsky, 'time becomes the very foundation of cinema' ([1986] 1987: 119); 'the cinema image is essentially the observation of a phenomenon passing through time' ([1986] 1987: 67; also cited in Schrader 2018: 8). It is about how much time the film-maker needs to tell a story, how much time the film-maker wants the audience to watch a story unfold and how much time the audience invests (or is willing to invest) in the film to be involved in the story. In practical terms, time also becomes a critical component in film-making because it facilitates the categorization of films for competitions or awards. Some prominent film bodies and institutions have set the minimum running time for a full-length or feature-length film. For the Academy of Motion Picture Arts and Sciences (AMPAS), British Film Institute (BFI) and American Film Institute (AFI), the film must go beyond 40 minutes (AMPAS n.d.: 2; BFI n.d.; AFI n.d.a). For AFI Awards submissions, however, the film should be more than 60 minutes long (AFI n.d.b). Meanwhile, Sundance Institute counts 50 minutes or more as feature-length (Sundance n.d.), and the Screen Actors Guild-American Federation of Television and Radio Artists classifies a film that runs for 80 minutes or more as full-length (SAGindie n.d.: 1).

While it can be confusing because the prescribed minimum running time varies and there is no agreed global definition or standard, it can be observed that a conventional full-length film shown in commercial movie houses runs between 80 and 200 minutes on average. Time is again a crucial factor here because of the temporal economy attached to film exhibition. A longer film costs more to screen because it requires more energy consumption (among other things) per screening, and the movie house will have fewer screenings of that film per day. Hence, the film's running time also determines the film's ticket price.

Given the independent nature of how Diaz operates and that most of his films (*short* films included) are unusually long and slow – running between four and eleven hours (see Table 1, at the end of chapter), it poses a great logistical challenge to distribute and exhibit his works in commercial theatres (Çağlayan 2018: 26). Hence, it is important to ask: How does one access Diaz's films – especially since these types of slow films are usually (if not only) seen in film festivals, arthouse cinemas, cinematheques but rarely in regular movie houses (Schrader 2018: 10)? However, this may not be entirely true in the case of Diaz because some of his lengthy films have had limited commercial runs in theatres.

Marketing and distribution strategies, and experiencing the cinema of Lav Diaz

What makes a film distributable? The answer is rather subjective because it is relative to the deciding distributor. In the world of film distribution business, distributors generally look at the film's commercial viability or (mass) audience appeal in deciding to distribute a film (or not). The film's running time is also a factor. If the film falls within the usual *standard* running time and appeals commercially to a wide audience, then the film is considerably *easy* to distribute. Any film that falls outside these parameters – such as short and (very) long films, documentaries, experimental films and the like – is poised to face a distribution hurdle. In the case of Diaz, his long films pose a creative business challenge – that is, within the realm of the formal film distribution economy.

Diaz's more conventional films (the four films he made with Good Harvest) have enjoyed commercial theatrical releases because they are distributed by a major studio that can consistently supply films – an important factor that exhibitors take into account in their decision-making process (Lim 2019: 138). Meanwhile, Diaz's long films have mostly been distributed informally because of inadequate institutional and infrastructural support through networks of cinephiles or film groups that organize non-theatrical screenings in alternative spaces, sometimes even in piratic modes of viewing among friends and social media interactions and later exhibited in various international film festivals and online platforms (Ingawanij 2017: 413, 421–25). In fact, Diaz is not against piracy (Guarneri 2013: n.pag.) because for him, it is part of the universe and propagation of cinema.

> I have met many people – mostly followers of my cinema, and they tell me that they have a complete set of my films. When I ask how they got hold of them, they say that they bought them in the black market. Actually, the films that I own the copyright – those that I don't earn from – are the ones being sold underground.
>
> (Diaz 2018: n.pag.)

The official Facebook page of Sine Olivia Pilipinas is also confident that a cinephile friend or colleague will surely have a copy of Diaz's film/s and advises prospective film viewers to ask around (2019: n.pag.). This has generally been the circulation pattern of Diaz's films because of the unconventional characteristics of his works that cater to an unconventional audience group. The commonly given assumption is that Diaz's films have a niche market and that most of these screenings are regarded as non-profit in nature even if there are (minimal) admission charges. To a certain extent, there is no expectation to earn profit from the screenings because there is no investment to recoup based on most of Diaz's funding sources. This does not mean however that it should shortchange the film-maker's earning potential.

It was not until Diaz has gained more following and a growing audience base that some of his long films were screened in commercial movie houses (again). In a way, the development of his audience follows the slow pacing of his films, although this gradual audience growth is still considerably small by commercial standards. In exhibiting his films, no matter the length, Diaz requires that they be screened straight through with no intermissions. While this instruction is not always followed, Diaz also does not expect his audience to stay put during the entire film screening if it were to play continuously (Ingawanij 2017: 428). In instances where screening intervals are necessitated, Diaz identifies the scenes where the gaps would take place so the film is not cut abruptly. For Diaz, this is a 'winning compromise'.

In another published interview regarding the potential theatrical screening of *Norte, Hangganan ng Kasaysayan* in the Philippines, he is willing to screen the film in two parts but cautions, 'Just don't destroy the film.' He also has another idea of having two types of screening: 'The movie will be split into two parts in one theater and, at the same time, it will be screened full-runtime in another theater' (Guarneri 2013: n.pag.). In the case of *Hele sa Hiwagang Hapis*, there are two screening options. One can watch the eight-hour film either in two or three parts based on Diaz's recommendation to the producers and distributors. A special ticket pricing has also been arranged depending on the movie house, so that the admission cost does not equate to paying four times that of a regular two-hour feature film (de Jesus 2016: n.pag.). Given these possibilities of screening approaches, Ingawanij argues that there is really no appropriate method or a singular way of exhibiting Diaz's films (2017: 421) or perhaps any other film that exhibits strong durational properties. Hence, a film's long running time need not really hinder it from having a wider public screening.

Listed here are the marketing and distribution strategies utilized to distribute and exhibit some of Diaz's long films.

1. Eventization

Event is defined as 'a special set of circumstances; a noteworthy occurrence' at a designated place and time (Getz 2007: 18). It is well planned and publicized in advance, cultivates a once-in-a-lifetime image of the affair (2007: 19), and emphasizes the specialness or uniqueness of the happening (2007: 26). Events are organized 'to achieve specific outcomes, including those related to the economy, culture, society and environment' (2007: 21). Eventization is the process of turning something into an event. In this case, it is the eventization of the screening of Diaz's films, where the objective is not just to gather cinephiles to experience the (slow) cinema of Diaz but also to develop and increase his audience and populate the movie houses.

While cinemagoing can be considered an event in itself because it entails the physical act of going to the theatre and attending the screening at a specific time, a regular film screening does not have the specialness of an eventized movie, which is targeted to a specific audience and specially promoted as an event movie – something different from the usual full-length feature film screened in movie houses. It has an element of focus and rarity – the idea of a limited engagement, unlike a regular movie screening that could even be extended depending on the film's box-office success. As Getz further describes, the specialness of an event occurs 'outside the normal programme' and 'outside the normal range of choices or beyond everyday experience' (2007: 27). To a certain extent, it is almost similar to a film festival except that there is only one film or a certain number of films by a particular film-maker/s. In this context, it is a celebration or a festival of Diaz's film/s.

The case of *Norte, Hangganan ng Kasaysayan* is generally considered a breakthrough in the film distribution scene because it is Diaz's first long film that has been picked up for local and international theatrical releases. These include deals with Ayala Cinemas (Philippines), The Cinema Guild (United States), New Wave Films (United Kingdom) and Shellac (France). Diaz is reportedly 'shocked' by the news and finds it unbelievable that discriminating distributors have bought the film's distribution rights (Tomada 2014: n.pag.). Diaz attributes this outcome to the inclusion of *Norte* in one of Cannes's programmes, which means that the film is 'accessible enough' or, in the words of his producer Moira Lang, 'very watchable' despite its length. However, Diaz thinks that *Norte* is not necessarily an easy film to watch, but it got the biggest push among his works because it had its world premiere at the French Riviera. He adds, 'It's become the most popular option for the curious as well. And the effect of course is not some solitary blessing but it trickled down the other sleepy works' (2015: n.pag.).

Lang considers *Norte*'s distribution deals as a remarkable feat for Diaz because his long films have always been perceived as 'very hard if not impossible to release because of the length' (Tomada 2014: n.pag.). In a personal interview, she explains that the approach needs to be different for Diaz's films because they are generally not commercial movies, so they cannot be marketed and distributed the way one would a typical movie that is expected to be a blockbuster hit. For the limited Philippine theatrical release, *Norte* is promoted as a special event. The idea is to have a series of one-off screenings per week for one month in four different locations. These screenings are then marketed like a concert event where there is a pre-selling feature so that the number of prospective viewers can be identified. This technique eliminates the dependence on walk-in audience members and increases the possibility of having a fully booked theatre. Lang calls this as the 'buzz screening' where the attendees are regarded as the film's 'first audience'. The objective is to create a positive viewing experience because the first audience will be responsible in creating the buzz or hopefully a positive word-of-mouth to encourage higher film viewership. The strategy has proven to be effective for *Norte* in that three of the screenings in Manila were sold out while another in Cebu was half full. Eventually, *Norte* has secured a regular one-week (*commercial*) run in several cinemas. Lang further confirms that *Norte* has even fared better than other independent films that also had a regular run in various movie houses (2015: n.pag.). In that sense, *Norte* can be regarded as a hit because it continues to have screenings around the world, and some institutions are even buying copies of the film. According to Diaz, producers and distributors have trusted him even more after the considerable success of *Norte*'s theatrical release, because they now realize that it is actually possible to earn from a five-hour film (2018: n.pag.).

The eventization strategy employed by *Norte* is also what Wyatt refers to as the roadshow release strategy. It is the act of transforming a film screening into a special occasion or event (Wyatt 1998: 65), where the film opens only in selected movie houses in major cities for a limited time before going for a general release (Hall 2011: 193; Verhoeven 2011: 258). Similarly, this approach can be likened to the four-walling strategy, where the distributor rents out the four walls of the movie house for a designated fee for a specific time frame (Wyatt 1998: 73; Donahue 1987: 250). The producer and/or distributor can then market the film screening as a special event and sell their own tickets (Wyatt 1998: 76; Lent 2012: 17).

While Diaz does not involve himself in distributing and marketing his films, he has sufficient understanding of how it works but wants to leave these responsibilities to the experts. He asserts, 'I am a filmmaker. I make cinema. Everything is consequential in the end. If you make good cinema, then everything will just follow. Better films create better agoras' (2015: n.pag.). Diaz further shares that he has been fortunate enough that his first (studio) film *Serafin Geronimo: Kriminal ng Baryo Concepcion* was noticed by the late David Overbey of the Toronto International Film Festival, and that started his festival circuit route. Various festival programmers have since been on the lookout for his new films (2015: n.pag.). Many North American and European film institutions and museums, and small-scale film festivals have also organized retrospectives of his works (Ingawanij 2017: 421), including the online platform Mubi's first-ever online retrospective of Diaz's films (Guarneri 2016: n.pag.).

Diaz's recognition in major international film festivals has boosted his reputation as a film-maker and paved the way for securing film distribution deals and television sales (Ingawanij 2017: 421). Reputation is highly important in the film industry because it 'facilitates trust within their networks, marks competency' and 'serves as a source of stability in an industry whose networks may be unpredictable and turbulent' (Zafirau 2008: 124). Reputation is one's intangible résumé that accounts for one's past performance and perceived qualities. Reputation also carries economic significance because decision-makers can use this as the basis in making decisions where other key information is limited or not available (Ebbers and Wijnberg 2012: 231). In this sense, reputation is treated as a form of capital, and it becomes the 'currency of creative labour' (Drake 2013: 145). While good reputation is generally not a guarantee for success, it is still used as a predictor or determinant. In the case of Diaz, his high reputational capital has given him a certain star power and created a distinct identity and branding. It has also strengthened his unique directorial credit 'Sine ni Lav Diaz' (Cinema of Lav Diaz) in establishing himself as an auteur. This has generated the necessary distribution advantage and opportunity not commonly accorded to Diaz's type of cinema. Instead of Diaz or his team looking for a distributor, distributors now compete for his approval. They are the ones who approach Diaz now to get his nod for a distribution deal. According to Diaz, some distributors even offer pledges or advance payment just so they can be awarded the distribution rights even if his film is still at the conceptualization stage (2018: n.pag.). The power shift in this context is clearly evident and becomes favourable to the film-maker or copyright holder if the expected economic yield or bottom line is derivable and acceptable.

2. Endurance viewing

After the groundbreaking success of *Norte*'s theatrical screening in the Philippines (San Diego 2014: n.pag.), Diaz's succeeding films such as *Hele sa Hiwagang Hapis*, *Ang Babaeng Humayo* and *Panahon ng Halimaw* (2018) have also been widely released in selected theatres in the Philippines and abroad (de Jesus 2016: n.pag.; San Diego 2018: n.pag.; Vivarelli 2016: n.pag.). These films are not necessarily eventized like *Norte*, but their screening strategy picks up from *Norte*'s success of eventization. They are not eventized in the sense that their screenings are not one-off screenings held as special events because they have been given a regular theatrical run following *Norte*'s successful theatrical screenings.

In the case of *Hele*, the promotional strategy is hinged on the film's running time. The marketing team has created an eight-hour movie challenge dubbed as 'The Hele Challenge'. In a way, the promotion of this film is eventized because people will have to come together to participate in the challenge – in the same manner, for example, when people go to a fun-run event. The film's official Facebook page invites people to join the challenge and use the hashtag '#GiveLavAChance' (*Hele sa Hiwagang Hapis* 2016: n.pag.). Instead of having the long running time work against the film and discourage or drive away audience, the team has managed to turn things around by capitalizing on the film's long duration and using this as a unique selling proposition. Time is commodified by banking on the experience of ('slow') cinema and treating this as a form of capital. Generally, people like the idea of rising up to a challenge, so the strategy has worked and led to most of the screenings selling out. According to Diaz, *Hele*'s distributor Star Cinema was actually shocked that the eight-hour film made PHP 11 million and that it performed better than *Humayo* at the box office (2019: n.pag.).

Having been successful in filling theatre seats through the 'challenge' strategy, the marketing team has met its economic objective. However, this promotional technique also raises questions related to cultural understanding and artistic value in terms of whether or not the film has been effective in communicating the message it wants to convey. Are the audience members just there for the sake of completing the challenge? Have they received and understood the film's message? Has their view on ('slow') cinema changed? Have they better appreciated the art of Diaz's cinema after the eight-hour screening? Is this a compromise that Diaz is willing to take for the propagation of his emancipated cinema?

In this context, understanding the narrative or appreciating the film itself (as an art form) only comes second or becomes consequential to a successful marketing strategy. However, Schrader argues that in slow cinema, time no longer serves storytelling. Rather, '[t]ime becomes the story – or at least its central component. Slow cinema examines how time affects images. It's experiential, not expositional' (2018: 10). Following this argument then, the marketing team has gotten it right by highlighting the time and not the narrative. As such, the film's length becomes a spectacle, and the idea of 'surviving' a Diaz film becomes a badge of pride.

This concept of survival viewing is also related to other modes of watching such as endurance viewing, which is meant to test the audience's resilience and endurance and 'confront the very act of watching and consumption'. This idea goes back to the 1960s when Andy Warhol's eight-hour film *Empire* (1964) was screened across New York and forced viewers to face the passage of time and monotony (Çağlayan 2018: 61). This 'endurance test' is also conveyed in the official Facebook page of Sine Olivia Pilipinas, when it uploaded a six-point guide on 'how to watch a Lav Diaz film' a couple of days before his newest film then *Ang Hupa* (*The Halt*) was set to open the 2019 Cinemalaya Philippine Independent Film Festival. First on the list is: 'Endure. The point of long takes and long forms of cinema is to endure it the way the characters in the film do. Their narratives require that length; there is a reason as to why it is long. It is up to you to find out' (Sine Olivia Pilipinas 2019: n.pag.). As Schrader explains it: '[T]he long take is about "being there"' (2018: 8) and pushing the viewer away from 'immediate emotional involvement' (17). The viewer has to immerse one's self in the filmic environment and experience the emotions first-hand like the film characters do. Hence, the last point in the guide says, 'Don't watch a Lav Diaz film only to say that "I survived" in the end. Don't watch for the sake of "surviving". Experiencing a Lav Diaz film is way beyond just going through it to be able to tag yourself a survivor' (Sine Olivia Pilipinas 2019: n.pag.). The first and last points may sound contradictory, but they are actually not. The object of endurance here does not pertain to the act of film viewing but to the pain or struggle that the characters are going through. The cinema of Diaz is about enduring the experience of the characters and going through it with them and surviving the hardship in the end (if this happens) and not about enduring and surviving the experience of watching a Diaz film.

The notion of endurance viewing is also connected to the marathon viewing of a television series. According to Baker, television marathon viewing suggests 'a lengthy act of endurance on the part of the audience – a challenge that the viewer meets and overcomes rather than one that overcomes the viewer' (2017: 39). This behaviour is also known as binge-watching or the excessive indulgence of watching (television), and in Baker's analysis, it can also be considered epic-viewing or the act of watching an epic genre that is 'designed specifically to be viewed over several consecutive hours – thereby shares with marathon viewing this emphasis on endurance' (2017: 39). However, Baker (following Vivian Sobchack's argument) notes that it is this very endurance of the epic's extended duration that becomes the genre's pleasures. Hence, Baker also indicates that Amanda Lotz's use of 'successive viewing' is a more neutral term for marathon viewing, as it describes the viewing practice and not the viewing experience itself. This is also because marathon viewing carries a negative connotation that (excessive) viewing can be hard work instead of pleasure. It implies effort, exhaustion but also pride (Baker 2017: 39) upon its completion, which in a way is a form of survival.

In other words, the idea of watching a long, slow film (of eight or ten or more hours) can be likened to watching several (or all) episodes of a television series back-to-back in one sitting or over an uninterrupted period of time, where the whole series is treated as one epic text.

In the context of Diaz, his long film is an epic text that can be binge-watched. The idea of binge-watching a Diaz film becomes more accurate if his film is screened in multiple parts in such a way that the film becomes almost episodic. The act of viewing Diaz's film now becomes fragmented or segmentized like episodes in a series even if it is not really (meant to be) episodic.

3. The distributor's cut

A 'director's cut' is defined as the director's version of his/her film that is usually re-edited to reflect the director's (*real*) vision or intention for the film after the 'original studio' version for the general public has been released ('director's cut, n.' 2020). On the other hand, the 'distributor's cut' is the distributor's version of the film, which could also be the studio version for general release that aims to generate (more) ticket sales. This means that it is a cut that is approved by the producers and/or distributors, which most of the time has also been consulted and agreed with the director. 'Cut' here also implies the distributor's share in the profit pie that it eventually receives when the film's marketing and distribution strategies work. There are instances however that the 'director's cut' is used as a marketing tool to promote the film by generating a buzz or controversy that there is another version of the film. This induces curiosity from the audience and attracts and encourages more viewers to see the director's cut of the movie, which now includes the scenes that have supposedly been deleted or excluded from the initial cut or general release. In this section, the distributor's cut refers to Diaz's film trailers that are produced or cut by the distributors and/or producers.

In Diaz's subsequent films following *Norte*, he is able to cast big-name stars such as Piolo Pascual and John Lloyd Cruz, whose popularity and name recall are used as part of the promotions. Since the lead stars come from the major television network and big studio ABS-CBN Star Cinema, which is also the local distributor of *Hele sa Hiwagang Hapis* and *Ang Babaeng Humayo*, the promotional technique used to market these films does not really veer away from the way Star Cinema usually promotes its star-laden blockbuster movies – that is, to focus the spotlight on the actors. Although the emphasis on the actors is not strongly evident in the trailers produced by Star Cinema, an avid Diaz viewer will immediately recognize the stark difference between the Star Cinema–produced trailers and the usual Diaz film trailers.

Based on some trailers available online, one can say that a 'typical' Diaz film trailer includes only one long-take shot like the trailers of *Kagadanan sa Banwaan ning mga Engkanto* (Dissidenz 2015) and *Mula sa Kung Ano ang Noon* (TIFF Originals 2014) or a few long-take shots like the trailer of *Prologo sa ang Dakilang Desaparecido* (Dissidenz 2017) that only has four shots and *Norte* (TIFF Originals 2013) that only has seven shots. In the extended trailer of *Norte* (New Wave Films 2014) however, it adds one scene in the end where two characters are talking albeit very briefly. As trailers are meant to attract audience and provide a glimpse or a general sense of what the film is about, it is important that the trailer reflects the film-maker's brand of cinema. The selected shots in Diaz's trailers usually do not include any dialogue from the characters nor do the trailers use additional background music and voice-over, because that is just how Diaz's cinema is. As Schrader notes: 'There is no music to guide emotions, no close-ups to indicate importance, no acting to affect feelings, no fast motion to distract the eye' (2018: 17).

Looking at the international trailer of *Hele*, as uploaded by one of the film's producers TEN17P (2016), it only uses a total of six shots within 88 seconds. There is the usual opening and closing credits, including Diaz's directorial signature, 'sine ni Lav Diaz', towards the end. There is no additional background music and voice-over. One only sees a succession of black-and-white images without hearing any character talking except for the actual sound of cries or wails of some characters. It is a producer's-cut trailer, but it still exudes a certain feel or aura that embodies the spirit or essence of a Lav Diaz film. One can conclude that this trailer follows the 'conventions' of a Diaz film trailer. In contrast, ABS-CBN Star Cinema's cut of *Hele*'s 90-second trailer (2016b) opens with a character talking off-screen, as the opening credits are shown. The selected shots in the trailer are those of the characters talking. There is an additional background music and voice-over that somewhat explains or provides an overview of what the film is about. There are two separate shots that just bear the names of the two lead actors on black background and then followed by the names of the other cast members superimposed on their respective solo shots in the film. The trailer then highlights the Silver Bear Alfred Bauer Prize on one shot. This is followed by a voice-over: 'From master director Lav Diaz', with an on-screen text that reads, 'A Film by Lav Diaz', instead of Diaz's directorial signature. The trailer utilizes several shots and is cut faster than the usual Diaz-paced film. The drama and tension can still be felt in the trailer but the 'slowness' of the film seems to dissipate as the trailer tries to invite a new set of audience for Diaz's film. Without any mention of the film's unusually long running time, a regular Star Cinema viewer will think that it would be like any other serious drama films of Star Cinema, only more artsy. According to Schrader, however, the purpose of slow cinema is to 'retard time' and 'withhold the expected' (2018: 11). The slow cinema director knows what the audience wants and expects and will do the opposite because s/he is after something else and will use the audience's expectations to get it (2018: 17).

There are also differences in the way various distributors cut their respective trailers of *Ang Babaeng Humayo*. The Berlin-based international sales company Films Boutique (2017) makes use of only five shots (with no dialogue) for the film's 60-second trailer. There's no additional background music or voice-over. It is a distributor's-cut trailer that maintains the mood of a Lav Diaz film. Meanwhile, the trailer uploaded by New York–based arthouse film distributor Kino Lorber (2017), which acquired all the film distribution rights for North America (McNary 2017: n.pag.), puts together a total of nine shots in 146 seconds. It begins with the usual opening credits, including the directorial credit 'A FILM BY LAV DIAZ'. The selected shots are scenes with characters talking, which are intercut with shots that quote the critics' commendation for the film, and scored using a character singing a cappella off-screen towards the end of the trailer. This is a distributor's-cut trailer that tries to retain the Diaz touch but compromising a bit on the characters in conversation and the off-screen singing. Last, ABS-CBN Star Cinema's version (2016a) opens with quotes from critics praising the film and then followed by a voice-over that highlights its Golden Lion win at the 73rd Venice Film Festival. Star Cinema once again uses several shots with mostly talking characters, adds background music and voice-over and cuts the trailer faster than the usual Diaz-paced film. The trailer then flashes the names of the two lead actors in two separate shots, including Diaz's directorial signature, 'sine ni Lav Diaz', towards the last 30 seconds, and then ends with the film's release date. Among all the trailer versions cited here, only Star Cinema's cut features the actors in the trailer. While the film's critical acclaim is emphasized at the beginning of the trailer, a star-driven approach is Star Cinema's common if not standard way of film promotion. In one of its press releases, ABS-CBN underscores the fact that *Ang Babaeng Humayo* is the comeback film of Charo Santos, one of the network's top executives who started out as an actor and hosts a popular TV drama programme (ABS-CBN Corporate Communication 2016: n.pag.).

Star Cinema has always used an actor-driven marketing strategy because it generally has a star-driven spectatorship. Hence, the company usually begins with casting when it conceptualizes a movie (Lim 2019: 137). Diaz knows about the strategy and advises against it because he believes that veteran actors no longer have the same audience pull as they used to because their fans have long stopped going to the cinemas. This means that the approach will not draw in as much crowd as the distributor hopes for. Diaz also points out that even if Santos has her share of fans and millions watch her long-time running weekly drama anthology *Maalala Mo Kaya*, they did not go to the theatres to watch *Humayo* (2019: n.pag.). However, Star Cinema's approach does not rely heavily on the stars but is geared more towards niche marketing because the target market of Diaz's films are not really the mass audience or the movie fans who would usually watch the movies of these actors. Nonetheless, Star Cinema has its own conventions to follow, and veering away from them means losing its branding. Distributing Diaz's film is already an extraordinary undertaking for the company; changing the way it cuts its trailers will be totally revolutionary.

Conclusion

This chapter highlights the role and importance of film marketing and distribution – without which a film will not reach its audience, even if it is within the conventional running time. Marketing and distributing the films of Lav Diaz can be a daunting task because of his films' unconventional characteristics that are defined primarily by their remarkable length. There are also scenes in Diaz's films where his characters engage in a rather philosophical or highly cerebral conversations. Diaz also uses an aesthetic style that employs long takes and long shots, which makes watching his films seem like watching a play or a live theatre performance – except that the stage is a (big) screen. As such, Diaz's cinema is something that the general mass audience is not accustomed to seeing. However, there is always a way to distribute a film no matter the length or style or content, as evidenced by Diaz's films. This just means that the marketing and distribution strategies need to be more creative and targeted.

Unconventional films do not necessarily require unconventional promotional approaches. The strategies used in all Diaz's films that have received a regular theatrical run are not entirely new. They are all about finding the right angle to focus on, defining the saleable elements of the films and packaging the films accordingly to make them attractive to a new set of audience or potential market. The cinema of Lav Diaz may have a niche market, but if the existing market – no matter how small – and the untapped market are targeted properly, there is no such thing as an unmarketable film, only unmarketed and mis-strategized films.

REFERENCES

ABS-CBN Corporate Communication (2016), 'Charo Santos' film comeback "Ang Babaeng Humayo" to be screened at the 2016 Venice Film Festival', abs-cbn.com, 28 July, https://ent.abs-cbn.com/articles-news/9872816-charo-santos-film-comeback-ang-babaeng-humayo-to-be-screened-at-the-2016-venice-film-festival-1715. Accessed 28 February 2020.

ABS-CBN Star Cinema (2016a), 'Ang Babaeng Humayo official trailer | Charo Santos and John Lloyd Cruz | "Ang Babaeng Humayo"', YouTube, 21 September, https://www.youtube.com/watch?v=jiciSsltTFw. Accessed 28 February 2020.

ABS-CBN Star Cinema (2016b), 'Hele Sa Hiwagang Hapis TV trailer | Piolo Pascual, John Lloyd Cruz | "Hele Sa Hiwagang Hapis"', YouTube, 12 March, https://www.youtube.com/watch?v=akPt3ZK7U9U. Accessed 28 February 2020.

Academy of Motion Picture Arts and Sciences (AMPAS) (n.d.), '92nd Academy Awards of Merit', https://www.oscars.org/sites/oscars/files/92aa_rules.pdf. Accessed 28 February 2020.

American Film Institute (AFI) Official Website (n.d.a), 'AFI Fest 2020 Film submissions', https://fest.afi.com/submit-your-film/. Accessed 28 February 2020.

American Film Institute (AFI) Official Website (n.d.b), 'AFI awards submissions', https://www.afi.com/afi-awards-submissions/#. Accessed 28 February 2020.

Baker, Djoymi (2017), 'Terms of excess: Binge-viewing as epic-viewing in the Netflix era', in C. Barker and M. Wiatrowki (eds), *The Age of Netflix: Critical Essays on Streaming Media, Digital Delivery and Instant Access*, Jefferson, NC: McFarland & Company, Inc., pp. 31–54.

British Film Institute (BFI) Official Website (n.d.), 'FAQ', https://www.bfi.org.uk/archive-collections/bfi-filmography-faq. Accessed 28 February 2020.

Brown, William (2016), '*Melancholia*: The long, slow cinema of Lav Diaz', in T. de Luca and N. B. Jorge (eds), *Slow Cinema*, Edinburgh: Edinburgh University Press, pp. 112–22.

Çağlayan, Emre (2018), *Poetics of Slow Cinema: Nostalgia, Absurdism, Boredom*, Cham: Palgrave Macmillan.

Diaz, Lav (2015), e-mail to author, 1 May.

Diaz, Lav (2018), in-person interview, 7 November.

Diaz, Lav (2019), in-person interview, 20 August.

'director's cut, n.' (2020), *OED Online*, Oxford: Oxford University Press, https://www.oed.com/view/Entry/53311. Accessed 28 February 2020.

Dissidenz (2015), 'Teaser DEATH IN THE LAND OF ENCANTOS de Lav Diaz', YouTube, 16 December, https://www.youtube.com/watch?v=JKzoKjDz1qY. Accessed 28 February 2020.

Dissidenz (2017), 'Teaser "Prologue to the Great Desaparecido" by Lav Diaz', YouTube, 22 March, https://www.youtube.com/watch?v=yVBpi_rLRYk. Accessed 28 February 2020.

Donahue, Suzanne Mary (1987), *American Film Distribution: The Changing Marketplace*, Ann Arbor, MI: UMI Research Press.

Drake, Philip (2013), 'Reputational capital, creative conflict and Hollywood independence: The case of Hal Ashby', in G. King, C. Molloy and Y. Tzioumakis (eds), *American Independent Cinema: Indie, Indiewood and Beyond*, Oxon: Routledge, pp. 140–52.

Ebbers, Joris J. and Wijnberg, Nachoem M. (2012), 'The effects of having more than one good reputation on distributor investments in the film industry', *Journal of Cultural Economics*, 36, pp. 227–48.

Films Boutique (2017), '*The Woman Who Left* – trailer (FR)', YouTube, 3 February, https://www.youtube.com/watch?v=daOFe7ctquc. Accessed 28 February 2020.

Getz, Donald (2007), *Event Studies: Theory, Research and Policy for Planned Events*, Oxford: Elsevier.

Guarneri, Michael (2013), 'Militant elegy: A conversation with Lav Diaz', *La Furia Umana*, 17, 7 July, http://www.lafuriaumana.it/index.php/29-archive/lfu-17/16-michael-guarneri-militant-elegy-a-conversation-with-lav-diaz. Accessed 28 February 2020.

Guarneri, Michael (2016), 'Long story long: An introduction to Lav Diaz's "Free Cinema"', Mubi.com, 8 October, https://mubi.com/notebook/posts/long-story-long-an-introduction-to-lav-diaz-s-free-cinema. Accessed 28 February 2020.

Hall, Phil (2011), *Independent Film Distribution: How to Make a Successful End Run around the Big Guys*, Studio City, CA: Michael Wiese Productions.

Hele sa Hiwagang Hapis (2016), 'The Hele challenge', Facebook, 9 March, https://www.facebook.com/helesahiwaganghapis/photos/a.424660417739202/438887312983179/?type=3&theater. Accessed 28 February 2020.

Ingawanij, May Adadol (2017), 'Exhibiting Lav Diaz's long films: Currencies of circulation and dialectics of spectatorship', *Aniki: Portuguese Journal of the Moving Image*, 4:2, pp. 411–33.

Jesus, Totel de (2016), 'Lav Diaz's "Hele sa Hiwagang Hapis" ticket prices range from P150 to P500', *Philippine Daily Inquirer*, 23 March, http://entertainment.inquirer.net/192725/ticket-prices-oflav-diazs-8-hour-hele-sa-hiwagang-hapis-range-from-p150-to-p500. Accessed 28 February 2020.

Kino Lorber (2017), '*The Woman Who Left* – official trailer', YouTube, 2 May, https://www.youtube.com/watch?v=MOopZgQuYz0. Accessed 28 February 2020.

Lang, Moira (2015), in-person interview, 29 January.

Lent, John A. 2012. 'Southeast Asian independent cinema: Independent of what?', in T. Baumgärtel (ed.), *Southeast Asian Independent Cinema*, Hong Kong: Hong Kong University Press, pp. 13–19.

Lim, Michael Kho (2019), *Philippine Cinema and the Cultural Economy of Distribution*, Cham: Palgrave Macmillan.

Luca, Tiago de and Jorge, Nuno Barradas (2016), 'Introduction: From slow cinema to slow cinemas', in T. de Luca and N. B. Jorge (eds), *Slow Cinema*, Edinburgh: Edinburgh University Press, pp. 1–21.

McNary, Dave (2017), 'Kino Lorber buys Venice winners "Woman Who Left". "Woman's Life"', *Variety*, 24 February, https://variety.com/2017/film/news/kino-lorber-venice-festival-winner-woman-who-left-1201995441/. Accessed 28 February 2020.

New Wave Films (2014), 'NORTE, The End of History, official UK trailer', YouTube, 1 July, https://www.youtube.com/watch?v=WwLGmYkdv20. Accessed 28 February 2020.

Orencio, Hazel (2020), e-mail to author, 4 April.

SAGindie Official Website (n.d.), 'Screen Actors Guild – American Federation of Television and Radio Artists agreement for modified low budget theatrical motion pictures', https://www.sagindie.org/media/Modified_Low_Budget_Agreement_1_7.pdf. Accessed 28 February 2020.

San Diego, Bayani Jr. (2014), 'Lav Diaz's "Norte", 4-hr Filipino film hailed overseas opens in PH', *Philippine Daily Inquirer*, 9 March, http://entertainment.inquirer.net/136945/lav-diaznorte-4-hr-filipino-film-hailed-overseas-opens-in-ph. Accessed 28 February 2020.

San Diego, Bayani Jr. (2018), '"Halimaw" and the sound of subversion', *Philippine Daily Inquirer*, 30 May, http://entertainment.inquirer.net/276631/halimaw-sound-subversion. Accessed 28 February 2020.

Schrader, Paul (2018), *Transcendental Style in Film: Ozu, Bresson, Dreyer*, California: University of California Press.

Shaw, Angel Velasco ([2002] 2013), 'An artist's prerogative: Excerpts from a conversation with Lav Diaz', Asian CineVision, https://www.asiancinevision.org/lav-diaz-and-batang-west-side/. Accessed 28 February 2020.

Sine Olivia Pilipinas (2019), 'How to watch a Lav Diaz film', Facebook, 31 July, https://www.facebook.com/sineoliviapilipinas/posts/880378468993877. Accessed 28 February 2020.

Sundance Institute Official Website (n.d.), 'Films and episodic content', https://www.sundance.org/festivals/sundance-film-festival/submit. Accessed 28 February 2020.

Tarkovsky, Andrey ([1986] 1987), *Sculpting in Time: The Great Russian Filmmaker Discusses His Art* (trans. K. Hunter-Blair), Austin: University of Texas Press.

TEN17P (2016), '*Hele Sa Hiwagang Hapis* (2016) – international trailer', YouTube, 13 February, https://www.youtube.com/watch?v=SXhCGMx5JoA. Accessed 28 February 2020 [no longer available].

TIFF Originals (2013), 'NORTE THE END OF HISTORY trailer | Festival 2013', YouTube, 23 August, https://www.youtube.com/watch?v=nzpfJrlL4SE. Accessed 28 February 2020.

TIFF Originals (2014), 'FROM WHAT IS BEFORE trailer | Festival 2014', YouTube, 19 August, https://www.youtube.com/watch?v=79EtADrXuvk. Accessed 28 February 2020.

Tomada, Nathalie (2014), 'Norte picked up for international distribution,' *The Philippine Star*, 24 March, http://www.philstar.com/entertainment/2014/03/24/1304251/norte-picked-intl-distribution. Accessed 28 February 2020.

Verhoeven, Deb (2011), 'Film distribution in the diaspora: Temporality, community and national cinema', in R. Maltby, D. Biltereyst and P. Meers (eds), *Explorations in New Cinema History: Approaches and Case Studies*, 1st ed., Malden, MA: Blackwell, pp. 243–60.

Vivarelli, Nick (2016), 'Venice Golden Lion winner, almost four hours long, to get Italian theatrical distribution', *Variety*, 19 September, http://variety.com/2016/film/asia/woman-who-left-venice-winner-lav-diaz-to-get-italian-theatrical-distribution-1201864718. Accessed 28 February 2020.

Wyatt, Justin (1998), 'From roadshowing to saturation release: Majors, independents, and marketing/distribution innovations', in Jon Lewis (ed.), *The New American Cinema*, Durham and London: Duke University Press, pp. 64–86.

Zafirau, Stephen (2008), 'Reputation work in selling film and television: Life in the Hollywood talent industry.' *Qualitative Sociology*, 31:2, pp. 99–127.

Appendix

TABLE 1:

| | Title | Year | Running time (minutes) | Distribution | |
				Theatrical	Non-theatrical
Good Harvest Unlimited	*Serafin Geronimo: Kriminal ng Baryo Concepcion (Serafin Geronimo: The Criminal of Barrio Concepcion)*	1998	132	Regal Films	
	Burger Boys	1999	103	Regal Films	
	Hubad sa Ilalim ng Buwan (Naked under the Moon)	1999	110	Regal Films	
	Hesus, Rebolusyunaryo (Jesus, the Revolutionary)	2002	112	Regal Films	
Short Films	*Walang Alaala ang mga Paru-Paro (Butterflies Have No Memories)*	2009	59		
	Pagsisiyasat sa Gabing Ayaw Lumimot (An Investigation to the Night That Won't Forget)	2012	70		Mubi
	Prologo sa ang Dakilang Desaparecido (Prologue to the Great Desaparecido)	2013	32		
	Mga Anak ng Unos: Unang Aklat (Storm Children: Book One)	2014	143	Zomia Films (expired)	Grasshopper Film, Mubi

TABLE 1: Continued

	Title	Year	Running time (minutes)	Distribution	
				Theatrical	Non-theatrical
	Ang Araw Bago ang Wakas (The Day Before the End)	2016	17		Grasshopper Film
Independent / Sine Olivia Pilipinas	Lakbayan (Journey): Hugaw (Dirt) segment	2018	36	Solar Pictures	
	Batang West Side (West Side Kid)	2001	315	Zomia Films (expired)	
	Ebolusyon ng Isang Pamilyang Pilipino (Evolution of a Filipino Family)	2004	660		
	Heremias (Unang Aklat: Ang Alamat ng Prinsesang Bayawak) (Heremias: [Book One: The Legend of the Lizard Princess])	2006	540		Amazon
	Kagadanan sa Banwaan ning mga Engkanto (Death in the Land of Encantos)	2007	540	Dissidenz Films	
	Melancholia	2008	450		
	Siglo ng Pagluluwal (Century of Birthing)	2011	360		Mubi

Title	Year		Production	Distributor
Elehiya sa Dumalaw Mula sa Himagsikan (Elegy to the Visitor from the Revolution)	2011	80		Mubi
Florentina Hubaldo, CTE	2012	360		Mubi, Rai 3 (TV, 2015, Italy)
Norte, Hangganan ng Kasaysayan (Norte, the End of History)	2013	250	Origin8 Media (Philippines), The Cinema Guild (United States), New Wave Films (United Kingdom), Shellac (France)	Shellac, Amazon
Mula sa Kung Ano ang Noon (From What Is Before)	2014	345		Grasshopper Film, Mubi
Hele sa Hiwagang Hapis (A Lullaby to the Sorrowful Mystery)	2016	485	ABS-CBN Film Productions/Star Cinema	Films Boutique

(continued)

Title	Year	Running time (minutes)	Distribution	
			Theatrical	Non-theatrical
Ang Babaeng Humayo (*The Woman Who Left*)	2016	227	ABS-CBN Film Productions/Star Cinema (Philippines), ABS-CBN International (2016, United States), Kino Lorber (2017, United States), Films Boutique (Germany), Grandfilm (Germany), World Sales: Hassala Films (Egypt), Microcinema (Italy), ARP Sélection (France), Contact Film (2017, Netherlands), Magic Hour (2017, Japan), Zeta Filmes (2017, Brazil)	Kino Lorber (all North American rights), absolut MEDIEN (DVD, 2018, Germany), iWant (Philippines)
Panahon ng Halimaw (*Season of the Devil*)	2018	234	ARP Sélection (France), Films Boutique (Germany)	
Ang Hupa (*The Halt*)	2019	282	ARP Sélection (France)	

TABLE 1: Filmography of Lav Diaz (as director)
Sources: https://www.sineoliviapilipinas.com; Orencio (2020).

PART 4

INTERVIEW WITH LAV DIAZ

11

A Lav Affair with Cinema

Michael Kho Lim and Parichay Patra

INTERVIEWER: How was it like the first time you tried your hand at film-making?[1]

LAV DIAZ: It was during a film-making workshop in 1985, at the Mowelfund Film Institute. I was part of that month-long workshop called 'The Total Filmmaking Workshop'. It was a very mixed and varied film exercise because everything was crammed, unlike today when you'd have specialized workshops on directing, cinematography, screenwriting, production design, acting, editing and sound. Christoph Janetzko was one of the facilitators. He showed us a lot of works from Germany – experimental, avant-garde works; and of course he taught us how to use the 16-millimeter camera. There were only two camera units to be shared among 40 of us participants.

It was my first time to touch a movie camera. I was only able to touch it (*laughs*). But there were enough Super 8 cameras. I think the institute had seven of them then, and I was able to shoot a Super 8 short. You won't be able to shoot without money then; you'd have to buy rolls of film. Raymond Red was kind enough to give me three Super 8 rolls. I didn't have money to buy them. It was the rich workshoppers who were able to shoot at will. For poor students like us, nothing was there. We just watched, hanged out and touched the cameras (*laughs*). The ones who were able to shoot used us as actors or we'd assist in their shoots or we'd drown our sorrows with the gin *bilog* and Tanduay rhum. There was that class issue. I think Mowelfund provided one roll. I made a short film called *Banlaw* ('Rinse') out of that roll and the rolls given by Raymond.

But even with the dearth of materials and money, it was an important moment in my life. Just to touch and look at those cameras, the Bolex 16mm, the Super 8s and the beautiful Kodak rolls – those were defining moments for me; it was a very tactile yet transcendent experience. That encounter created a lasting kinship. It created that sensation, a bond, and from then on, I've committed myself to cinema. It was a very spiritual experience in a way. Back then, seeing and being able to hold a camera was really something; it can be life-changing. I experienced epiphany, enforcing the possibility that I could really be a film-maker. I knew that I'd be a film-maker, even though I was so poor that I couldn't even buy a roll and a cigarette. I was only able to attend the workshop because Ricky Lee sent me there. I was part of Ricky's screenwriting workshop then, and he chose three of his students to go to the Mowelfund Workshop, and I was lucky enough to be one of them. I didn't even have PHP 500 to pay the Mowelfund fee then. I still owe them that money.

INTERVIEWER: Would you recall how much a roll cost at that time?

LAV DIAZ: It was very expensive. The standard 100-feet 16-millimeter roll was around USD 50–60, while the 400-feet roll would cost almost USD 200. With the 100 feet, you can shoot only three minutes of footage. It's really expensive. And Raymond Red, who just arrived from a film festival, nonchalantly threw three Super 8-millimeter rolls at me, and I was able to do my very first shoot. Raymond was one of the facilitators/teachers of the workshop.

The facilitators and teachers were Christoph Janetzko, Ricky Lee, Raymond Red and Mac Alejandre. Of course, Nick Deocampo was the head of the institute at the time. They invited other facilitators and instructors and teachers like Peque Gallaga. Even the great late Lamberto Avellana came. He was hilarious and extremely intelligent. Ed Infante was also there. Other veteran film-makers were also invited to facilitate during that month-long workshop. It was a defining moment for my batch. Some of my batchmates were Larry Manda, Ricky Orellana and Mel Bacani. That batch was a great group. We were very close and made a commitment to become film-makers.

INTERVIEWER: How did the experience of touching the camera (and using it) influence you, as you made the transition to the digital medium?

LAV DIAZ: We had a purist perspective, the pure cinema bullshit, that cinema is celluloid. Admittedly, I was part of that hardcore with a very naive mentality that cinema can only be celluloid, and to go digital is Faustian. It was hard when digital film-making arrived. We resisted, and we actually said bad things about digital like it would finally be the death of cinema, it was cheap cinema, it was only a new toy, it was only for those who have poor taste in cinema, it was only for the weak film-maker, the uncommitted, the compromising.

But then ultimately I had to embrace it. I didn't have money, that reality confronted me really hard, but it was clear. Pure cinema? And in the case of the Philippines, it was a period when there were no laboratories anymore, or film laboratories were being phased out fast. And we don't have film rolls. They had to be ordered abroad, and worse, we don't even have film cameras. So what would you do? You had to embrace this new medium, this new development. It's part of the evolution of cinema after all. That's the nature of the medium. It keeps evolving. You have to be open about it. As Andre Bazin said, 'Any development in cinema is a step towards understanding its nature.'

INTERVIEWER: How long did it take you to accept the transition?

LAV DIAZ: Well, what pushed me to really embrace it was the film *Evolution of a Filipino Family*. I'd been shooting it for years. I couldn't finish it because it was being shot in 16-millimeter. The process became very protracted and tedious because I shot only when there was money, and most of the time, there was really no money. The coming of digital gave me an option, a new medium to pursue and finish it. It's affordable, there's more room when it comes to the durational issues. There's greater flexibility, I can actually shoot longer. With the 16-millimeter format, with a 100-feet roll, you're limited to less than three minutes shooting on 24 frames, and there's 400 feet that gives you eleven minutes. It's the longest you could do, eleven minutes – and it's really expensive. Another difficulty is that you couldn't buy a roll in the Philippines. It had to be ordered from America or Japan. Practicality was a big reason for the decision to use digital. And I had to be practical. There was this film that I couldn't finish, and maybe I wouldn't be able to finish at all if I kept dreaming of 16-millimeter. And the coming of digital offered some reprieve, telling me: 'Hey, you can finish it. Use me'. The decision gave me that big realization as well, that cinema, this medium, will keep on evolving, that's including theory and praxis.

Digital appropriated my being poor, my process, my methodology, the long takes, the one frame, one take, static shots. You can't do that with the 16mm. I've tried it in New York during the early days of the shoot because I actually started shooting *Evolution* in New York, Maryland and Virginia. I had to do two, three jobs to be able to afford the rolls. I was practically killing myself to exhaustion. I'd been working at this Filipino newspaper weekdays, and on weekends, I'd be waiting tables, and did other odd jobs so I could buy those rolls. I was able to do that because it was New York. Just work and work. So every weekend, I'd buy two to three rolls. I raised money from tips at the bars and other jobs. I also did proofreading. I could afford that kind of privilege while I was in New York. But when I got back to Manila, it was impossible. There's nowhere to buy the rolls. There's no job, too. There's nowhere you could get a camera. By then, Mowelfund had only one functional 16-millimeter camera left and you'd have to compete with so many people just to be able to use it. Only a few rich film-makers had 16-millimeter cameras in the Philippines then.

When I decided to go with digital, I had many doubts, many fears. It's a new medium and I don't really like the look. It's flat, it's 30 frames per second. You don't see the grain, you'll notice lines instead. You're frustrated all the time with the look (*laughs*). But it's created that kind of ideology, the kind of stubbornness, the kind of toughness; digital will give you that. *Okay, let's push this thing, let's push this thing.* We'd see the raw material and it looked 'terrible'. But at the same time, it creates that kind of friction, or tension. It creates something in your head, some kind of discourse or dialogue like, okay, if this thing will work and if you're poor, well then, use it. It's become dialectical. That kind of ideology, that this is what I have, and I'll make it work. Enough romanticizing. But if you have money, by all means, buy the rolls.

The purist notion is very romantic for me now. It's a realization, that sticking to the purist perspective – it's very romantic. Embrace the medium as it evolves. If you want to be part of the revolution, then embrace it. It's a romantic notion to film in 16-millimeter when you can't even afford it. If you looked at it from the Marxist perspective, you'd embrace digital technology, right? It's part of the evolution. You embrace it. You use the tool. The romantic notion just dried up.

We were like a tribe at Mowelfund. We'd converge, talk cinema shit, we'd drink in the evening, talk more cinema shit, smoke pot and *talampunay* (Datura) and more cinema shit, ad infinitum. It was so cool and so romantic. *Long live 35mm! Long live 16mm! Long live Super 8! (laughs)*. But nobody was filming. No one was creating. We were all floating in a dream, rowing in the haze of our celluloid dreams. But there it was, right in front of us, history happening, the zeitgeist telling us to jump and to plunge and be part of it, right? And I took the plunge.

INTERVIEWER: Would you recall how much of *Evolution* was shot in film and in digital?

LAV DIAZ: The whole US shoot was done in 16mm and the early years of shoot in the Philippines, too. We were able to continue using 16mm because a friend helped fund it. His name is Paul Tañedo, a great photographer. He gave me USD 11,000.

INTERVIEWER: That's big enough?

LAV DIAZ: At the time, yes, for a modest production. We were able to buy a Bolex 16mm camera. Paul bought one for USD 5,000. We used that. Eventually, the USD 11,000 fund ran out. And so we finally shifted to digital in 2003. I borrowed digital cameras here and there, knocking on doors, begging, pestering and bugging people. Everything was borrowed. Until we finally finished it in early 2005.

INTERVIEWER: Would you be able to quantify that 30 per cent was shot in 16mm?

LAV DIAZ: We shot a lot on 16mm, but we ended up not using most of it. Like the entire US shoot didn't make the final cut. So there's another film right there, the US shoot. I have the Super VHS transfers. I still love VHS.

INTERVIEWER: You can make that film now?

LAV DIAZ: I can work on it again. The transfers are actually somewhere in my studio. I can do it, if mould and humidity haven't eaten them up yet. An upgrade has to be done on the digital transfers first though, to adapt to the new technology, so I can watch and revisit the project, and consider it for cutting. I'd have to be serious about working on it again, so it wouldn't have been for nothing. I will have to commit myself to watching a lot of footage that were shot a long time ago and have to go back to those zones and spheres. Not easy but at some point, I will have to do it.

The entire US shoot wasn't used at all as a result of the end-less writing and rewriting during the Philippine shoot. The idea was for the Philippine shoot to form the story's flashback, but the story just expanded, morphed and evolved, and in post, it became the entire film.

My process of writing the script during the shoot started with the *Evolution of a Filipino Family*. I was forced to write the script during the shoot, create and follow new threads.

I'd need to see the places, the locations so I can map out a geographical flow for the narrative, for the characters. I'd need to see the characters as well; they need to be with me, the actors must be there, for the story, the narrative, to flow nat-urally. That's how I work it out. I'm very comfortable with that process now.

Due to the intermittent long gaps, I needed to adapt and adjust every time we resumed the shoot. I had to rework and rework the whole thing. There'd be lulls in the shoot – more than a year's gap, three months, six months, another year. The actor Rey Ventura passed away, what would I do then? Another actor, Mike Fernandez, died, what would I do then? The kid has grown up, so you jump the story to where the kid is now. You'd be confronted by disasters and tragedies, the carabao is dead, they changed the look of the house where we were shooting major scenes, they wouldn't let us borrow the truck anymore, there's a new building beside the house of this character. When we started the film, El Ryan de Vera, who played the lead character, was just 9 years old. By the time we wrapped, he was 20 or 21. We started in 1993 and finished in 2005. Almost twelve years.

I realized a whole lot – that cinema really is free. It's a defining film for me.

INTERVIEWER: How does this mixture of form and aesthetics result in the film? That kind of combination, the digital and the 16mm?

LAV DIAZ: During the process of creation, my primary question always is, 'Will it work?' Whether it's the execution of a scene, the actor working on his character or the flow of the story. In the case of *Evolution*, I was forced to work in extremely difficult conditions. At the end of the day, my principle was to have faith, just trust my guts. And there's the film. People who earnestly experienced the film and continue to be inspired by it don't really see and talk about the elements, factors and forces that were combined and used to achieve it. They're into the vision and discourse of the work. Only a technical savant will notice the mix – there's the 16-millimeter footage, there's the digital – the grain versus the line discourse, it's dirty, they don't match.

INTERVIEWER: Now that you're always using digital, how do you approximate the specific colour that you're looking for?

LAV DIAZ: Digital post-production can do anything, there's really no limit now. We used to believe that digital would never be able to approximate the celluloid resolution. That's not true anymore. Digital is way, way better than celluloid now. In terms of resolution, we now have the 2k, the 4k, the 6k, even 8k. It's gone way past what celluloid can do. In fact, celluloid is very dependent on digital now. Technology is amazing.

INTERVIEWER: In terms of process, do you shoot in black-and-white mode?

LAV DIAZ: Both, I use both. There are times when you need to use a log, the flat mode so you can go deeper in range during grading in post. This is for when shots end up too dark, too bright or there's not enough light sometimes. A log is in full colour and then adjust it later on in grading. For the most part though, I shoot in black and white. But I'd really need to know the camera first before I do that. Sometimes the settings aren't right. You really have to know the camera, have a relationship with it like a musical instrument, familiarize yourself with its settings, its attributes. I'm using Panasonic GH5s and S1H now. These small cameras can shoot 4k to 6k. The depth is amazing. But at the same time, the limitations still present themselves when there's too much light or when it gets too dark. But then, you can play and work around the settings. And working around these cheap and small digital cameras, I often experience déjà vu – being transported to struggling again with 16-millimeter Bolex camera.

The other day, maybe three days ago, Black Magic introduced a new, very small camera. And it can be set to 8k (*chuckles*). It's only USD 1,200. Very cheap, but it's really good. I think this year many cameras will be coming out with a 6k to 8k resolution. These resolutions are much better than the celluloid. You can do a lot when it comes to grading, changing colour, mixing, everything. You can be a one-man army nowadays with a cheap camera that comes with 8k, 6k, 4k. We're privileged to have powerful computers nowadays. Some are a bit expensive, but still much cheaper than the celluloid process, ten times cheaper, even twenty times cheaper. So this is really liberating for film-makers.

With the so-called film looks or filmic looks, there are LUTs [look-up tables] now, where you can easily have the look of your favourite film roll or the look of your favourite movie. I can approximate the beautiful black-and-white Kodak 7222 (my favourite 16mm film stock) look by using an LUT. Approximation of the looks of film stocks or even your favourite movie is easy now. But I really haven't taken that route yet. I don't want to do it because that would practically be copying and seems like lazy work. I want to use digital technology based on its own attributes, struggle with it. I want to do it that way, be tactile and dirty with it, have a deeper and earnest relationship with the medium.

INTERVIEWER: So you rode the digital wave. You had no choice?

LAV DIAZ: I had to. That's why I made the commitment to make one film a year. That's important. Sometimes two. I have four to five unfinished works. It makes me busy. I want to keep myself busy. I have friends who end up not making anything. They're too nostalgic, oftentimes too self-absorbed, and they end up with lulls, slumbers and gaps and ultimately biting the dust. That's difficult and heartbreaking because I know so many brilliant friends who suffer the paralysis of inaction. Your cinema will end up not just lazy but dead. Film-making, specifically for directors, requires an inordinate discipline of mind.

INTERVIEWER: Would you like to comment on the way you compared digital cinema to liberation theology?

LAV DIAZ: Digital gave us the tool to be able to fight. Cinema is also a class issue, issues of struggle and resistance, it has had a very feudal and fascistic system and set-up before digital came, that is, the studio system and imperial Hollywood. If you don't have money, you can't create cinema, or it will take a long hard struggle before you are able to create one. If you have no connections and uncompromising, it was hard to enter the system. I attach the coming of digital to the idea of liberation theology because just like many marginalized and poor film-makers, I was liberated by digital film-making. I wouldn't have been able to make my first long film without that. *Batang West Side* was shot in 35-millimeter because there was a producer: Tony Veloria, an independent producer. He produced it, which enabled me to shoot in New York. But the *Evolution of a Filipino Family* was different. It was an act of resistance and subversion, a defiant one, a liberation movement, it became my manifesto. With digital, the peasant, the proletarian and the working class can now fight. I was able to do it. I was able to change my miserable situation. I was able to create on my own terms. It's empowering. It freed us from the class issue. Digital is the great equalizer.

INTERVIEWER: Your consistent engagement with the 1970s dictatorship(s) and their reappearance form the crux of your cinema, but more often than not it manifests through sexual violence. Is that a conscious choice?

LAV DIAZ: It is the curse of the history of the Philippines, and I call it the Filipino struggle. Emilio Aguinaldo, Ferdinand Marcos, Rodrigo Duterte. They form the three faces and the three phases of that curse. They form that cycle of dictatorship and megalomania that imposed devastating effects on the Filipino psyche. They are the greatest executors of the Filipino's cultural debacle. The other evils are colonialism, imperialism and hegemony (Spain, America, Second World War Japan and now, with Duterte's shameless capitulation and cowardice, China). Sexual violence in my cinema is rooted on imposition, oppression, exploitation, vindictiveness, opportunism and trauma.

The engagement/discourse with the subject of dictatorship and its underlying effects just comes out naturally, like the one that I've recently shot called *Historya ni Ha* (*History of Ha*). The initial premise was simple. But once I anchored the story on a particular epoch, the discourse became bigger. It is set in 1957, the year President Ramon Magsaysay died; also the epoch when the Hukbalahap (*Hukbong Bayan Laban sa Hapon* [The Nation's Army Against the Japanese]) movement ended and the heyday of *bodabil* (Filipino vaudeville). It all happened in the 1950s. And so again, it's something I couldn't avoid. It's about fascism again, loss of ideals, sociocultural dysfunction.

My cinema is set in historical time. Every story that I make is anchored in a certain period of Philippine history, like *The Woman Who Left* is set in 1997. And *Season of the Devil* is set during the Martial Law period. And then *A Lullaby to the Sorrowful Mystery*, the Philippine Revolution of the late nineteenth century. They're all epochal.

It is something that comes out when I make cinema. During the writing process, the discourse would become dialectical. I never intentionally set out to do a film set in 1957, but when I started writing, somehow I remembered my father's stories, and there is that immediate referencing and discourse on the past. My father was a courier during the Hukbalahap movement in the Second World War. He was a young man during the war. He was courier for the guerillas. When the war ended, he continued being a young courier for the Hukbalahap that evolved into a very strong socialist/communist movement. My father became a teacher and a social worker eventually, and he worked and lived with the indigenous peoples of Mindanao.

The film became anchored in the 1950s because of my father's stories about that period. It was a very progressive time, the post-war perspective of reconstruction and rebirth, but suddenly it crashed. In 1953, the Hukbalahap politburo decided on an all-front offensive, to encircle Manila and hit the jugular; some were against it, including Hukbalahap chairman Luis Taruc, who contended that they were not ready. Some said that the result was a devastating failure because of the hastiness of the decision, but others said it was because of internecine strife and betrayals in the movement; and that America's CIA played a big part in it. Most of the leaders were rounded up, they were caught, and the movement was crushed. Eventually in 1954, Luis Taruc, out of disillusionment, surrendered, opting for a prison life rather than pursuing a dysfunctional struggle, and then, the very popular president, Ramon Magsaysay, died in a plane crash in 1957. This was also the period when Filipino *bodabil* was at its height especially in the Avenida/Quiapo/Escolta area of Manila. The *bodabil* was patterned after the American vaudeville, but this Filipino version was more farcical and absurdist, sometimes politically charged (the 1950s), sexually charged, and this was where the so-called Filipino toilet humour had its beginnings as well. *Historya ni Ha* revolves around those backdrops and events. When I started writing the characters, there's the fascist again represented by a village chief. It's a very conceptual film, but it's anchored again in an epoch, a historical period, the post-war Filipino struggle.

INTERVIEWER: Your engagement with the epic novel in cinema features literary figures such as Dostoyevsky and Jose Rizal. How much influence do those figures have on your cinema?

LAV DIAZ: Rizal, of course. His work has really influenced me a lot; his commitment to educate and liberate our people during the Spanish period. His mind is so prescient, so brilliant, so generous, he has no equal. As did Russian works, because of my father's obsession with Russian literature and history, his interest in the Bolsheviks. Eventually I myself got into the Russian works: Dostoyevsky, Tolstoy and Chekhov; all these guys. Even my name is Russian: Lavrente. I was named after Lavrentiy Beria, who was very close to Stalin. The two of them were the architects of the Russian slaughter, where around 20 million died, and the Ukrainian famine that claimed the lives of 3.9 million Ukrainians.

So the way I work on my cinema is I write them as if I am writing novels. That's why they're long. I want everything contextualized. I want fulfilled characters. I want a fulfilled narrative. For me, if you tell your story quickly, you're just scratching the surface of it. It's a shallow film. You don't see a lot of things. You don't feel a lot of things. You miss the nuances. These things are more important. Just like the novel. I want space. I want details. I want more space in my cinema, just like the novel. I want poetry and I want more music, not a score. I don't want to make the stories run really fast because you lose so many things.

That's what has always frustrated me about cinema. I watch a two-hour or an hour-and-a-half film, and it feels like it's all surface; oftentimes, it's all gimmickry, manipulated by very noisy soundtrack and fast and flashy editing. At the end of the movie, there's nothing.

INTERVIEWER: How would you comment on the idea of showing and not telling? For instance, a scene with too much dialogue, with no cuts.

LAV DIAZ: Showing is directly connected to seeing, and telling is connected to hearing. Showing and telling are essential to cinema. Either you want to show and not tell or you want to tell and not show. Or you can do both, show and tell. Or do not show and do not tell, nothing. Everything is valid in cinema.

INTERVIEWER: Much has been written on the walkers/walking figures in your cinema. Relatively scant attention has been paid to your exploration of the landscape. This landscape has certain qualities that are not to be experienced in mainstream narrative cinema; you have never presented it as something exotic for a foreign audience. As we all know, landscape plays a rather important and cerebral role in certain experimental films. You hail from Mindanao, the backyard of the Filipino nation, infamous for the Islamist militants ravaging the countryside. For your new film, you are exploring obscure locations in Palawan. Would you like to elaborate on your association with the landscape?

LAV DIAZ: Nature is a big actor in my works. I grew up in a place where nature played a big part in our lives. I grew up in Maguindanao, in the south-western part of the main island of Mindanao, in the middle of a forest, in the middle of a farm, in between two formidable mountains and a majestic river. There was no electricity. Nature's presence is integral to everything that we do. We're attached to the ways of nature. And it's all nature really, just commandeering our lives. I grew up in a place like that. And it manifests in my works. The culture I grew up with shows in my work.

INTERVIEWER: How have film festivals influenced your film-making style?

LAV DIAZ: Festivals don't excite me, really; it's a love-hate relationship, but I acknowledge their importance, their role in cinema propagation. They've taken care of cinema, even my cinema, and I deeply appreciate that. The other side of festivals is decadence. I couldn't take the circus, the hedonistic atmosphere surrounding it. Oftentimes, they become festivals of big egos, arrogance, pomposity and greed. They forget cinema. But I do love attending the better-programmed ones because I get to see a lot of works from other cultures, from fellow film-makers. It educates me. And I really can learn from the works of other film-makers, past and present. The interaction is great. You'll really learn. It can really help you. Festivals have really helped open my mind. I focus on watching a lot of films every time I go to a festival; otherwise, I stay in my hotel room, play guitar, read and sleep, then do my duties, which is always part of the deal when invited, introduce the film I'm representing, do question and answers, interviews and the so-called master classes. And I've juried in so many festivals, so there's the great bonus of watching really good works and have some healthy, sometimes bloody and cumbersome discussion. But if it's up to me, I'd prefer to just make cinema and stay in the background.

INTERVIEWER: But in terms of cinematic style or the way you work, does it have any influence like that?

LAV DIAZ: You can't escape influences, especially when you're still trying to develop your own language in the medium, you're an alloy, an amalgam. Watching a lot of cinema, the canons, they help in defining your own footing; and not just cinema, the little things that you see in life every day, great essays, history, books, the news, the regular visit of wild doves atop your neighbour's wall,

Russia, the *taho* vendor, these things shape your aesthetic. A big inspiration to my cinema language is the novel form. I always want to approximate the novel. I'm speaking for myself, my own experience with cinema. I always feel there's something lacking. I want to see more. I want to read more. I want to experience more. I want it to be the way I experience novels, how you get deeper and deeper into it that you end up seeing things between the lines. Even in the blank spaces, sometimes there's something there. I want to approximate that with cinema. I want to see that.

INTERVIEWER: Would you like to comment on your cinematic predecessors or successors from the Philippines and abroad?

LAV DIAZ: Lino Brocka is a big influence of course, because of *Maynila: Sa mga Kuko ng Liwanag*. But through my father I was able to watch a lot of films as a kid. That was a big thing, it was my film school, really. Watching a lot of black-and-white films when I was a kid. There were four cinemas back then in a town called Tacurong; it's two hours of jeepney ride from our place. These cinemas offered a double feature. We'd watch eight movies a week. My father was a cinephile; we'd watch and he would discuss cinema over dinner. My father was such a good teacher. He's a really, really committed person. Instead of raising us in the city, he brought us to the mountains, lived with the poor, educating the tribes, the Maguindanaos, the Manobos, the B'laans. My siblings and I resented it then, but we eventually realized how lucky we were, living with our people. You know, witnessing the struggles of Filipinos, seeing poverty, neglect, the dysfunction of our society. I saw all these as a boy, and it really shaped my perspective. My parents taught me the issues of sacrifice and education.

INTERVIEWER: You lived there since your childhood?

LAV DIAZ: Up till high school. We got displaced because of the Muslim-Christian war and the Martial Law. We left the place in 1972 and never returned. We transferred to Tacurong, the cinema paradise of my youth.

INTERVIEWER: That was the time you moved to Manila?

LAV DIAZ: I stayed in Manila with my young family in 1980. But my mother, my brothers and relatives are still in Cotabato, in Maguindanao, in Sultan Kudarat. Our farm is still there. They didn't leave. They're all teachers, my brothers and my late sister. They took after my parents, who both taught in public schools. They never left. Only I did, because of my young family. We went to Manila and I pursued law, and cinema. I didn't finish law, though I tried. I gave it a year at the University of the East, but all the reading and memorization exhausted me. I couldn't memorize those thick civil and criminal law books. All I did was drinking. So did my classmates. I couldn't handle it. I almost died, drinking alcohol every night. I ended up in the hospital.

Then I attended Ricky Lee's workshop. And just like that, cinema was back in my life.

When I got sick, I felt paralyzed. I was a writer/contributor then for *Masa*, the Filipino edition of *Malaya*. That's where I saw the announcement for Ricky Lee's screenwriting workshop. That's how my world opened up: attending Ricky's workshop, then going to Mowelfund. That's how cinema got me hooked again. There was no going back. My gratitude to Ricky Lee is immense.

INTERVIEWER: What's your view on the 'Filipino New Wave' and Khavn dela Cruz's manifesto?

LAV DIAZ: Khavn is a good friend; we have a rock band called The Brockas. And we had a small gang of film-maker friends then. We'd gather, talk cinema shit and shoot. I like our group's credo of just going at it on your own, just doing it by all means necessary. To use what's available to you. That's cool. Like Lars Von Trier's Dogme group back then. They were drunk and laughing when they concocted the so-called commandments of new cinema, The Dogme. They were able to convince the world with their bullshit (*laughs*). They were actually shocked that the world took them seriously. They were just having fun. But they created something magical and universally influential, almost akin to the French New Wave. Sometimes it's all just rhetoric, but it affects things when there's application. Like the Dogme group, they really created things, good works. They showed us digital films shot without lights, without production design, like 'found object' cinema, and a return to cinéma vérité. It's really inspiring to see their works, and it inspired us. Looking back, the so-called new movement here in the Philippines that started in early 2000 was very much inspired by Dogme. Of course, the digital was the biggest push on the birthing of the so-called Philippine Independent Movement or the indie. There was no organized group; we just started shooting and shooting.

INTERVIEWER: How would you describe your engagement with the Filipino Diaspora abroad?

LAV DIAZ: Well, I was part of it. I lived in New York. I worked in New York starting in 1992, while my family was in Manila. I was an Overseas Filipino Worker (OFW). I was sending them money. I did odd jobs in New York so I could send money and start my cinema at the same time. I lived in dangerous basements and colonies of desperate and displaced artists. I lost the only copy of my first film, the Super 8 *Banlaw*. I've experienced the struggles of the Filipino abroad because I was one of them. So I know it first-hand. *Batang West Side* is a testament to that.

INTERVIEWER: All these years, your film-making career, how would you describe its evolution?

LAV DIAZ: I still feel like a fraud, man (*chuckles*). I can't still anchor myself, in a way, in this universe we call cinema. I'm still searching. I still feel that cinema lacks something, and I profusely lack so many things, and there is that acceptance that I am nothing. I feel that I just got lucky I was able to make cinema, I was given the chance, and I'll just do what I can do, what I can contribute. That's what I can say. After all these years, I still do not know cinema. It's frustrating, as a cultural worker, on the issues of education and responsibility, I question my being: Am I really helping with the struggles of our nation? Is cinema of help at all? With the struggle of humanity? That's my frustration. I want to be part of the struggle. I want cinema to be part of the nation's struggle. I want cinema to be a big part of humanity's struggle. These are some of the reasons why I do cinema, but I feel it's not really effective. But I'll keep making cinema. I question it, but my faith in it remains pristine. I am still that kid from the boondocks who would see eight movies a week.

Beyond existential discourse, we know the reason/reasons why cinema is still not really reaching its full potential in relation to its greater role in culture. Systems are really bad. There is a great disparity of support for commercial and serious works. Most theatres are given to Hollywood and mainstream movies while serious films are always relegated to small and obscure venues or there are no venues at all. Add to that the ignorance of the masses that we have to contend with. They only see cinema as entertainment, a form of escape, reprieve and furlough from their miseries. They don't see it as a medium that can help them. We have to break through these walls. My frustration with cinema stems from there. I want cinema to be part of the struggle, but there's only so much we can do. The nation's struggle is what keeps you moving. Humanity's struggle will keep you moving.

That's why I want to involve so-called big actors in my films; I want to push cinema more, push it to be part of the greater cultural struggle. I ask popular actors to collaborate with serious film-makers, to get involved in the struggle, to get people to watch the better works and realize that cinema is not just entertainment. And some of these actors' eyes have opened. Their view of the medium changed in a big way.

INTERVIEWER: The first big name was Piolo Pascual?

LAV DIAZ: Piolo Pascual, John Lloyd Cruz, Shaina Magdayao. I would like to think that after working with me, and with other progressive film-makers, they have a better understanding of their roles now, that they are not just actors, that they are cultural workers, that it's not just vanity and money and that they have a responsibility to educate people. In the case of John, especially after *A Lullaby to the Sorrowful Mystery* and *The Woman Who Left*, he began to withdraw from the limelight. I am not saying that I influenced his decision to take a hiatus or to almost turn his back. He has his own mind, his own reasons. And I believe that he'd seen the problems in the system, he'd seen the industry's malevolent side, greed, exploitation and decadence. Now they're more open to working in independent cinema. Piolo turned to producing and helping other film-makers, which is a commendable step. Even Shaina has changed. She said so many things had changed since she had started working with us. She has transformed like, *oh these aren't just vanity projects. I can actually be a tool for change.*

I've made many films. But it hasn't worked. They aren't reaching the people.

INTERVIEWER: When you say, 'It hasn't worked. They aren't reaching the people', do you mean that few people have seen your films?

LAV DIAZ: Yes, that's true. But I always knew that the struggle to reach the masses will take time considering their mentality and the system's negligence. The ignorance of the masses and the system just keeps worsening. You realize that through the years, the quagmire created by a dysfunctional system has become so thick that it has pushed the masses deeper and deeper into ignorance. How do we fight this? How do we destroy man's biggest enemy, ignorance? Sometimes I'd think that it would be easier to just turn my back on cinema and just focus on my grandkids, put up a coffee shop somewhere in Cotobato, go back to our farm. But the thing is, no matter how small my contribution is, or anybody's contribution, it can at least help in affecting change. But it's frustratingly limited. That's why I'm involving big actors in my projects now if they're available. Please, help. That's what I ask them. Please, come and help. I tell them, look, Rodrigo Duterte is elected president of our sad republic. That is one devastating result of ignorance.

INTERVIEWER: How did you choose them? Piolo and John, for instance? How did you meet them?

LAV DIAZ: In 2005, during the shoot of *Heremias, Book One*, Ronnie Lazaro said John wanted to work with me. Then eventually, John became friends with Erwin Romulo, who's also a friend of mine. That started it. We met and talked about doing projects. Piolo also reached out through another film-maker friend Joyce Bernal: *Oh, he says he wants to work with Direk Lav.* I said, well, if you want to give my films a shot, let's go.

John suggested a long, long time ago that they wanted to work with me. But I think initially they did so out of some romantic notion: Who the fuck is this bum? When I met with them, I told them they need to be responsible. They had a responsibility to their country, to humanity, to give back. I told them that they are cultural workers. What's a cultural worker? I said, your world revolves around culture. You are artists. And there are two kinds of artists – there's Narcissus, the self-absorbed one who just works for his ego, for himself, he's so in love with his image and his hedonistic ways; and there's the altruistic artist who wants to help humanity, the cultural worker. Cinema is part of the cultural struggle. Let's use cinema as a tool to educate people on humanity's struggle, on history, on truth. That as cultural workers they had an important role to play in the bigger scheme of things. If they get past vanity, then they'd be of use to our country. They can use their stature to do good works. That's the only thing. It's simple, I told them. Help out when it's a meaningful film. That's it. If their names help bump up the number of viewers, that's already a huge contribution. Don't just think of the box office. Some films may be 'small', but they have more impact. We can change someone's perspective. So don't be afraid if a film only reaches a small audience. If it's a good film, it will outlive all the theme-park movies of DC and Marvel. With *Hele*, the audience was really small. But Piolo and John were cool with that. I thanked them

for putting their names on the marquee of an eight-hour historical film. I told them that their film will be studied and viewed by
historians, history students and social anthropologists for years
and years to come.

INTERVIEWER: How about your work with Charo Santos? How did that start?

LAV DIAZ: Star Cinema is the distributor of *Hele*. So when the film won the
Silver Bear Alfred Bauer Award in Berlin, they had this big celebration at ABS-CBN. We were seated next to each other. I just asked
her, 'Do you still want to act?' She said, yes, if the material is good.

That very night when I rode a taxi going home, this Tolstoy short story came to mind: *God Sees the Truth but Waits*.
I thought the story suited Charo. I'd just need to make the character female. I read the story again, then wrote a storyline based
on that, inspired by that. I sent it to her that same week, and she
said okay. Yes, she agreed right away. I asked her to read the short
story, I sent her the link. She read it. She liked it. *This is the inspiration for our material*. I didn't have a script, just an outline. She
was okay with that. It was fine. She was eager to jump back into
acting after a 30-year hiatus.

When she asked me where I intended to shoot, I said, *Well,
I've gone to Mindoro; I want to shoot in Calapan*. She said, *I
grew up in Calapan. That's my hometown. My father was the
hospital doctor*. She lived there till high school. So again, landscape played a great role; it was a place familiar to her. When we
went to Calapan, she saw all the people from her childhood and
the places she grew up in. She had an attachment to the land, and
to the people, and that helped her turn in a beautiful performance. It wasn't an alien place to her. She truly embodied the role.
Whenever I'd shoot in a certain location, she'd go, *Direk, I used
to run here*. One time we shot at a place and she turned to say,
There's our house. She pointed out where she used to live. And
we found her nanny. She's still alive, very old, and they cried and
hugged when they met again. I said, *Wow, this is something else*.
The shooting of *The Woman Who Left* was amazing, truly an
amazing and magical experience.

When we were shooting, she was surprised to see that it was
just the sound man and me doing the camera, and I'm using a
small camera and two small lights. She was concerned about it,
Will we be able to see anything, Direk? Hear anything? I said,

Yes, Charo. Don't worry. And she said, *Pwede pala ang ganitong shoot. We should do this in Star Cinema and ABS.*

INTERVIEWER: She wasn't used to it, coming from Star Cinema.

LAV DIAZ: Yes, but she saw for herself that it could be done. I kept reassuring her, but she kept asking if anything was registering on the camera or if the sound was okay. She was fascinated by the simplicity of the shoot. So for her, the Golden-Lion win in Venice came as a shock. That was a treat for her. She came to many realizations about cinema. The experience really woke her up. She said she wanted to introduce to ABS-CBN and Star Cinema what she experienced with us. Smaller budgets. Fewer people. But of course, the studio is supporting a lot of employees. So they'll be maintaining the status quo. They'll maintain their model of doing cinema. I don't think anything's changed there, but it's their call. They have money.

INTERVIEWER: But did you have conversations about those?

LAV DIAZ: Yes, she was very excited after we won the Lion. We went to Venice. She represented the film in Toronto. What she saw inspired her. It got her thinking of putting up a festival and a film school through ABS-CBN because of what she'd experienced. We had a lot of conversation on how to go about it; she wanted to talk to people about the idea, those who could help set them up, the school and the festival. People I know from MoMa wanted to help. And people from Venice, from Berlin. But she didn't push through with it. I don't know what happened. She didn't pursue it. She's just too busy, I think.

I have an unfinished work, *Henrico's Farm*, where she plays one of the main characters. She is joined by actors Hazel Orencio, Angeli Bayani, Shaina Magdayao and Karen Haniel. They're OFWs in the film. This is based on real stories, as I did a lot of interviews through the years. I had many conversations and encounters with OFWs in Milan, Rome, Hong Kong, Singapore, New York and other cities. I met some in Moscow. It's almost done. We shot in Singapore and here in the country. It was funded by the Singapore Arts Council. But I don't want to rush it, because there are still parts unfinished. I feel it's still missing something. Maybe by next year I'll get it done. Or maybe late this year (*laughs*). I want it finished.

Charo was able to meet with people at the Singapore Arts Council during our shoot in Singapore. We had interactions with the massive talents of the Council; we watched some of their shows, they came to our shoot, and Charo once told them, 'I'll invite you to my future school, to conduct talks and workshops, when it's set up'. I hope she pushes through with it, the film school and the festival. They're good ideas.

INTERVIEWER: So with that kind of involvement with the big names, the big stars, will this be the new norm for you?

LAV DIAZ: Not in all films, of course. Every film has different demands and attributes. I can't put them in my documentaries of storm children and rebel returnees and a short film about frogs and in films that only needs non-actors. In some films, I will invite them if they want to join and help. I want to encourage other film-makers to do it this way as well. That you can actually invite John or Piolo and other so-called celebrities, now that they're open to this. Having them on board won't make you less cool. I know people who harbour that prejudice on popular actors. I heard them attacking me, some are even my friends. But I'm cool with that. It's not cool when you shut out the big names, especially if they were offering help. Just look at society where there's the greater struggle; these stars can be of help, I can assure you that. Don't just create art for art's sake. I want that, too, but don't think that it makes you less cool if you have Pokwang in your film. Or Vice Ganda. They're cool.

I actually invited Vice Ganda to work with us. He was just busy. He was supposed to be in *Ang Hupa*. I want these big names involved because they pull in audiences. This needs to be done. There's that urgency, the zeitgeist calls for it.

INTERVIEWER: Some scholars have also described your work as philosophical, that there's a lot to dig into. In that aspect, is there such a thing as a Lav Diaz philosophy of cinema?

LAV DIAZ: I think it goes with the issues of discourse on history, anthropology, politics, ethics, truth, morality, culture, dialectics and the verisimilitudes that they see in my works. My films investigate life, existence. Once you question life, say you pick a specific theme such as colonialism, or a period like the Philippine Revolution, there's a lot to ask there, there's a lot to see and not to see. Once you discourse earnestly on things, that's already threading on philosophy. My cinema creates discourse, or it struggles to create greater discourse. They ask a lot of questions, especially about humanity's struggles; struggles of specific individuals, or that of a specific nation like the Philippines. And I always see Socrates walking by the side street every time I do a work in some obscure island. I follow him, offer him a drink, which he always refuses, and see him stop by the agora and say, *any praxis is dialogue.* And so, my struggle: *Can cinema see the truth?*

NOTE

1. The interview with Lav Diaz was conducted by Michael Kho Lim and Parichay Patra at Marikina on 20 August 2019. It has been translated by Rachelle Tesoro and transcribed by Jing Racelis.

PART 5

TRIBUTE

12

Indictment and Empowerment
of the Individual:
The Modern Cinema of Lav Diaz

Alexis Tioseco

> *"The salvation of this human world lies nowhere else than in the human heart,*
> *in the human power to reflect, in human meekness and human responsibility."*
> —Vaclav Havel

From the first frames of his first feature-film—a memorable long shot of a man on his knees amidst an open field in the Dostoevsky-inspired *Serafin Geronimo, Kriminal ng Baryo Concepcion* (1998), to the final frames of his last—the epilogue *A Story of Two Mothers* that closes *Ebolusyon ng Isang Pamilyang Pilipino* (2005), Lav Diaz has been chronicling the crushing weight of guilt on those who seek redemption. Diaz's cinema is modern in many respects, but none so much as in relation to the norms and history of Philippine society, culture, and cinema. In seven years and spanning seven feature-films (including the forthcoming *Heremias*), he has developed a body of work that stands alone in contemporary Philippine cinema, seeking out new ground both formally and thematically, and challenging the legacy left behind by the great Lino Brocka.

* * *

As a country, the Philippines has had a troubled and arduous past. Initially struggling to free itself from Spanish and American colonizers, it now, independence gained, wrestles with itself in search of identity and direction, pointing fingers when it ought to take responsibility. The shadow cast by Ferdinand Marcos' imposition of Martial Law stills looms prominently over the country, nearly twenty years after the dictator's reign has ended. Marcos created a legacy; not only of fame and wealth, but of stifled hands and silenced voices; a legacy of disempowerment.

Filmmaking in a country is often at its most gripping when its citizenry are in their most dire straits. Many Filipino filmmakers, from Ishmael Bernal (*Nunal sa Tubig*, 1975, *Manila By Night*, 1980 and *Himala*, 1982) and Mike De Leon (*Kisapmata* and *Batch 81*, both made in 1982) to Peque Gallaga (*Oro, Plata, Mata*, 1982 and *Scorpio Nights*, 1985), created their best works during Marcos' rule. The most prominent filmmaker in the country during this period, both cinematically and vocally, was Lino Brocka. Brocka's was, when granted the opportunity, a cinema of opposition; one that challenged the status quo, and painted a horrifying picture of society at its most desperate. Fighting to be heard amidst a crassly commercial industry and strict censorship, Brocka often had to sacrifice making several commercial features in order to make one work of substance.

It is from these two strains—Martial Law and Brocka—that Diaz both gained his inspiration and begins his point of departure.

Diaz first encountered the power of cinema watching Lino's *Maynila* as a college student. "That film changed my perspective on cinema", Diaz imparted to me in a 2002 interview, "[It made me realize that] this medium is very powerful: you can use it to change people's minds; their conditions; their perspectives. From then on I said I want to make good art films; for my people."

* * *

Debuting to critical acclaim in 1998, Diaz's *Serafin Geronimo, Kriminal ng Baryo Concepcion*, announced the arrival of a major talent, and a possible new direction for Philippines cinema. Where Brocka had examined society's effect on the individual, Diaz's *Kriminal* looked at the effect of the individual's actions on his conscience. His Russian influences written on his sleeve—the film begins with a quote from *Crime and Punishment* translated into Tagalog—Diaz's hero was akin to that of Dostoevsky but atypical of Philippine cinema; a quiet man with a guilty past seeking redemption in the present. With *Kriminal*, Diaz laid down his archetype character and began to plot the path of his aesthetic.

In 1999 Diaz completed two more films for Regal films (producers of *Kriminal*), the farcical *Burger Boys*, whose shooting actually began before *Kriminal*, and *Hubad Sa Ilalim ng Buwan*. *Burger Boys*, about a group of youths writing a screenplay about a group of youths planning a bank robbery, is a curious film, and one that seems most out of place in the context of Diaz's oeuvre. Filled with close-ups, quick cutting, conscious camera angles, strange costume design, and oddball characters, it is most interestingly seen as a genre experiment by an anti-genre filmmaker.

Hubad Sa Halim ng Buwan brought Diaz back to more familiar territory. An ex-priest and failed husband (Joel Torre), whose daughter (played by starlet Klaudia Koronel) sleepwalks in the nude plagued by memories of being raped, questions his decisions and examines his past, as his life slowly crumbles before him in the present. Again, we have a hero, quiet, introverted, searching. The film received favorable reviews, and screened in the Berlin International Film Festival, but was also re-cut with additional sex scenes (shot without Diaz) inserted at the producer's behest.

It was in the independently produced *Batang West Side* (2001), arguably the first modern Filipino masterpiece, that Diaz fully realized his aesthetic and first tackled, indirectly, the theme of Martial Law. At a startling five-hours, then the longest Filipino film ever made, and shot almost entirely in the US (save for brief but powerful dream sequences), *Batang West Side* dealt with an issue close to home for Diaz and many in his country, that of the Filipino diaspora abroad. The subject matter had been dealt with before (Laurice Guillen's *American Adobo*, 2001), but here the issues and characters were more than melodrama and caricatures. Brilliantly sketched and cast, so fully realized on the screen; allowed to sit, stand, breathe, and exhale (a key motif throughout the film, including its final scene), they became cinematic equivalents of people you knew—your mother, father, brother, sister, cousin, lover, or grandfather. Diaz's quiet unobtrusive camera registered every detail of Filipinos from all walks of life in the US. Treating every minute as precious, he utilized the films long running time to masterful effect, allowing scenes, moods, and relationships to sink in as deep with his actors as with his audience. *West Side*'s plot, revolving around the death of a Filipino youth on a New Jersey street corner, served as a metaphor for the state of Filipinos today. Officer Mijarez, himself harboring a dark past, interrogates the entire Filipino community in search of the murderer, in search of truth, of a face on whom to place the blame. By the films end Mijarez's investigation has drawn to a close, but nothing conclusive about Hanzel's death has been determined. "If I push for the case, I'll be killing a lot of Filipinos", Mijarez says, and as the last frames roll out we understand why: *we are all our responsible.*

Diaz followed *West Side*, with another Regal Films production, *Hesus Rebolusyonaryo* (2002). *Hesus* was an ambitious science-fiction film set in a future not so dissimilar from the past (the year is 2010). Using as a recurring theme a song by the rock-band The Jerks that comments on the circular nature of history, Diaz projects his concerns, nay paranoia, for what the future will hold for a society that has not yet learned from its mistakes. The films complex story plays out less as a traditional futuristic thriller, than a psychological mind-game, as we witness the interplay of action and discourse between the three main characters—Kumander Miguel (Ronnie Lazaro), Col. Simon (director Joel Lamangan) and the revolutionary Hesus Mariano (Mark Anthony Fernandez). "Future Tense": the title of film critic Noel Vera's review of the film, aptly sums up its mood.

In April of 2003 Diaz returned to nine-year old unfinished work. Using DV in place of 16 mm film due to lack of budget, he set out to complete an intimate epic set just before, during, and after martial law. In January 2005, the final cut of his 11-hour masterwork, the beautiful confusion *Ebolusyon ng Isang Pamilyang Pilipino* (2005), premiered at the Rotterdam International Film Festival. *Ebolusyon* recreates scenes of rural life splicing them between and with harrowing historical footage from the period. "Is there a direct correlation between the historical footage presented and the lives of the characters in the film?", one begins to ponder, watching the film. While it is not hard to imagine the psychological implications a state imbued with fear brings, the direct connection between the two appears missing, a telling clue as to the point Diaz is making. One would commonly expect a film that deals with such an important period of a county's history to focus on large-scale events. Boldly, Diaz points his camera in another direction, choosing not to make a reductive statement indicting the former leader, but instead demonstrating and dramatizing the effect individual choice has in the face of societal forces. At the same time that Diaz sympathizes with the burden that his people have borne, he also appears to declare the futility of placing blame for ones woes entirely on society. It is for this reason that such a disparity exists between the illustration of historical events and Diaz's depiction of fictional lives. Diaz chooses not to show us the direct effects of key moments in history on the lives of the characters, but rather the role that their own choices played in determining the courses of their lives. Puring's strength, her deep belief in the fertility of the land and the importance of education, Kadyo's good-natured but misguided attempts at supporting his loved ones, Reynaldo's departure from and return to his new family, the moving epilogue *A Story of Two Mothers* that ends the film; these are all sketches coalescing into a grand collage, a work of art that both indicts and empowers the individual in the face of oppression; declaring him responsible for his own salvation.

* * *

You can feel the weight of history, of the past, in every frame of a Lav Diaz film. It's written in the worn wrinkles on the faces of his characters, in their stammered speech, their furrowed brow; their moments of silence. This is the key to Diaz's cinema, and the well from which it draws its strength and importance. While many filmmakers in the Philippines, having been bred and influenced by the films and words of Lino Brocka (correct for their time, out of place now) seek to emulate the path of his career, Diaz has adapted and grown, stepped back and attempted to understand the present picture of our country and its people today. Twenty years ago, when under the rule of a sole dictator, we knew well whose wrists deserved to feel the sharp ends of our knives. Today, in a society so quick to judge and pass blame, the only flesh that remains to be examined is our own. Diaz's camera, steadfast, unwavering, reveals the truths only found beneath the surface, and points us on the path to deliverance.

ACKNOWLEDGMENT
Originally commissioned for the 2005 Torino International Film Festival Catalogue for their retrospective of Lav Diaz.

Contributors

WILLIAM BROWN is an independent scholar. He is also an honorary fellow for the School of Arts and Humanities at the University of Roehampton, London. He is the author of *The Squid Cinema from Hell: Kinoteuthis Infernalis, The Emergence of Chthulumedia* (with David H. Fleming, Edinburgh University Press, 2020), *Non-Cinema: Global Digital Filmmaking and the Multitude* (Bloomsbury, 2018) and *Supercinema: Film-Philosophy for the Digital Age* (Berghahn, 2013). He is also the maker of various films, including *En Attendant Godard* (2009), *Selfie* (2014), #randomaccessmemory (2017) and *This Is Cinema* (2019).

* * *

CLODUALDO DEL MUNDO JR is professor emeritus and university fellow at De La Salle University. Some of his screenplay credits are *Maynila ... Sa mga Kuko ng Liwanag (Manila ... in the Claws of Light), Kisapmata (In the Blink of an Eye), Batch '81, 'Merika, Mulanay, Aliwan Paradise (Entertainment Paradise), Bayaning 3ʳᵈ World (3rd World Hero)* and *Markova*. He also wrote and directed *Pepot Artists (Pepot Superstar)* (2005) and *Paglipad ng Anghel (Flight of an Angel)* (2011). His film essays and documentaries include *People Media, Maynila ... Isang Pelikulang Pilipino (Maynila ... A Filipino Film), Komiks, Lupa* ('Land'), *Pahiyas* (or *Exorcising the Ghosts of St. Louis), Maid in Singapore, Ehem!plo (Corruption and Integrity in the Philippines)* and *Tinitingnan, 'Di Nakikita (Looking without Seeing)* on urban poverty. His books include *Native Resistance: Philippine Cinema and Colonialism 1898–1941* (1995), *Spirituality and the Filipino Film* (editor, 2010), *Direk: Essays on Filipino Filmmakers* (editor, 2019) and *Riding the Waves: Fifteen Years of Cinemalaya* (editor, 2021).

* * *

MARCO GROSOLI is assistant professor in film studies at Habib University, Karachi, Pakistan. He has published the first Italian-language monograph on Béla Tarr and a book on the early stage of 'politique des auteurs' trend in French film criticism ('Eric Rohmer's Film Theory', Amsterdam University Press, 2018).

* * *

MICHAEL GUARNERI has a Ph.D. in film studies from Northumbria University. He is the author of the books *Questi fiori malati: Il cinema di Pedro Costa* (Bébert, 2017), *Vampires in Italian Cinema, 1956–1975* (Edinburgh University Press, 2020) and *Conversations with Lav Diaz* (Massimiliano Piretti Editore, 2020). A Locarno Critics Academy and Berlinale Talents alumnus, he freelances as a film critic for several outlets, including Film Comment, MUBI Notebook, Débordements and BOMB.

* * *

MAY ADADOL INGAWANIJ is a writer, curator, teacher and professor of cinematic arts at University of Westminster where she co-directs the Centre for Research and Education in Arts and Media. She works on decentred histories and genealogies of cinematic arts; avant-garde legacies in Southeast Asia; forms of potentiality in contemporary artistic and curatorial practices; aesthetics and circulation of artists' moving image, art and independent films in, around and beyond Southeast Asia. Recent publications include articles on Karrabing Film Collective, Nguyen Trinh Thi and Araya Rasdjarmrearnsook. Curatorial projects include *Animistic Apparatus* and *Lav Diaz: Journeys*. May is writing a book titled *Animistic Medium: Contemporary Southeast Asian Artists Moving Image*.

* * *

MICHAEL KHO LIM is lecturer of media and cultural policy and acting course director of the master's programme in cultural and creative industries at Cardiff University, United Kingdom. He is the author of *Philippine Cinema and the Cultural Economy of Distribution* (Palgrave Macmillan, 2019), co-editor of *Re-imagining Creative Cities in Twenty-First Century Asia* (Palgrave Macmillan, 2020) and co-author of *The Media Kit: A Frame-by-Frame Guide to Visual Production* (Anvil Publishing, 2008). He presently sits as assistant secretary on the National Committee on Cinema under the Sub-commission on the Arts of the National Commission for Culture and the Arts. He is also an independent film producer and a freelance writer, who has extensive experience in the management of cultural and creative industries.

* * *

KATRINA MACAPAGAL earned her Ph.D. in film and media studies from Queen Margaret University, Edinburgh. She previously worked as instructor at the University of the Philippines, Diliman. Her monograph on slums and spatial justice in Philippine urban cinema has been published by Edinburgh University Press. She is based in Edinburgh and works in charity communications and research.

* * *

ADRIAN MARTIN is a film critic and audiovisual artist based in Vilassar de Mar, Spain. He is also an adjunct associate professor of film culture and theory at Monash University, Australia. From 2013 to 2015, he served the Goethe University in Frankfurt, Germany, as a distinguished visiting professor. Apart from several books, translated works, 70 audio commentaries and 200 audiovisual essays, some of his recent publications include *Mysteries of Cinema: Reflections on Film Theory, History and Culture* (2018 and 2020) and *Mise en Scène and Film Style: From Classical Hollywood to New Media Art* (2014).

* * *

PARICHAY PATRA is an assistant professor of film studies in the Department of Humanities and Social Sciences, Indian Institute of Technology Jodhpur, India. He is currently working on his monograph on the Indian New Wave of the 1970s.

* * *

TOM PAULUS teaches film history and film aesthetics at the University of Antwerp. He is co-founder of the research group Visual Poetics. His edited collection *Slapstick Comedy* (with Rob King) has been published by Routledge in the AFI Film Readers Series. His research centres on the history of film style, a topic explored in book chapters and essays on silent film pictorialism, Ford, Ozu, Hou Hsiao-hsien and Godard. Tom is the editor of the online journal *Photogénie*, an environment devoted to the history and theory of cinephilia.

* * *

ALEXIS TIOSECO was a Manila-based film critic who published a number of essays on Lav Diaz in particular and Filipino cinema in general. In 2009, he, along with his Slovenian partner, was murdered under mysterious circumstances in Quezon City, Philippines.